THE FALCON
DIARIES

To Sam and Kristie Furrow
Best Regards,

Emily Lodge

AN
AMERICAN
IN
JORDAN

Aug 21, 2019

EMILY LODGE

Published in the United States of America

FIRST EDITION

ISBNs: 978-0-692-10011-0 (Hardback)
978-0-692-10012-7 (Paperback)
978-0-692-10013-4 (eBook)

Library of Congress Control No.: 2018904399

DEDICATED TO my father, who encouraged me
to take an interest in the world and to my husband,
who took me there.

CONTENTS

ACKNOWLEDGEMENTS

A T A PARIS BOOK PARTY for Maureen Dowd, op-ed columnist in *The New York Times*, my friend, Marlise Simons, of *The New York Times*, told me about Agatha Christie's *Come Tell Me How You Live*, an autobiographical account of Christie's time in the Middle East in the 1930s. I am grateful to Marlise for her suggestion that I keep my own record and to her husband, Alan Riding, of *The New York Times*, who has been helpful in editing the manuscript. I am also honored to have had the comments of Diane Johnson, prodigious novelist, notably of *Le Divorce*, an essayist with the *New York Review of Books*, and a finalist for both the National Book Award and the Pulitzer Prize. Another inspiration was *The Berlin Diaries 1940-1945* by Marie Vassiltchikov, and indeed her daughter, Sandra Harnden, was herself inspirational.

Although we were in Amman eight years, this book is mostly about our first year, when the differences and similarities between our cultures became stunningly evident. I will be forever grateful for the kindness of all our Jordanian friends who welcomed us so generously. I am particularly obliged to Nyla, our Arabic teacher and friend who taught me so much, including how one would translate this book—"Muthakarat Issaqer: Amerkeeye fil Urdun." (I also considered the title *The Innocent American* so much did the wisdom of the Arab people become revealed to me.) My agent, the late Charles Everitt, and editors, Catherine Tanzer, Sally Arteseros and Karl French, were of invaluable help in improving the manuscript. Lastly, I would like to thank my husband for his endless patience, ideas and support and my father, my lifelong editor, who inspired me to take an interest in the world.

INTRODUCTION

O N NOVEMBER 11, 2005, suicide bombers struck the Hyatt, Radisson and the Days Inn hotels in Amman, Jordan, killing 60 people and wounding 115. A few minutes after the attack, just before the government shut down the internet, my husband Bobby managed to call me at our house in Paris to tell me he was safe. "Don't worry, I'm alive. Turn on the television," he told me.

Bob, a consultant for European power companies in Iraq, had been at the Amman Hyatt with his group at the same time that the U.S. Army Corps of Engineers were, "figuring out ways to pay less for more," as he put it. At the last minute, he had decided to avoid the U.S. contingent dining in the back, and had moved the meeting to the Intercontinental a block away. The suicide belt of the Al-Qaeda attacker, containing nails along with explosives, had ripped through the Hyatt lobby, killing dozens, including Moustapha Akkad and his daughter, Rima. Syrian-born Akkad, one of the most illustrious Arab filmmakers, ironically, had produced *The Message* (1976) about the history of Islam, a religion of peace and tolerance. A few days later, Bobby sent me a photograph showing him partying in the streets with the locals to celebrate the monarchy's control of the situation.

Bob was impressed by how well run the country was, that it didn't feel chaotic. We both knew there were tensions under the surface, knew that the Muslim Brotherhood was influential, and that Al-Qaeda attracted a small following. But under the monarchy, people enjoyed a kind of freedom. King Abdullah can dissolve the parliament and is therefore not a constitutional monarch but a benevolent ruler, who "has never made a mistake," according to Israeli Ambassador Jacob Rosen in an interview at the end of this book.

After the fall of Saddam Hussein in 2003, the US government occupied Iraq for at least two and a half years and Bob had been commuting from Paris to Amman during that time. The European power companies that had worked with Saddam found themselves without contacts in the US government and called on Bob, former director of the Chubb Insurance Company France, to see if his consulting business could help them build electrical sub-stations in Iraq. While Bob told me he was going to Amman, Jordan on business, he was actually riding fourteen hours in a big SUV across the desert to Baghdad to try to negotiate a deal with the Army Corps of Engineers "who were like Thomas and Sir Richard in *Downton Abbey*."

When we told our family that Bob was going to help with the reconstruction of Iraq from Amman, our children naughtily called their father a war profiteer. As director of Republicans Abroad Europe, based in Paris, during the Bush administration, Bob was well known on French radio and television. His work was generally limited to Europe so this new assignment came as a surprise. We liked to think of ourselves as "forward deployed," helpful to Iraq after the fiasco of a war that the Bush administration created at the behest of neo-cons in support of Israel to bring democracy to the Middle East. (Thomas Ricks' *Fiasco: The American Military Adventure in Iraq, 2003 to 2005*, is a startlingly complete history of that period.)

Initially, the electrical consortium that Bob represented built mobile home-sized units (by brave Iraqis they had employed) with wires running underground (suited to hospitals and small villages), rendering them less vulnerable to attack. One courageous and crazy Frenchman was riding around alone in a car without his seat-belt on. "They always know you're a foreigner if you wear a seat-belt," he would say. The insurgency bombed the units as they were being built and then they'd have to start over. But eventually, electrical sub-stations named for the heroes of the Arab golden age were operating all over Iraq—Baghdad, Fallujah, Ramadi, Sulaymaniyah, and Basra, among other places.

One of the substations outside Baghdad to the north to supply Kurdistan was called *Al Malik* after the Umayyad king Abd al Malik (691-2) who built the Dome of the Rock on the Temple Mount in Jerusalem; the other substation to the south of Baghdad supplying Basra was called *Al*

Rachid after the caliph, al Rachid (786-809) whose reign is considered the apogee of the Abbasid dynasty, when the Arabs controlled all of the Middle East, North Africa and Spain. One of Bob's associates hired one of Saddam's former bodyguards for *Al Rachid*. "Was he friendly?" I asked. "He called me 'my teacher'," Bob replied. "He was a killer."

During the construction of one Baghdad electrical plant, Bobby received an email from Al-Qaeda explaining that their grievance had to do with our role in injustices against the Palestinians and with the "Western crusaders"; they threatened to cut off the heads of his European-UK-US team. Bobby's advice to his colleagues was "stay low in the boat" and security was increased. Although Bobby managed to blend in easily—a regular Mr. Magoo (the cartoon character who ingeniously and distractedly manages to escape danger)—he did have a scare in 2003 in Fallujah, on one of his business trips when he stopped to relieve himself in the bushes behind a service station. Two clearly armed Sunni Iraqi Bedouins hiding there, said, "Hey mister, what you doing in my country? You make politic? You make business? Maybe I kill you." Eventually the U.S. government refused to pay for war insurance so Bob's consortium stopped working for them.

Bobby once worked with France's premier water company, who had the plans to the city of Baghdad water works from the Saddam years, to set up new treatment plants and to repair the old system. The U.S. Army Corps of Engineers asked for the plans. In a reversal of roles, Bob, an American, refused to hand over the plans to the U.S. government unless the French company was given the contract. "Why should we, after all?" he said. They didn't get the contract for a sewage treatment plant in Baghdad but they did manage to get a treatment facility to treat the water from the Tigris River. The opening of the plant was a grand affair. Little children carried flowers in celebration. The next day the plant was bombed and they had to start over again, a common occurrence in the early years.

It had been three long years of watching and waiting. So when Bob suggested we move to Amman four months later, I was both happy to share the adventure and was concerned about security. In the end, I felt it would be better to worry with him than without him. A journalist, daughter of a professor and granddaughter of an ambassador, I enjoyed living abroad, first in Brussels in 1985, then Paris in 1987. Where Europe is the most likely cultural destination, Mark Twain, in *Innocents Abroad*, conveyed the importance to innocents of seeing the West from the East.

In this slice of upper class Jordanian life, a restricted circle opened up for us. Once accepted, the generosity was altogether American in spirit, though perhaps it helped that Jordanians admired my grandfather, Henry Cabot Lodge who, while ambassador to Vietnam, hired foreign service officer Philip Habib, a Lebanese Christian Arab, to advise him. The Jordanian or Palestinian university-educated social set close to us—Christian or Muslim—didn't fit the stereotype. Our Arabic teacher, always beautifully coiffed with perfect nails, drove a Lexus and her sons, attired in Hugo Boss suits, a Mercedes and a Porsche.

Whereas for Bob Iraq was his subject, mine was Jordan. Among those I met were many middle class Palestinians whose families were displaced by the "Nakba", the catastrophe of 1948, the creation of the Israeli state. My first awareness of the Israeli-Palestinian crisis came from U.S. news media broadcasts of the '67 war which featured the heroism of Moshe Dayan riding in a tank conquering the Palestinians. I hadn't known any Arabs or Jews as a child, though I had read of the Jewish exile from Palestine in 71AD by the Romans, as well as later, the Ottoman Empire control of Palestine until WW I, and, finally, of the horrors of the Holocaust and of Eastern European Jews returning in the late 19th and early 20th c. Thankfully, I came to have a more nuanced view of the region. Once in the region, I became aware of Walid I, the Umayyad Caliph who continued the work of his father, Abd al Malik in building the Dome of the Rock in Jerusalem as well as the Great Mosque in Damascus and went on to conquer all of North Africa and Spain (705-715AD). I also learned of Harun al Rachid, one of whose presents to Charlemagne in 802 was a water clock that marked the hours by dropping brass balls into a bowl as miniature mechanical knights emerged each hour from little doors which shut behind them. As I waded into the history and culture of the country, the proverbial scales fell from my eyes. Distinctions between Arab Muslims or Christians didn't matter; that conflict had been addressed centuries before. But the one with the Israeli Jews has not. It is tragic that a people treated so badly would then treat their Palestinian "brothers" likewise (as Jordan's Prince Hassan called the late Yitzhak Rabin.)

Our son, Maxwell, had been to the American School of Paris with a member of Jordan's royal family and the boy came to our apartment in Paris for dinner with his parents, Faazi, a former ambassador to France and Hana.

Of Lebanese origin, she had a regal demeanor—strong, independent but caring—with long dark blonde hair teased high on top. Unconventionally chic, she wore a turquoise mohair skirt fastened with a broach. She spent a long time saying goodbye, the mark of especially good manners. Bostonians tend toward quick goodbyes and I realize I began to learn from Arabs then and there. Her dress and looks and funny quirks appealed to me.

Amman was depicted reassuringly as a safe and fast-growing city emerging from poverty with a secret service that offered protection. In subsequent dinners with my guides and other Jordanians, the deep-seated grievances toward America for not addressing the Palestinian issue and always taking Israel's side became a constant thorn in my side. In spite of this bias, the over-riding emotion was always one of welcome: *as a foreigner, you are welcome in our country.*

A few weeks after that dinner, Hana invited me for lunch at the Hotel Plaza Athenée in the lounge that is actually a long hallway like a fashion runway where you can observe everyone walking by. She motioned to the young man standing next to us in jeans surrounded by bodyguards. "Do you know who that is?" she asked me. "Rafic Hariri's son, Saad," she confided, referring to the son of the heroic Lebanese PM who had been assassinated the year before, the man who reconstructed Beirut after the 15-year civil war, restoring its status as "the Paris of the Middle East." "Another bomb attack," I murmured quietly, but my confidante assured me, "Jordan is not a security risk," she said.

"But why not?" I asked.

She only smiled and said, "You'll see."

As the falcon, a bird emblematic of the Middle East, casts his gaze from above, our travels took us to countries on Jordan's borders—Syria, Lebanon, Israel, Iraq and Egypt, an exciting journey across Jordan's geopolitical and historical landscape. In ancient Egypt, the falcon symbolized the eye of the dead person, the soul or consciousness that survives death in a transcendent visionary state, as Susan Brind Morrow describes in *The Dawning Moon of the Mind: Unlocking the Pyramid Texts*. This odyssey into the Arab world aims to understand the collective consciousness here, however difficult a task that may be. As our candid and strikingly beautiful friend, Gabriella, correctly put it, "You are in over your head." Nevertheless, my ambitious hope is that a candid look at this vital part of the world will humanize the cruel face often depicted of the Arab world so that they are recognized as the credible partners for peace that they are.

In my interview with him at the end of the book, Prince Hassan, the Jordanian Hashemite prince, uncle to Jordan's King Abdullah, brother of the famous King Hussein, describes a unique three-state solution to the Middle East to bring together Israel, Jordan and Palestine, on the Benelux model with its roots in a centuries-old pan-Mediterranean, multi-ethnic, inter-faith model. Unfortunately, the very next day, Israel's Ambassador Jacob Rosen's position floated comfortably above the search for peace, and almost diametrically opposed the important plan.

Whenever I tell people I lived eight years in Jordan, they ask, "Were you afraid?" I answer no. Fear is born of ignorance and fosters mistrust. I discovered the apprehension toward the Arab world to be overblown, made worse by the advent of ISIS and heightened by Hollywood. In those pre-ISIS days, there was something inherently ironic about our life there, both very luxurious and at the edge of something dangerous. During our time in the Middle East, I came to understand relatively obvious ways to repel the terrorist threat that would be consistent with our foreign policy and democratic principles. My hope is that in the blend of the small and large scale, from the tiny details of quotidian life to issues of the vital global significance that the book will produce the promised falcon's eye view of life there.

CHAPTER ONE
April

ONCE PAST THE MEDITERRANEAN SEA from the plane flying in at sunset, the vast red desert stretches out for miles with little patches of green here and there. Jordan, in the Levant area of the Fertile Crescent, sits at the edge of West Asia. At the farthest eastern edges of Europe, Greece and Turkey, she is the cool center of the Middle East hotspot with Syria to the north, Iraq to the east, Saudi Arabia to the southeast, Israel to the west; her port at Aqaba on the Red Sea is only a short ferry ride away from Egypt and the African continent. While flying over Israel, a prerogative obtained from the 1993 Oslo accords, the lights are dimmed for a minute or so; we were told to remain seated. From the skies, the Arab-Israeli landscape is homogeneous and I was later to learn that their "cousinage" also includes linguistic similarities and dietary preferences and restrictions.

A magnificent bouquet of pink flowers setting off the pink marble in the lobby greeted us at the Hyatt where we were staying (despite the bombing) while looking for a place to live. From our room, low white concrete villas and a few apartment buildings interspersed with palm trees gave the aspect of a peaceful suburban village. It brought back memories of our first move abroad to Brussels, another April twenty years earlier with our four-year-old and four-month-old sons—except with full sun instead of incessant rain, hail and snow.

One of the two newly redecorated restaurants—with seafood from as far away as Australia—was bathed in blue light with modern white leather banquettes and small metallic beads hanging between tables while the other was Italian, with seating in cozy amber niches and dark red walls with antique stone ceiling motifs. The wine was excellent (and we later discovered locally grown) although alcohol is excessively taxed. Men eat together in the restaurants at one end of the table while the women, dressed to the nines, do the same at the other end. It struck me that mixed company must be a Western invention and the Levant custom of men being served first alerted me that I was on new turf.

Bob took me to the newly renovated piano bar/restaurant in the lobby. "It was here," Bob said quietly, placing me at the exact spot of the bombing, now filled with the happy sound of quiet laughter and the tinkling of glasses. An open hearth with a warm fire glowing seemed to me an eternal flame to their memory.

For four centuries, the entire area—Transjordan, Syria and Palestine— was known as 'bilaad issam', the Ottoman Empire's 'country of Damascus,' the largest city and the center of culture. At the turn of the century, with growing Arab nationalism and resentment toward Ottoman authorities, Sharif Hussein of Mecca, of the Hashemite tribe of the Hejaz led the great Arab revolt of 1916 which had the support of Bedouins, Christians, and Circassians as well as the British and French.

Through a mutual friend at the *Financial Times*, we met Teresa posted to the Jordanian Embassy in Washington. Her mother, Katya, an auburn-haired Circassian beauty, became an invaluable friend and guide. The family had migrated to Jordan in the early 20th century and become the first King Abdullah's royal guards. I noticed that the screensaver on Katya's cellphone was a pen and ink sketch of a woman in a Circassian encampment on the Russian steppe, Muslims hounded by czarist forces in the diaspora of the late 19th century. Most went to Turkey but some were able to make the trek further south into Syria and Jordan. (The blood of this non-Arab Muslim tribe can be found in the Vikings, Celts, Galicia, Spanish, and even in New Jersey, when the U.S. took them in during the '67 war.)

"When my grandparents came to Jordan at the turn of the last century," she said, "we became the royal guards of the king because loyalty in our culture is the greatest virtue." Katya, an intuitive child, was only a toddler when she announced to her father, a Jordanian diplomat in

Damascus, that she was going to see the Pasha; the next year they were in Egypt. Katya's mother, who was ninety-two years old in 2006, remembered her grandmother, downtown by the stream on their property near the Roman amphitheater. "They lived in mud huts in the late 19th century," Katya said, "and the Ottoman Empire gave them the land downtown."

After World War One in 1921, under the Sykes Picot agreement, the British gave Transjordan (as it was then known) to the Hashemite tribe, and the Circassians welcomed King Abdullah into a little train car (preserved to this day) to sign the kingdom over to them and housed the new king in their newly built stone mansions. They owned much of the downtown oasis in the desert kingdom giving her a significant amount of property. "I am as proud of being Jordanian as I am of being Circassian. We are more reticent by nature than the Palestinians but we have a similar history, " Katya added, with the relentlessly positive spirit combined with a teasing little laugh that makes everyone want to be with her.

When Katya picked us up in her teal green Mercedes to look at apartments, she had the *take charge* air of someone who knows what she wants and gets it. Most of the houses here are boxy single-family dwellings. One property whose roof resembled an ice-cream cone had two huge living rooms—one for men and the other for women—with a small, dank pool in the basement. (Evidently, mixed company cannot be taken for granted in every house.) We never found anything we liked to rent and in the end chose to buy an unfurnished 360-square-meter apartment on the third floor of a building on a hill with a 65-square-foot 4th floor penthouse surrounded by a roof terrace, with a 180-degree view of all the hills leading downtown.

After living in New York City and Paris for thirty years, I had a house with a garden in mind, but Bob (known here as Mr. Robert) found a view of all Amman; in the end, I agreed that the wrap-around terrace was too spectacular to turn down. The 3rd and 4th floor duplex sits next to a security unit for the king. The building—called Saqer, meaning falcon (hence the book's title)—backs onto the Zahran palace and garden of Queen Zein, the late queen mother, King Abdullah's grandmother, with its forest of pine trees full of large crows. Bob drolly remarked that an apartment bordering a "nest of Hashemites" was prime real estate. King Abdullah, the eldest son of King Hussein and British-born Princess Muna, and king since the death of Hussein in 1999, is the great grandson of the King Abdullah who founded modern Jordan in 1921.

When Hana asked our assurance that we would not be looking down into the king's security police next door—so close to a royal estate—it occurred to me that we were able to buy our apartment through her. I replied in the negative which of course turned out not to be true since every day there was a new commotion that drew my attention.

We were living out of suitcases in the larger apartment on the third floor facing west toward the security unit while the penthouse was finished; my nerves were on edge. Our cat, Puffie, looked confused as there were no soft cushions for sleeping. The crows in the neighborhood noticed Puffie, gray and white striped with big green eyes, on the terrace and as they flew to the railing, she gave out little anxious squeaks, and backed away facing the crows, as with predators. Besides the ordinary birds, there were some with headdresses—spindly feathers parted in the middle and curling, as if their hair had been blow-dried, to each side. The next morning I heard a loud chirp and there on the railing were a pair of large green parrots.

Being a neighbor to the national police station (like the French Gendarmerie) facing us to the west, built five years ago (by the CIA) after Queen Zein's death, turned out to be a mixed blessing. When greeting fellow officers, men kiss each other first on one cheek then the other, two or three times, followed by a little chest bump-hug. The sexes spend a lot of time together, men hold hands in the street, and marriage often occurs between cousins as dating isn't allowed. One can guess what else this means.

During the first three mornings after my arrival, with my coffee and toast, as I looked out at the medieval fortress replica complete with battlements, soldiers were rappelling off the roof of the station across the street, yelling, "Allahu Akbar!" *God is great!* The first day was an exercise in getting down the fastest; the second day was under gunfire and on the third day they went down headfirst. There were also martial arts practiced in the yard accompanied by ear-piercing screams.

Every morning before dawn, at 4:30 am, a loudspeaker woke the troops and the call to prayer began, repeated again an hour later, in a higher voice, followed by a new lower voice reading verses from the Holy Qur'an. Neighbors said this would never be permitted if Queen Zein were still alive. The mysterious, eerily beautiful sound of the muezzin calling the faithful to prayer is the celebration of all that has passed between midnight and 4 am when God's heart, they say here, is most open to the human heart. The muezzin, amplified in unison throughout the city, broadcasting the "adnan" was lauded for his mystic resonance. After a few weeks, the subconscious became accustomed to the call to prayer five times a day.

On our street in the 7th arrondissement of Paris, there were many small religious orders nearby—bells calling the monks to vespers and the other hours of prayer during the day. I was told that the prophet devised the Islamic call to be heard over the sound of the liturgy of the Hours dating back to the desert fathers of Egypt: Matins, Lauds, Prime, Terce, Sext, None, Vespers, Compline. Jordan is now almost completely Sunni Muslim, with a small percentage of Circassian Muslim and Christians including Greek Orthodox, Greek and Roman Catholics, Syrian Orthodox, Coptic, Armenian, and Protestant; there are a few Buddhists, Hindus and a factsheet claims Jordan is 0.1% Jewish which surprised me as I never met a Jew except as a visitor.

Soon after our arrival, I realized I needed cookware and had no idea where to buy it so I called Hana. She arrived with her driver the next day, dressed in beige pants and a white blouse with a collar and cuffs that resembled cutout paper. I told her how fortunate it was that we, mothers of sons at school in Paris together, got along so well for it is not always the case. "How true," she said and we laughed comfortably together. When we arrived, the valet recognized the Mercedes (the car of preference in the region) and touched his forehead in respect, allowing us to park in front. I needed a mixer and started removing the pieces to make sure the set was complete. When I started putting it back, she said, "Oh don't bother, it will give them something to do," a rather mirthful approach to service that is definitely not the custom in Paris where salesgirls give you stern looks if you unfold a sweater. On the way out, the store gave me a present of a large crystal candy bowl. I learned that if you ask, the stores give their customers a little gift.

Afterwards, Hana and I had tea at the Four Seasons. She asked me again, "So now that you are here, how do you feel about security?"

"So far, so good," I admitted, "thanks to your kindness."

I later discovered that friends are enlisted to help with security. A professional journalist with experience as an investigative reporter as a *60 Minutes* researcher and as a columnist and feature writer in Brussels and

Paris, I told her I was keeping a journal of my experiences. My feeling was that she was keeping an eye on me but what I am not sure she realized was that I was all the time learning from her, collecting thoughts that would later become this book.

On our arrival, we didn't entirely grasp how deeply we were stepping into an angry bees' nest surrounding Western colonialist treachery and treason, made worse by the ongoing Iraqi war. An art exhibit we visited soon after our arrival featured millions of tiny wax figures, refugees streaming out of Palestine. At a local theater, a silent documentary film showed Israeli soldiers removing belongings from a Palestinian's house in Jerusalem—there was a gramophone, a library of books; the film showed the soldiers opening a beautiful white embroidered tablecloth, playing with it and laughing.

An American couple buying an apartment was, it emerged, highly controversial. One society lady confessed this was more discussed than the king and queen. Our real estate broker asked if we were Jewish, claiming— incorrectly—that it is forbidden for Jews to buy property in Jordan. There is no difference in the Jordanian mind between being an American and being Jewish. Since the United States is widely considered a colony of Israel or Israel is considered the fifty-first state of the U.S.A., there is a good deal of concern that Israel will decide that Jordan is part of their "Eretz" vision which includes at least all of the West Bank, ancient Judea and Samaria, and take over. In the 1930s, Menachem Begin had his eyes on all of Canaan and the West Bank. Laughing at the presumption of it, Bob said, "Begin even called Jordan 'East Israel'."

In the only newspaper in English, the *Jordan Times,* Rafi Dajani writes in 'Making One's Voice Heard,' that Americans identify with Israelis as "us" while considering Palestinians as "them." Here, the Palestinians are "us" and the Israelis are "them." In the U.S. it is assumed that in the Middle East the most evolved society is Israeli not Palestinian, and I began questioning my own assumptions. When ISIS or Al-Qaeda refer to the creation of a caliphate they are partly speaking of the 8th century conquests after which for seven centuries Arab armies straddled all of North Africa and reached into Spain and France. They are also referring to the Ottoman Empire, from the 14th to 17th centuries, at its height under Suleiman the Magnificent and to the Hashemite leaders of the early 20th century Arab nationalist movement, as featured in *Lawrence of Arabia*—not that the monarchy would ever consider creating a caliphate.

JORDAN WAS CARVED OUT of the Ottoman Empire, Germany's wartime ally, by the British in the 1920s and called the Arab Emirate of Transjordan because it was a major crossroads between Iraq (another British mandated territory) and Palestine. Before the First World War, Sharif Hussein, the Hashemite father of King Abdullah and King Faisal, with ancestry to the prophet Muhammad (570AD-632AD), was the guardian of the sacred cities of Mecca and Medina and governed western Saudi Arabia before the rival tribe of Saud drove out the Hashemites. The first Hashemite King Abdullah I took power at a time when his brother, King Faisal, who fought with Lawrence of Arabia to drive the Turks out of Aqaba, was attempting to create a greater Arab state—Syria, Transjordan, Palestine and Iraq. The British, with T.E. Lawrence as their go-between, promised "larger Syria" to the King in return for leading the Arab revolt against the Ottoman allies of Germany.

Meanwhile, the Balfour Declaration (1917)—a gift of Lord Balfour to Lord Rothschild— agreed to the establishment of a homeland for the Jewish people within Palestine, another Ottoman territory, without violating the civil and religious rights of the non-Jewish people. Balfour's negotiating partner was a Russian-born scientist, Dr. Chaim Weizmann:

"A Russian immigrant, wandering around Whitehall and dropping into the offices of the most powerful statesmen in the world for romantic conversations on ancient Israel and the Bible, managed to win the backing of the British Empire for a policy that would change Jerusalem as radically as any decision by Constantine or Saladin and define the Middle East to this day."[1]

Still, Israel's founding father, Theodor Herzl, founder of the Zionist movement, understood that Jerusalem *was* Palestine and should be a shared city, a status unique to the entire world (later affirmed by Weizmann and the Sykes-Picot treaty): "We shall extra-territorialize Jerusalem so that it will belong to nobody and everybody, its Holy Places the joint possession of all Believers."[2]

---

[1] Simon Sebag Montefiore, *Jerusalem*, Knopf: 2011, p. 427
[2] Ibid, P. 398

Columbia University historian Rashid Khalidi has argued that following the Balfour Declaration there ensued "what amounts to a hundred years of war against the Palestinian people." The Sykes Picot Treaty (made in secret in 1916) took effect in 1920, when England occupied Palestine, Jordan and Iraq and France colonized Syria and Lebanon. After the Sykes-Picot treaty and the Balfour Declaration came the League of Nations mandate in 1922, that the British would rule Palestine, formerly part of the Ottoman Empire.

At the end of the First World War, King Faisal tried to realize his dream to establish a provisional government in Damascus as the nucleus for a pan-national state. But in 1920, the French insisted the terms of the Sykes-Picot agreement allowed them to force King Faisal to abandon his dream of a pan-Arab regional state directed from a Damascene court. In this tale of treachery and betrayal, the British installed Faisal as King of Iraq, another ex-Ottoman territory as a consolation prize. "T.E. Lawrence [of Arabia] knew the secret of the Sykes-Picot carve-up of the Middle East and it shamed him: 'We are calling them to fight for us on a lie and I can't stand it.'"[3]

In 1921 after a meeting between Emir Abdullah and Winston Churchill, Palestine became the area to the west of the Jordan River. To the east, Transjordan, "Winston Churchill's sandbox," was specifically excluded from the clause concerning the establishment of a Jewish homeland. Between 1921 and 1946, the Emirate of Transjordan was part of British-mandated Palestine, until it became fully independent in 1946. But while the British did have a military presence here, they never wanted Jordan to be under their mandate the way Palestine was. On May 25, 1946, Jordan obtained full independence from the British and every year that date is marked by fanfare and fireworks. The British insistence on Palestine turned out to be a poisoned chalice.

Israeli historian Ilan Pappe in his groundbreaking 2006 work, *The Ethnic Cleansing of Palestine*, explains how the Palestinians, a peaceful agrarian society used to one invading force after another, and inclusive toward all immigrant groups, had initially been welcoming, employing Jews in their citrus industry, and even accepting Jewish leadership. They had no idea of the catastrophe that awaited them. Small groups of Jews had been emigrating to Israel since the 1930s and were increasingly intent on taking

---

[3] Ibid, p. 425

power from the British and getting rid of as many Arabs as possible under their ethnic cleansing policies.[4]

The empire struggled to maintain peace but after a series of bombings from both Israeli and Arab factions, in September 1947, the British announced the end of their mandate in Palestine on 14 May, 1948 and their plan to give it to the UN. On November 29, 1947, the UN voted in favor of the controversial Resolution 181 to partition Palestine into two states—a Jewish state and an Arab state. Naturally, the Arabs refused to accept the partition of Palestine giving the Jewish settler population 55% of Palestine when the indigenous Palestinian population comprised 70% of the population and owned 94% of the land. The morning after the resolution was adopted, the 75,000 inhabitants of the port city of Haifa were singled out for a campaign of terror by the Hagana (army) and the Irgun gang. The ethnic cleansing of Palestine began in earnest in early December

---

[4] "In [The Red House], on a cold Wednesday afternoon, 10 March, 1948, a group of eleven men, veteran Zionist leaders together with young military Jewish officers, put the final touches to a plan for the ethnic cleansing of Palestine. That same evening, military orders were dispatched to the units on the ground to prepare for the systematic expulsion of the Palestinians from vast areas of the country. The orders came with a detailed description of the methods to be employed to forcibly evict the people: large-scale intimidation, laying siege to and bombarding villages and population centres; setting fire to homes, properties and goods; expulsion; demolition; and finally, planting mines among the rubble to prevent any of the expelled inhabitants from returning...This plan was both the inevitable product of the Zionist ideological impulse to have an exclusive Jewish presence in Palestine, and a response to developments on the ground once the British cabinet had decided to end the mandate....Once the decision was taken, it took six months to complete the mission. When it was over, more than half of Palestine's native population, close to 800,000 people, had been uprooted, 531 villages had been destroyed, and eleven urban neighborhoods emptied of their inhabitants...under international law today a crime against humanity. After the Holocaust, it has become almost impossible to conceal large-scale crimes against humanity. Our modern communication-driven world... no longer allows human-made catastrophes to remain hidden from the public eye or to be denied. And yet, one such crime has been erased almost totally from the global public memory: the dispossession of the Palestinians in 1948 by Israel." Ilan Pappe, *The Ethnic Cleansing of Palestine*. One World Publishing: 2006. P. 2-4.

1947.[5] The massacres that occurred at Deir Yassin became a rallying cry against Jewish atrocities. In December, 1947, the Arab countries—Egypt, Jordan, Lebanon, Syria and Iraq—declared war against Israel, sending "the Arab Liberation Army" (Jaish al-Inqath, literally 'Rescue Army', 'to rescue from imminent danger.')

When the Israeli police came in 1948, the coffee was still warm, the food half eaten on the table. Even Golda Meir, who saw these scenes, lamented they reminded her of the pogroms in Russia. I came to know those Palestinians displaced from their beautiful homes in Jerusalem—the Dajanis and others—and Katerina, Nyla and Emad from Jaffa (to the south of Tel Aviv) and Haifa (to the north). Miko Peled recounts in *The Israeli General's Son* how his father had the right to one of these houses but that his mother refused it, telling her husband, "What right do we as Jews have to dispossess another family because we ourselves have been dispossessed?" She couldn't bear to look into the eyes of the woman forced to leave her house. When I see an Israeli postcard from Jaffa or Haifa, they have a different meaning for me now—that this country should be called Palestine/Israel. Those who found themselves in Gaza still had the keys to their houses in Jerusalem, Nablus, Nazareth or Caesarea, planning to return. Refugees streamed into Jordan and Lebanon from the newly created Israeli state—something that is called the "Nakba", in Arabic, or "catastrophe"—an exodus of almost one million Arabs.

On the same day the British left, May 14, 1948, Ben-Gurion declared the establishment of the state of Israel. By May 26, 1948, King Abdullah of Transjordan had conquered Jerusalem's Old City and all the West Bank. UN mediator Count Folke Bernadotte, grandson of a Swedish king, was sent to administer the partition and proposed a new version giving all of Jerusalem to King Abdullah. But when this made the Jews furious, the Swede suggested that Jerusalem be internationalized, as Theodor Herzl had suggested thirty years earlier. Yitzhak Shamir, a Lehi extremist (and future Israeli prime minister) had Bernadotte assassinated.

The Armistice Israel signed with all five Arab states in April, 1949 divided Jerusalem between Abdullah's forces who kept the Old City, East Jerusalem and all the West Bank and Israel who received the territory to the

---

[5] Ibid.

west on Mount Scopus, the Mount of Olives cemetery, the Kidron Valley. (They were promised access to the Wall but this was not in fact allowed for nineteen years and why it was called the Wailing Wall, because they could see it but not touch it.)

Besides East Jerusalem, Transjordan occupied the West Bank including Bethlehem, Jericho, Hebron, Ramallah, and Jenin. Egypt administered the Gaza Strip; in 1950, Transjordan annexed the West Bank of Palestine, ancient Judea and Samaria, to which Israel acquiesced essentially because they had no settlements there at that time. Our friends tell us that before the '67 war they used to drive to Jerusalem for dinner and come home that night. What used to take forty-five minutes now takes eight hours with all the border and security checks.

In 1951, history took a different turn: a Palestinian extremist assassinated King Abdullah at the Al-Aqsa mosque in Jerusalem, missing his eighteen-year-old grandson and heir, Hussein. Abdullah's position toward Israel was perceived to be too accommodating—after all, a fraction of the population (the Jews) received the majority of Palestinian land. After a brief reign by his son, Talal, who had a mental illness, Hussein (b. 1935) assumed power in 1952 and became the sovereign beloved by all until his death in 1999. In 1958, Iraq's King Faisal II, Hussein's cousin, was assassinated in a bloody coup. Various sects vied for power until 1978 when Saddam Hussein became president. In the same year, King Hussein married an American from New Jersey, Lisa Halaby who was re-named Queen Noor.

In 1967, with the Six-Day war, Israel's goal was to *"finish the job,"* according to Miko Peled, in *The Israeli General's Son*—to take possession and occupy all of Palestine (East Jerusalem, the West Bank, Gaza and that part of Syria overlooking Israel, the Golan Heights). Although the Arab countries were overtly hostile to their neighbor, the war was initiated by Israel and the air forces of the Arab countries were decimated. Thousands of people were left homeless and sent to refugee camps, a kind of no man's land.

The Israeli occupation from 1967 to the present day is illegal. According to international law of the 1920s, no state could take territories by conquest. On November 22, 1967, the UN Security Council unanimously passed the famous Resolution 242 which affirmed the "inadmissibility of the acquisition of territory by war" and the need to work for a just and lasting peace in the Middle East including the withdrawal of Israeli forces from territories occupied in the conflict. It specifically excluded the phrase "all territories," a sticking point for the Arab states. Subsequent decisions by the International Court of Justice have affirmed that this means Palestinians have a right to their territory and Israel to theirs (2003 Resolution 1515) and to the Quartet's Road Map toward a permanent two-state solution.

As George Brown, British Foreign Secretary in 1967, said:

"The Israelis had by now annexed de facto, if not formally, large new areas of Arab land, and there were now very many more Arab refugees. It was clear that what Israel, or at least many of her leaders, really wanted was permanently to colonize much of this newly annexed Arab territory, particularly the Jordan valley, Jerusalem, and other sensitive areas. This led me into a flurry of activity at the United Nations, which resulted in the near miracle of getting the famous resolution – Resolution 242 – unanimously adopted by the Security Council. It declares 'the inadmissibility of territory by war' and it also affirms the necessity 'for guaranteeing the territorial inviolability and political independence of every state in the area'. It calls for 'withdrawal of Israeli forces from territories occupied during the recent conflict.' It does not call for Israeli withdrawal from 'the' territories recently occupied, nor does it use the word 'all'. It would have been impossible to get the resolution through if either of these words had been included, but it does set out the lines on which negotiations for a settlement must take place. Each side must be prepared to give up something: the resolution doesn't attempt to say precisely what, because that is what negotiations for a peace-treaty must be about."

In the months leading up to the Resolution vote, U.S. Secretary of State Dean Rusk stressed to the Israeli government that no settlement with Jordan would be accepted by the world community unless it gave Jordan some special position in the Old City of Jerusalem. The U.S., who presumed Israel would abide by international law, assumed Jordan would also receive the bulk of the West Bank as that was regarded as Jordanian territory even though it was Palestine. Instead the Israelis occupied it; even the Old City is under their control. Jordan disputes Israeli occupation of the West Bank and East Jerusalem (almost 200,000 Israelis are living in occupied East Jerusalem). The Jordanian/Palestinian Islamic *Waqf* remain the administrator of the Al-Aqsa mosque, the third holiest site in Islam where the prophet Muhammad traveled on a night journey from Mecca to Jerusalem, prayed at the mosque and was then taken to heaven by the angel Gabriel.

Although there are 2.2 million Palestinians in Jordan, out of a total population of 6,269,285 (now more than 10 million). With no reliable census, many believe the ratio of those of Palestinian origin to East Bank Jordanians is closer to 70%. Although the vast majority of the Palestinians who came to Jordan after the '48 and '67 wars with Israel enjoy close ties with Jordanians, have Jordanian passports, and are among the most educated and respected Jordanian citizens, some 400,000 refugees were not allowed Jordanian citizenship and are still confined to camps. Some chose not to accept citizenship, believing it would affect their right to return to their homeland. Most of our friends and neighbors are refugees from both the '48 and the '67 wars, though we know some Jordanians as well. There are also currently over 500,000 Palestinian refugees in Lebanon.

Although the majority of the fortunes made in commerce are Palestinian and although many ministers in government are Palestinian, the army is strictly the province of the Jordanians. The reason for this is that thirty years ago, the Palestinian Fedayeen (meaning *opening up*) movement, with the aid of Syria, tried to take over the country from the government of King Hussein (the father of the current King Abdullah) in order to attack Israel and take back their land. The king pleaded with Nasser, the Egyptian leader, to help him defuse tensions with the PLO. The dispute came to a head in September 1970 when three international airplanes were hijacked. Skirmishes took place in Irbid, Zarqa and Mann, and there was an assassination attempt on the king. In 1972, "Black September," a particularly violent PLO faction, attacked the Israeli Olympic team and among other people, mortally wounded our friend Katya's husband, the Jordanian ambassador to India. The insurrection was put down and the PLO in Jordan ceased to exist but it is still a source of resentment in some quarters.

Abdul Nasser's defiance of colonialist hegemony over the Suez Canal in 1956 and his wider message of social egalitarianism made him a hero in the entire Middle East. Thankfully, President Eisenhower refused to side with the British, French and Israelis in the Suez crisis, possibly the only American decision in the Middle East that the Arabs genuinely admire. Nasser was so loved by the people of Jordan that on one state visit the crowd lifted him *in his car* into the air. He chided fundamentalists for assuming he could impose the veil on his wife and daughters. If ever there was a vision of a secular caliphate, it was Nasser's with Egypt as the ruling political-cultural-historical center of the Middle East. He provoked the '67 war by insisting that UN forces leave Egypt's border with Israel. Since Israel knew Egyptian pilots didn't get to the airbase before nine am, they simply destroyed their air force at eight.

In 1978, Sadat, Nasser's heir, tired of war with Israel, concluded a separate peace treaty with Menachem Begin at Camp David with the help of President Carter under which the Sinai Peninsula was returned to Egypt and diplomatic relations with Israel were established, angering the Palestinians, the Jordanians and other Arab states. Ayman al-Zawahiri, a leader with the Muslim Brotherhood who conspired to murder Sadat, has been head of Al-Qaeda since the death of Osama Bin Laden, in June 2011 (with a $25 million bounty on his head). I was shocked to learn from a 2009 *Jordan Times* article that a little over one in four Jordanians had confidence that U.S. President Barack Obama "will do the right thing" while a little under one in seven Jordanians had confidence in Al-Qaeda leader, Osama Bin Laden, according to a Pew Research Global Attitudes Survey. The comparison seemed odious.

In 1993, in the Oslo Accords, Israel acknowledged the PLO as the negotiating team of the Palestinian people in return for Palestine recognizing Israel's right to exist, the acceptance of UN Resolution 242 and the rejection of violence and terrorism. In 1994, Jordan renounced its claims to the West Bank in favor of the PLO, formalizing a 1988 agreement, and signed the Israeli-Jordan Peace Treaty establishing the River Jordan as the boundary. The Palestinian Authority governed the West Bank and Gaza until 2007 when Hamas won an election in the Gaza Strip; this left Palestinians divided until a unity government was formed in 2014.

The perception in the West of Palestinians is of a destitute, helpless, emotional, disorganized, desperate and volatile people. In fact, the majority of the Palestinian diaspora—Christian and Muslim—is just as cultivated as we are and as is the Jewish diaspora. There is a sophisticated, educated Palestinian élite at work in many different fields and in Egypt, Kuwait, the United Arab Emirates, and Saudi Arabia. The articulate and focused Jordanian Queen Rania is a Palestinian who grew up in Kuwait; in Jordan, in the West Bank and in Gaza, there is a strong network of highly successful doctors, nurses, lawyers, teachers, journalists, statesmen, all of whom have the same goals and aspirations for their children as do their counterparts in the West.

FINDING HOME
Amman

AMMAN, LIKE ROME, is a city of seven hills—Jabal Amman, Jabal Al-Lweibdeh, Jabal Al-Hussein, Jabal Al-Jofeh, Jabal Al-Ashrofiah, Jabal Al-Taj, Jabal Al-Qala'a. We live close to the fourth circle of the Jabal Amman, a thoroughfare of eight circles running east and west. But beaming off the north-south axis, from one side of the city to another, one must find the street that snakes its way into the "wadi" (valley) and then the street that makes its way up the opposite "jebel" (hill), a maze of intricate and hopelessly confusing streets. Until the early 1980s, there were only three circles with wild hyenas roaming around the periphery. Then suddenly in Amman, what were goat paths up hillsides turned into streets and neighborhoods, growing ever outward seemingly without any sort of city planning.

Grocery shopping is surprisingly pleasurable. Most anything one can find in Paris or New York is available here (even pork) and the service at the Cosmo supermarket is superior—the valet takes your car, a friendly employee offers an empty cart in exchange for the one that is full; at the checkout line, the cart is unloaded, provisions are bagged, brought to your car, and loaded into the trunk by attendants.

On our first visit to the supermarket, I realized how ambivalent Arabs are toward the West. A man buying a Barbie doll in traditional Arab garb—a long black dress, embroidered with red and gold on the chest, with gold shoes and gold bracelets—approached me. He was holding it in his hand a long time, wondering if it was the right choice. Standing in line at the cash register he told me it was the only outfit available—that all the Western style outfits had sold out and, hesitantly and sweetly, he asked me if I thought his daughter would like it. I felt awkward that an Arab man was asking the opinion of a Western woman about buying this doll, this symbol of the West. Did he mean that he didn't want his daughter to think he wanted her to wear traditional clothes? Or was he worried that she would think he wanted her to? In the end I said, "It's a beautiful choice. She will love it," deciding it really doesn't matter one way or another what I said because she would choose for herself—she is Jordanian and here women have the freedom to choose the way they dress. The horrible black chador is almost non-existent here and it is common to see families at the local mall with the mother in traditional headscarf and long dress and the daughter wearing Western clothes.

Another day at the supermarket, I saw our painter Mohammad, who works in Western clothes in long white robes. I didn't recognize him at first but he made a point of saying hello, showing off his new month-old baby girl. His wife, in a headscarf and a long dress, was open, sweet and cordial, oblivious to the fact that I was dressed differently than she. His easy style and happy recognition made me aware of how fearful I was in that first month, a fear born of ignorance, of course, of men wearing long white robes. I gazed at the fascinating phenomenon of a month-old baby; all babies have that same look of being old and wise—as if they have been reincarnated from their old selves, selves not yet fully shed. I have sometimes thought it a curse to be born female and yet, looking into the parents' shining faces full of pride and joy with their baby girl, I was touched by their assumption that she would be happy.

While the penthouse must be built like a boat, the huge terrace is our ocean. From this desert perch, with fine sand coming in whirlwinds off the desert, we would create a roof garden with palm trees, boxes of gardenias, and bougainvilleas, eventually nicknamed the "hanging gardens of Amman" by one of our Muslim friends – (though I was told making distinctions between Muslim and Christian annoy people because they are unimportant here). Mansour, a great giant of a man and grandson of a prime minister, who always used to arrive with an enormous bouquet of flowers, extravagantly dubbed our terrace parties "Gatsby parties" for the food and music and lively crowd. The consistently dry weather from May to October is conducive to terrace dining and so, the nights are full of wonder—with bright stars and often fireworks on Thursdays, a popular day for weddings.

We found furniture to fit our "boat" at May Khoury's award-winning *Badr Adduja Arts & Crafts* shop: an artisanal dining table with two crossed ancient plows making the base to support a glass-top, wood thresher-backed chairs and a carved wooden bar from India to separate the living room from the kitchen. We had cupboards on the underside of the Bauhaus glass facing west, and designed two small sofas to go around the fireplace. We were told it was to be finished by Easter. Eventually, once our terrace garden was in flower and the tables set up to dine outside, this small inner sanctum became known as "party central."

Technicians told me that it would take five months to get an internet connection! Eventually, Sayel, an enterprising Palestinian, taught me how to check to see if the router was "down" or not. The system may show a strong wireless signal but the router is sometimes blocked (or "down.") Everything was strictly controlled by the secret service, the dreaded Mukhabarat, reputed to be among the best in the world, and perhaps situated in the building across the street, a suspicion that caused some anxiety. "Voicemail" doesn't exist. You call back, and usually, on the third ring, they pick up. Everything is spontaneous and hopefully, by the will of God, "in sha Allah" things will work out. The letter I must send my editor will, in sha Allah, take anywhere from ten days to six weeks by the regular mail and, in sha Allah, four days to three weeks by FedEx.

At the crossroads between Lebanon, Israel, Syria and Iraq—countries (intermittently) at war—Amman was becoming a new center for the Middle East, a safe haven. The increasing value of land was the topic of every dinner party here. Real estate was increasingly big business. In Amman—a 1,000-square-meter apartment here now cost about $1.5 million compared to a 400-square-meter apartment on the Avenue Foch in Paris that cost the equivalent of $6 million. When I told this to my friends here, everyone touched wood. Besides the huge increases in property values, it was just our decision to come that made them curious. Once, running late to a party, I ran into a famous pastry shop in the evening light and on my way out, in the dark I noticed a beggar-woman outside and gave her a dinar (pegged to the dollar). Suddenly she asked, somewhat menacingly in English, "What are you doing in my country?" It gave me pause to think about how little I really knew about Bob's work and why we were there. Although Bob had considered working from Beirut, Jordan's proximity to Iraq made it possible for his construction contacts to slip across the border and meet in Amman with greater ease.

Between 2006 and 2007, the country switched from leaded to unleaded fuel but many cars still emit huge plumes of black smoke. The aggressive driving style is not as bad as Cairo or Baghdad, but drivers sway over road markings as if following camels on caravan routes. Perhaps in an effort to evoke fear, the policemen directing traffic wear the German spiked helmet of the pre–World War I period with a back flap to protect against the strong sun, perhaps adapted from the Ottoman model.

It is impossible to walk around Amman because there are few overpasses and fewer sidewalks. The sidewalks that *do* exist are in terrible disrepair, forcing pedestrians to use the main streets and there are no parks to speak of. A friend was recently paralyzed from the neck down after being hit by a car. There is no subway system and the only public transportation were old buses with attractive purple curtains fringed with gold in the windows—the kind you see in American hearses. Six months after our arrival, new buses were introduced but they must be for the laborers because the maids take taxis, which are reasonably priced.

Travelers tend to listen more carefully to sounds. Trucks carrying goods drive through the neighborhoods advertising their wares. I chided myself for imagining that the one broadcasting "Battiix" from a loudspeaker, was a call to arms; in fact, he was selling "watermelons"! Another with a little bell sound, like an ice cream truck, sold gas canisters for the oven or barbecue. Gas isn't piped into houses here and replacing your gas tank is a monthly, spur of the moment occasion. Two tanks are generally bought and when one is used up, you call the gasman on his cellphone or hail his truck.

Three topics kept resurfacing here in the news: the Arab-Israeli conflict, the debacle of the Iraqi war, and water-deficiency. Jordan is the fourth water-poorest country in the world. It mostly comes from the Sea of Galilee (lake of Tiberias) they "share" with Israel. (More on this later.) Town water is rationed to a weekly supply and if you go over the amount, you might find yourself without water (as we do the night I am writing this, because of the construction) in which case a private company comes and fills your tank. But in the Jordan Valley, near the river, delicious fruits and vegetables are grown and brought to Amman's roadside stands and sold for nothing.

Strangely, the telephone company leaves its bill off at your house with the Egyptian night watchman who is supposed to deliver it to your door. But if you are not there, he might forget and your telephone service is cut. Or sometimes the bill never arrives and the service is cut and it takes days to get the line back on. Direct payment with the bank takes months.

The construction all around us adds to the noise pollution. The pounding of jackhammers during the day and even into the night could be coming from the wadi where they are extending the hospital or from the a fourth circle bridge near the prime minister's residence, connecting Jabal Amman with Abdoun, a chic suburb, which is mentioned in the Bible as Abaddon, a "place of destruction," a crematorium in ancient times (Job 26:6, Proverbs

15:11, Revelations 9:11). Today Abdoun is filled with palm trees and handsome villas proving the truth of the legend of the phoenix—out of the ashes, life springs eternal. The peacock, symbol of immortality, renewal, resurrection and royalty, is depicted on ceramics in the region. The Palestinians here believe deeply in their renewal and resurrection.

With the noise upstairs and construction around us, the Four Seasons spa has been one of the great saving graces and has made the move bearable and restorative. The hotel has the look of a palatial fortress—a garden of Babylon—with huge pillars rising from the top of a hill and twelve enormous palms backlit at night and swaying in the breeze. It is a kind of eyeball on the world; when I pull up in our rental car and give my keys to the valet, there are usually six or seven black Mercedes there already, and sometimes armed soldiers, tanks, and cement roadblocks. There are few black chadors.

The desire to please among the Arab people reminds me of American hospitality to the power of ten. The Four Seasons training is over the top. As I was getting out of my car, the back to my new black Nokia cell phone fell off accidentally as we were entering the Four Seasons. When the car valet saw the back to my phone was missing, he immediately took out his own—the same make and model—and offered me the back of *his* phone! We were passing through the metal detectors where the attendant was checking us through. The woman at the security checkpoint welcomed me by saying, "The world is shining now that you are back."

After a lengthy exchange of greetings with the personnel at the Four Seasons Hotel—the tradition in Arab countries—I entered into the turquoise (which, when worn as a stone, protects you from envy) and wood Zen-like environment of the spa where I work by the pool, studying essential Arabic—among others, "Allah yatik el afyeh," *May God give you health and strength* and "As-salamu alaykum!" *Peace be with you.* The Four Seasons had become a refuge away from the incessant flooding at our house, a problem that would last our entire first year here.

Spring rainwater was leaking into the living room from the roof through the ceiling and electrical sockets. The living room was a wading pool, and, as it turned out, we lived out of boxes an entire year! We had to re-paint the décor three times. Eventually we went to court to be remunerated for the damages and we won. I learned that I should have called him every day—in a fit of rage—if I had wanted it done. As to fixing it, everyone's favorite word here is "*boukra*" (*tomorrow*) followed by the dreaded "in sha Allah," the perfect excuse if God does not will it. Even Lisa Haleby, or Queen Noor, the American (fourth) wife of King Hussein, (the father of the current king, Abdullah), a graduate of Princeton in urban planning, discovered on her first date with the king that the palace was leaking. During her tenure as queen, she was able to help create the first building codes, we learn from her memoir, *Leap of Faith,* but they don't work. There are no building inspectors so the builders ignore the law and construct with cheap materials without insulating the roofs against the rain with disastrous results.

MY FOUR GUIDES

AT A TEA KATYA ORGANIZED, I was happy to meet some other outspoken, educated women: Yolaine, the French wife of the Brazilian ambassador; Donatella, the Italian wife of the French ambassador; and Katerina, of Palestinian and Russian background, a close friend of King Hussein. These four became my inner circle within The French Group, mostly wives of ambassadors here or distinguished visitors. Thanks to my fluency in French, I was admitted, allowing me, week by week, a unique viewpoint into Arab culture. From time to time when the anti-Americanism started to grate on my nerves, I would leave but I always came back. For the departing wives of ambassadors there would be a "Livre D'Or," hand-written messages from the whole group, who would also organize dinners to see them off.

Yolaine, a pretty blonde, majored in English at Paris Nanterre receiving her masters in American Literature, with her thesis on Philip Roth. As a child, vacationing in La Rochelle, a seaside port, Yolaine observed the wives of NATO's American naval personnel chewing gum and smoking, and wearing Bermudas and pointy sunglasses—everything a French girl was not supposed to do—and she fell in love with the freedom of Americans and was happy to serve in Chicago at one time. Donatella, a vivacious Venetian countess and *savante*, author of XVIc. art history, felt the absence of a library here. Katerina a legendary dark-haired beauty of yore, won the admiration of King Hussein. Widely read, her open-mindedness rendered her somewhat enigmatic—it is hard to see where one stands with someone so accommodating—noted that there were many Lebanese-Palestinian marriages here. Many of the elite here went to the American University of Beirut before, during and after the wars with Israel. Being "the culture-vulture" of Amman, she pulled a stack of tickets to concerts out of her bag to sell. I learned from them that the Arabs have a problem with Turkey because of her alliance with the U.S. and Israel; also because the Ottoman Empire controlled the entire Middle East until the Arab Revolt of the early 20th century.

Katerina's father was born in Nazareth; in the 1920s, he went on horseback to Beirut every day to study law. "Most of the lawyers here started with my father." In 1970, he was one of the first 4,000 lawyers to be chosen to be part of the society "Peace Through Law Around the World." Her mother was born in Kiev but grew up in Iran because her father was a banker there. Afterwards, Katerina's mother moved to Aleppo, Syria, and then to Haifa, Palestine where Katerina was born. After the 1947 war, the Israelis occupied their beautiful three-story villa, the mayor's house.

Katerina, (a Christian) and Katya, (a Muslim), discussed how, increasingly, Jordanian women cover their heads and don long robes. They said that women had greater freedom in the 7th century when the Qur'an was written, than they have today. I mentioned that the president of Iran had just banned women from stadiums, and from attending soccer matches. They shook their heads. They told me they hoped American women would speak up for Muslim women; and that America would open a dialogue with Iran, with whom the U.S. has not had positive diplomatic relations since 1979. They also agreed that Hamas should recognize the state of Israel as the world community does, excluding Iran, Syria, Saudi Arabia, Iraq, Lebanon, all of Muslim Africa, Indonesia, etc.

Later, Bob and I watched a documentary about Israeli military preparations for an attack on Iran, and about Iran test-firing rockets in the desert that could easily reach Israel. He jested, "Isn't Armageddon great!" The absurdity of it called forth humor but we both knew it was comic relief.

MAJID, MAMDOOH AND EMAD

FROM MY DESERT PERCH I often found myself pondering the terrace, inspecting the tiles and wondering what was wrong and why so much water was getting through. One day, Emad, our carpenter referred by Katya, and Majid, our driver, whom Bobby used in previous visits, came at the same time to inspect the terrace. Both had become protective of me: Emad insisted that I was *his* sister and Majid responded, "No she is *my* sister." I supposed it was permissible to speak with a married woman if she was your sister. And then they told me happily that in the Muslim faith, a man can take four wives. I asked, "And can a woman have four husbands?" With that, they looked away.

MAMDOOH

MAMDOOH, OUR EGYPTIAN GARAGE attendant, made the trio of three of the most help. A jolly young man in his thirties, he made sure the water tanks on the roof were filled, brought fresh bread and the *Jordan Times* in the morning, carried groceries from the car to the apartment, tea to the workmen, and washed the cars in the evening. As was the case with those in his position working in most buildings here, he had a wife and four children in Egypt dependent on his salary. His ever-present smile and comical temperament made him Bob's favorite. There was infighting in our four-story building over the six parking slots because the owner promised all of us two slots. (One downstairs neighbor employed by Microsoft had a Porsche, a Jaguar and a Kia.)

Here a woman is defined by her male relations. MamdooH called me Um Max, mother of our first son and Bob was sometimes called Abu Max. (Ummah, a near-homophone, meaning the Islamic community is the 'motherland.') On forms, my Jordanian name was Bint George and Um Max—daughter of George and mother of Max. In Syria and Egypt, if there are no sons, mothers are called by their eldest daughters' names but not here.

MAJID

WE NEEDED A DRIVER IN the beginning to become accustomed to the difficult geography, to learn you may have to go in the opposite direction to get somewhere, because a deep valley is obscured from view. Getting lost is part of the process. In 1978 the Ambassador Hotel in Shimesani was the only building apart from the International Traders Building. At the French ambassador's house, I met an American psychologist treating U.S. soldiers for PTSD, who expressed her sympathy for anyone driving in Amman and advised exploring small sections of the city surrounding our house then working outwards in concentric circles. I wished she had been able to tell me more about her life treating the soldiers; my anxiety paled by comparison. Even FedEx drivers had trouble finding out where we lived and packages took ten days to arrive. The surest postal method—the one used by embassies—is hand delivery. It took the Brazilian Embassy driver two or three days to locate us in order to obtain written acceptance of a formal invitation.

On a scouting trip months prior to our move to Jordan, I asked our driver, unaware he was a practical joker, if he knew how to get to the Dead Sea; he mused, "Oh no, I have never heard of it." After pretending for some time, Majid burst out laughing. A heavy-set man of medium height in his fifties with full cheeks, a long nose in proportion with his long oval face, Majid's bright brown eyes sparkled with fun, sometimes followed by a furtive glance. A Palestinian from Hebron, Majid came to Jordan as a baby in the early '50s when his father worked for Glub Pasha, the British officer and friend of Lawrence of Arabia, who ran the Jordanian army (called the Arab Legion) until King Hussein dismissed him in 1952—the British were "not well-liked," according to Majid. He remembered a time when a crowd attacked his father and Glub rescued him. I felt that Majid was one of our protectors here.

Adjacent to the urban sprawl that has engulfed Amman was Majid's favorite restaurant, a throwback to their desert village culture, Bedouin-style with tents outside for summertime. Passing a Damascene fountain, the Oriental welcome to visitors being the luxurious sound of water, a woman in Bedouin garb sat at the entrance making large flat loaves over a dome-shaped wood-fired bread oven. Inside the large round room, fifty large square tables, inset with brass Damascene trays, each one set off by eight low black leather chairs. Old doors with slats in them were fastened to the ceiling and antique lamps hung from them. Waiters in tuxedos swarmed around us with fresh vegetables, hummus, tabbouleh and baba ganoush, followed by grilled fish (on ice that you choose at the entrance) or lamb and beef on kebabs. One scooped up the food with the freshly baked bread, and the waiters brought heated jasmine water (available at supermarkets) at the end of the meal in little finger bowls. Both veiled and unveiled women socialized and at almost every table men, women and girls were smoking from hookahs, the social but deadly fruit-flavored tobacco water pipes, nargileh, or as the Lebanese say, 'hubbly-bubbly' (one pipeful is like smoking thirty cigarettes.) As we walked out, the owner proudly showed us his white Rolls Royce and Majid mentioned his house was modeled after a French chateau.

EMAD

MY CARPENTER, EMAD, WHOM I met thanks to Katya, appeared when it pleased him. There was my design of our furniture and then Emad's interpretation of my design. His two cellphones would ring constantly, with conversations sometimes conducted simultaneously. In his forties, of medium height with dark doe-like eyes, he had two furniture and re-upholstery workshops, and traveled to Istanbul and Pakistan regularly. Patient and thoughtful, Emad was able to mask an impressive temper with a ready laugh. I became aware of Arab intuition, as if an invisible antenna was attached to the back of their heads. The secret of his success, he told me, was that he didn't talk down to his employees. It is vitally important not to offend people's dignity. I told him I thought his temper did not hurt—this muffled anger creates an undercurrent of fear, a trait he shared with Bob. He was customarily courteous to foreigners, both a religious duty and the national creed.

Emad took me to the store called Kalha, with a breath-taking variety of fabrics—Indian-made green silk embroidered with gold and blue flowers and vines, and white silk with red and green wool flowers and vines—the fabled riches of the Orient—muslin originally came from Mosul, damask from Damascus, gauze (qazz), mohair (mukhayyer) and taffeta (Persian taftah, the Persians having brought the silkworm from China) attesting to the importance of the textile export trade in the region. Everywhere you do business here, tea or coffee is offered and you are expected to take the time to converse before you buy. Reconciliation between the tribes is performed over a ritual cup of coffee, "qahwa," first discovered in Ethiopia in the 15th century, introduced in the 16thc in Istanbul, Europe in the 17th century. It is considered rude to be in a hurry and refuse a cup, and was considered no less rude for me to refuse to envision myself as a foreign tribal leader, an ambassador without portfolio. Mr. Kalha told me that, like Emad, his family came from Jaffa, refugees of the '48 war; he started as an errand boy and worked his way up.

One day, driving past an oval-shaped park, we passed a house with a lovely lemon tree and saw a boy of eight reaching up to cut the fruit. As I was admiring the lush trees that give forth fruit even through the middle of winter, Emad said, "You know this is one of the oldest parts of Amman. When the first Palestinians came in '48, they went to an area known as Al-Mahatta meaning train station. I was born in Jabal Al-Lweibdeh in 1960 and then the family moved to Jabal Al-Hussein in '67. The city of Amman ended at the third circle and twenty years later, the fourth, fifth, sixth, seventh and eighth circles were built." Inspired by the boy, I grew my own lemon tree on my terrace garden, and later wrote a poem entitled, "Desert Fruit":

> How long the unripe fruit stays on the vine,
> This Mediterranean fruit in the desert.
>
> The green lemon buffeted by two winters
> And sprayed by storms, clings, steadfast.
>
> Full of the future, it burgeons from a source
> Of slow moisture and sweetness,
>
> Like the longing in love, ripening essences
> mingle in unconscious wonderment.
>
> Like the mother full of the heavy child, swaying
> In the slow dance of their shared destiny.
>
> A concept like trust does not belong, nor conscience,
> Nor forethought, nor virtue. Unconscious and pure,
>
> Life is called into being. The way a friend looks
> at another over some sentiment, quietly shared.
>
> No need to hurry, the lemon tree seems to say—
> "patience!"—not knowing, just being.
>
> And suddenly inside itself, full of its essence,
> It removes itself from the source, and drops.

WHAT ARE YOU DOING IN MY GARDEN?

THE KING RECENTLY VOICED support for a dialogue between Iran and the West, stressing that an arms race is the last thing that the Middle East needs. He also said that Jordan would do everything it could to support the newly established government of Iraq and, "We hope that others in the region will help the Iraqis also." I told Emad this book concerned peace in the Middle East and asked him what he thought of the problems between Hamas and Israel, the Sunnis of Syria backing the Sunni regions and the Shia of Iran backing the government of Iraq. His face darkened but his voice was hardly audible, "It is all the Americans' doing."

His eyes were hot but his temper cool.

"Excuse me?" I asked.

"The Americans created Israel and the other problems," he replied, from taking down Mossadegh in Iran to giving Israel carte blanche, to the disaster of the war in Iraq.

Emad said that what angers Muslims has more to do with the arrogance of the U.S.—with the attitude that it is the world's policeman. When speaking about Israel and Iraq, he voiced the same opinion of many Americans frustrated with politics: "You know when you go into somebody else's garden, they get angry. It's the same thing here. People in Iraq or Syria or Palestine are all asking America, **'What are you doing in my garden?'**"

We were driving through Jebel Webde in search of a light fixture and went into a local shop. I noticed the rapport with the owner and surmised, "You've known that man a long time."

"His father was a friend of my grandfather," he answered. "My mother and father came from Jaffa [the ancient Tel-Aviv port city] on vacation for one week in 1948, just before the war. After the war, my father didn't want to go back to his house in the downtown area of Abu Kbier. He couldn't go back, not with other people on his land. Before, he had once hoped to, but now there is no hope of returning."

Bob concurred, "Jaffa is not even on the table."

The Palestinians' land was confiscated within living memory and there hasn't been any compensation. Initially, the Palestinians didn't want compensation. As mentioned already, they all had their keys and they were planning to go back. They took their deeds with them. Whereas the rich

Palestinians and middle-class integrated into society immediately and have Jordanian citizenship, there are still three and four generations of Palestinians living in refugee camps in Jordan, who came from other Palestinian towns overtaken by Israelis in '48 and '67—without citizenship, unable to leave and living in hardship.

Palestinians dominate in commerce while Jordanians run the government and military. It is perhaps a human trait to live in quiet rivalry with one's neighbor, each believing they have more stature over the other. Palestinians, kings of commerce, believe they run the country, and Jordanians, believing that they are the aristocrats with roots in the original tribes, resent it. Nyla, our Arabic teacher, is also originally from Jaffa, the ancient and beautiful port town south of Tel-Aviv, and was schooled in Jerusalem. Her father started a tobacco company here in the 1920s when trade in greater Palestine, west and east of the Jordan, was peaceful and prosperous. She was married to a Jordanian ambassador who died young so their children are half and half.

It is taboo to discuss prejudices between Palestinians and Jordanians. Emad (whose last name is Azab) told me, "A policeman stopped me but before he wrote the ticket, he asked if I was an Azab from Salt [Jordan] or from [the West Bank town of] Nablus," because he was a Jordanian from Salt and he couldn't give a ticket to "his brother." He laughed and said, "Naturally, I told him I am from Salt. In fact there were many Palestinians [like Nyla] here before 1947." When I asked Nyla about the prejudice, she said, "Emad is right. There is a prejudice. Jordanians feel they are in the minority now so they become defensive which is why they speak the way they do about the Palestinians."

Emad drove Bob to the court of justice, to be judged an honest man and fingerprinted ("not necessarily in that order," said Bob). King Talal, who ruled Jordan briefly after King Abdullah's assassination, (and before he was diagnosed as a schizophrenic) created the current system of government—a Chamber of Deputies elected democratically, currently numbering 102; the Senate, also called the King's Council, has grown from twenty members since its inception to forty, and the Supreme Court is made up of five judges (more on the Justice system on p. 141).

That night we invited Emad and Majid to dine with us on our terrace. Emad brought his wife and five-year-old son, Racan. "My goal," Bob said, "is to speak enough Arabic to understand what Racan is saying." It was a beautiful, balmy night and there were fireworks one could see on the horizon, in various parts of the city. Majid got the hubbly-bubbly going and Bob and he smoked their apple tobacco contentedly. Majid got up suddenly to pray, standing, then bending at the waist and touching his forehead to the ground. The reason they pray with the head to the ground, he told me, is to thank God for all his blessings. Sometimes, Majid told me, he prays for others. "I pray for you, that you are strong. I mean it…I am very serious." The night before, Majid, typically poetic, told Bob he was lucky to have me because God is with me and that I was sweeter than the sweetest flower in the garden.

Majid told us about the custom that when Allah is very good to you, you sacrifice a lamb and offer raw meat to the poor. "I'll take care of it," Majid said. How biblical, I thought. "Where, and to whom do you give the lamb?"

"There," he pointed from our balcony, beyond the next wadi on the hills where the Palestinian refugees live. He told us we should distribute the warm, freshly slaughtered lamb with our own hands.

As in *The Great Gatsby*, the green light is a symbol of longing. At night from our terrace, the green lights of a thousand mosques light up in the distant hills. I considered the longing of thousands of Palestinians who still hold the keys to their houses in Israel, never expecting that their exodus would be permanent. One can't help but believe that the prayers of millions here are for a peaceful solution to Arab-Israeli conflict including compensation for property. They are a patient people. Indeed, in speaking of the leaks inside the house, "Mrs. Emad" whose name is Maram, serene and abstemious, calmly said, "In sha Allah," the way a maiden aunt from New England would say, "Patience, dear."

The commander of a police station across the street had asked to meet us. I asked Emad if I needed to accompany Bob. He said, "No need." (Emad never said no, just, "No need.") Mixed company is a foreign invention. The female is rare and exotic here. When I consider that women here are not discussed, I wonder if that's a blessing or a curse.

AL-QAEDA

A FEW WEEKS AFTER OUR arrival in the spring of 2006, in Hibhib, north of

Baghdad, Jordanian police tracked down and killed the terrorist responsible for the bombings of their three hotels. "It's George Bush, Emily," a friend told me. "Everything he has done has inflamed the Arab world. It isn't what happened in the time of Mossadegh in the '50s, it's right now. Osama Bin Laden is a hero to many people," he said shockingly.

His viewpoint was by no means unanimous: the news of the death of Zarqawi, the chief Iraqi Al-Qaeda leader, arch-foe of the monarchy, caused great celebration. Bobby happily joined the crowds gathered at the third circle. Great cheers went up, horns were honking and drums were beating all over Amman, and the fireworks, a common event for every wedding here, were more elaborate than usual. The prayers that night were particularly moving. There were two muezzins, their voices threading the night air.

In Zarqa, Zarqawi's hometown, police stopped a live Al Jazeera broadcast, confiscated their tapes and camera and detained Abu Hilala, the journalist interviewing Abu Qudama, Zarqawi's brother-in-law, as he was praising the dead Al-Qaeda leader and depicting him as a hero. Nasser Judeh, the government spokesman, said, "Some people felt that Al Jazeera's coverage or approach wasn't balanced and that emotions were charged, especially for the families of those who died in the November bombings." The authorities banned filming in Zarqawi's hometown and required the media to obtain permission, which Abu Hilala admitted he had not done.

Four Muslim brotherhood lawmakers paid condolences to the family of Zarqawi, whom the king described as a mass murderer. The king gave an interview to *Der Spiegel* in which he said, "I think people have to agree on zero tolerance to terrorism. I can't fathom making Zarqawi into a hero. The overwhelming majority of the Islamic movement in Jordan is moderate and peace-loving. There are some elements in Jordanian society who are misguided individuals. They have to redefine their relationship with us. They have been working in the gray area for the past decades," the king said, referring to certain members of the Muslim Brotherhood. "I think society throughout the world now has to decide what is good and what is evil. I believe the majority of the Brotherhood wants a good future for this country and a good future for their children. I think we can work together as a team."

I tried to imagine George Bush working "as a team" with the Muslim Brotherhood. Whereas many in the Brotherhood renounced violence decades ago and supported elections, four of their parliamentary representatives here expressed sympathy for Zarqawi and were charged with "fuelling national discord and inciting sectarianism." It is evidently a tenuous balance for an enlightened monarch in a country governed by Sharia law (the law of the Brotherhood).

The king went on to say that the Palestinian issue remains the worm that eats at the core of Arab society, inciting extremism; that Israelis and Palestinians should be encouraged to concentrate on the great final goal of a genuine peace, with a secure Israel, living side by side with a viable, independent Palestinian state. The tension recently became evident when Hamas won a majority in the Palestinian elections. Weapons—missiles, explosives and machine guns—were smuggled by Hamas into Jordan, according to the *Jordan Times*, and the government "indefinitely" postponed a visit by Mahmoud Zahar, the Palestinian Foreign Minister. We were told that Hamas was increasingly popular here because Hamas helps people in extremis. There were "cells" here and they were growing. The discovery that Hamas aimed to destroy Jordanian military installations triggered training across the street—mock house-to-house searches followed by fake bomb explosions. Some generals came for a review of the troops.

EASTER SUNDAY AT MT. NEBO

YESTERDAY THE ANGLICAN CHURCH of Amman celebrated the Eastern Orthodox Easter at a dawn service at Mt. Nebo where God allowed Moses a glimpse of "the Promised Land" provided the Jews respect the covenant and the Ten Commandments. It was thrilling to finally be here where one can see the Dead Sea and on a clear day, Jerusalem. At a simple ecumenical service in a cloister—a ruin of Roman columns and mosaics of crosses—birds shrieked their greeting of trumpet and song from the rafters of the tin ceiling, diving for the bread of Christ on the altar.

After the service, I met U.S. Army Captain Mary Kay whose job was to help Western relief agencies help civilians in Iraq. Dressed in a yellow suit, she had the relentlessly positive look of a woman who is never in a bad mood. She said she had no operating budget, making me wonder if the army, occupying a foreign country, realized that not having any budget for civilian relief would fuel the gathering terrorist storm.

Anton and Salwa invited us to lunch to sample Mansaf, Jordan's national dish—boiled spring lamb and rice with a yoghurt sauce. The intuitive and jocular Anton, heavy-set with half-lidded eyes, a professional skirt-chaser, knows everyone and works for no one, or so he made it seem. Salwa invited the ladies to sit at the dining table while Bob, ever adventuresome, joined the men in trying the Bedouin tradition of forming the lamb and rice into balls and popping them in their mouth. Anton, irreverent and amiable to foreigners, vaguely claimed to have been among the first to introduce information technology to Jordan in the 1980s; he is now the owner of Nobile, among other restaurants. His wife, Salwa, an English professor at the University of Jordan, is pert, short, sharp, and, I noticed, has pretty legs—in a country where it is rare to see legs. Neither of their two accomplished daughters—one a journalist and the other a comedian—were there but we met their niece and her husband (whom Anton called her "roommate"), a surgeon who operates on emergency cases—soldiers with head wounds flown out of Iraq. The enemy, of course, aims for the head so he is very busy. Diana, an American from Maryland, a redhead with a ready laugh, has spearheaded Basra Prosthetics. The continuous Al-Qaeda bombings are due to the military presence and civilians in cars behind the convoys are also hit. Dr. M.A. Yousif, director of the Basra Prosthetics Clinic and a rheumatologist—a gentle man with light copper skin, told me that just this year, since the beginning of 2007, there have been 5,000 civilian amputees—men, women and children—and that the numbers will increase. Currently, he is using the cheapest type available supplied through the Red Cross or Red Crescent and he is looking forward to receiving new materials from Diana—an MRI scanner, the latest prosthetic tools, carvers, machines. Bob reminded me that the ICRC, the International Committee of the Red Cross, has not been able to supply the region; their doctors and nurses have had to withdraw from Baghdad after their lives were threatened.

CHAPTER TWO
May

I AM TOLD THAT THE reason that Muslims adhere to their tradition of praying five times a day is not just religious but to discipline a Middle Eastern spirit inclined to in-fighting and prone to the frustration that accompanies unemployment and poverty. Once I told a Muslim businessman that I too pray five times a day. He looked shocked, as if all Westerners are by definition degenerate and dishonest (failing to enforce UN resolutions on the Israeli land grab of Palestine, starting a crazy war in Iraq, etc.).

The degeneracy that springs from selfishness (avarice, and lack of compassion) is the root of the ethos that created the fanatical Islamic sect, Al-Qaeda, according to Reza Aslan in *No God but God*. When the Jordanian Al-Qaeda leader, the Sunni, Zarqawi, declared war on the infidel, he meant both the so-called "heretical" branch, the Shia and, like our Puritans, non-believers in general, the near and far enemy. The populist cry, "resistance," or "muqawamah," Hizbollah's battle cry, resonates in Palestine, the Sudan, Egypt, and Lebanon. The Shias and Sunnis in Iraq may be fighting for dominance, but the call to "resist" the American occupiers wins passionate followers in both camps.

Friday is the Muslim holy day. The long sermon broadcast throughout the city on the first Friday of every month is the voice of an angry cleric that we first mistook for a brawl. The speech began with a reminder of the importance of Arab unity in an increasingly sectarian world; it went on to advise which foot to wash before you pray and other hadiths (a set of instructions interpreting the Qur'an, collected since the death of the prophet.)

In this very conservative country, I was much taken aback when at 8 o'clock one morning I heard loud knocking and stumbled to the door in my nightgown. I don't know who was more surprised. Three snipers in bulletproof vests and large rifles seemed to be asking for access to the terrace. Evidently the king and queen would be in attendance in the garden below our window at the Zahran Palace for the 60th anniversary of the independence of Jordan from the British (May 25, 1946). Not speaking their language but typically graceful, Bob made them laugh by putting his hands up in surrender. MamdooH brought a pot of tea and he, Bob and the snipers squatted down together in the shady part of the terrace and drank tea.

I asked Bob to request that the commander grant advance notice of such visits; we later discovered these were the king's personal guards, outside the commander's control. But since Bob's visit to the commander, the loudspeaker behind our house has been turned off. I had already been informed that between midnight and 4 am, when Bob comes to bed, God's (Allah's) heart is supposed to be most open to prayers. The 4am call to prayer, gently sung by a muezzin farther away, became a soothing antidote to Bob's lifelong battle with insomnia—just as others were waking up.

ARABIC

THE SOLDIER INCIDENT MADE us eager for our second Arabic lesson—an arduous process requiring much concentration. Nyla became one of our favorite people—someone who always sees the positive side of life. An Orthodox Christian of penetrating wisdom and common sense, she is honest, strong and kind, and with a ready laugh and effervescent charm. Well-dressed and elegantly coiffed, she takes charge immediately. If you are shy, as I am, she will draw you out carefully with encouraging remarks. Bob said, "If she were a WASP, she would have been a great debutante." Widely read and traveled as the widow of the former Jordanian ambassador to Chile, with a long roster of international students, she is insightful about culture and history. In other words, she is what the French call, "une grande dame" (a real lady) and Bobby dressed carefully for each of our lessons. Trained as a nurse, she is known for her medicinal wisdom. Her mother was Queen

Noor's tutor and after Nyla's husband died, her mother asked her daughter to help her teach the wives of ambassadors here, having been one herself.

The basics of Arabic are greetings and courtesy. Sharaf means *honor* in Arabic and Sharif means *the Honorable*. Islam is taken from *sallem*, the verb meaning *Give everything up to God*, and also, to *say hello*, and to *bless*. It is courteous to say, "mabsutiin bisallmu aleek" (*we are happy to say hello to you*) even if you don't mean it. That seems very American to me, a sort of pervasive friendliness without meaning. Laced through the Arab language is the word peace. I ponder whether as many American soldiers would have been killed had they known five (disarming) key phrases: "assalamu alaikum"—*peace be upon you*; "hamdellah allah essamalah"—*thank God for your peaceful return*, "Allah ysalmak"—*May God preserve you*; "salamtak"—*may the peace help you recover from fatigue or illness*, "kol sana wa enta salem"—*may there be happy returns of the day*; "wa enta salem"—*and to you, peace as well.*

Arabic, a language of consonants, seems so very foreign. Here vowels are unimportant where for us, a, e, i, o and u form the framework of our parlance. Nyla puts it in breezy sort of way: "We are liberal with our vowels," meaning an "a" or an "e" is interchangeable and sometimes they are invented. The word for fish is SMK with the vowels inserted—samak. We have asked everyone what the word for *maybe* is and they reply, "yimken" or "mumken". It turns out that yimken means *maybe* and mumken means *possibly*, a subtle distinction. The word for *husband* is the same as *walnuts*, "jauz" or, in classical, "zauj." Nyla tells us of the similarity between the Arabic word for *member* or *friend* (a9daa ?) and *enemy* (a9daa)—the question mark representing a glottal stop. This speaks yards about how quickly one could become the other. Likewise, the word for *mosque* is "jaame9" and *university* "jaame9a", one vowel, and *society* ("jam9ia"), one vowel more.

We learned that "sam" (pronounced "sham") means *Damascus*. A similar word, "sams", means *sun*. "Naturally 'sams' in Arabic, the word for sun, is feminine," Nyla told us, "because women are like suns."

"We Arabs find Damascus is more beautiful than Amman because it has water," she continued. "Foreigners like Amman because its hills have character." Jordan being historically *the country of Damascus*, ("bilaad issam"), there are group taxis there and back but the service is irregular. (We took one once but the Syrian lady returning with us to Amman thought Bob was "a pig" to assume he could sit on the same seat with her.) There is also a daily ferry service from Aqaba to Taba, Nuweiba, or Sharm El Sheikh (Egypt).

BILAAD ISSAM

JORDAN IS AN ARCHEOLOGIST'S paradise and it became a hobby of ours, along with the history, during our time here. There are at least 200,000 archaeological sites—biblical and otherwise. Jordan is in the center of the Great Rift Valley, a geological schism that runs from northern Syria to Lake Victoria in east Africa. Early humans—*homo erectus*—literally walked up this valley over a million years ago from Africa. In the 1990s, Dr. Gaetano Palumbo, an Italian archaeologist who is currently the World Monuments Fund's Program Director for North Africa, the Middle East and Central Asia, excavated fossilized mammoth bones and flint objects dating to a million years ago in Zarqa, north of Amman. Now Jordan can be added to the list of countries outside of Africa with the earliest evidence of *homo erectus* (the others being Ubeidiya in Israel, Georgia, China, Pakistan, Spain and a controversial one in Java). Civilizations in Jordan are layered here over millennia (with a somewhat inexplicable abandonment of the settlements during the Bronze Age.) Barbara Porter, the director of the American Center for Oriental Research, reported the discovery of an Iron Age sculpture in downtown Amman and added that there hadn't been nearly enough done about our earliest origins. The beautiful downtown Amman Roman ruins of the Citadel are considered "late" here.

Agrarian life began in the Fertile Crescent about 10,000 years ago, in Palestine, Phoenicia, Assyria and Sumeria. The idea of a God emerged here even before that, 14,000 years ago. The Jordan Valley was Christian before it was Muslim, having emerged from the influence of Judaism, and became part of the Byzantine Empire—Christian Orthodox Empire—the heart of Eastern Christianity until Istanbul fell. Muslims and Christians have lived in peace for centuries. We are constantly told, "When you have President Bush talking about the Crusades, you rub an old wound, and are getting it wrong historically and every other way because the thing was healed a long time ago."

In the U.S., Arabs are typically thought to be Muslim. In fact, Palestinian Christian Arabs are descended from those that carried the first cross out of Jerusalem and across the Jordan River for safety. Arab Christians and Muslims pray to the same God, Allah.[6] Historians date Amman—or Rabbath Ammon in the Old Testament—to 6500 BC. This land of the Ammonites, the Moabites and the Edomites (Genesis 19:37-38) trace their origins to Lot, a nephew of Abraham. Abraham, the patriarch of all three religions—Judaism, Christianity and Islam—was born in Ur, in what is now Kurdistan. Lot's cave is perched on top of a mountain overlooking the Dead Sea, east of the Jordan River.

From pre-Roman times to the 19ᵗʰ century, caravan routes connected Damascus—the largest city and a cultural center—and greater Damascus ("bilaad issam"), as Jordan used to be called, with the entire region. When the Arabs took over Amman (Philadelphia) from the Romans, the silk routes went toward Jerusalem and Beirut from the Medes in Persia. Jordan was not on the silk route although the part that intersected with the silk route may have come through Amman on the way to Damascus. It is on the incense and spice route, however, and this is what made the Nabataeans of Petra so wealthy. Incense, of major use in Greco-Roman temples (including embalming) and later by Christian churches, grew in southwest Arabia (now Yemen and Oman) and was originally brought by the land route—camel caravans—through Petra and then on to Gaza. One of the three wise men, Melchior, might have come from Yemen, but most people believe the Magi came from Media, the Medes region of what is now Iran but which was then Persia. Everything was interconnected. Historically speaking, all our religious

---

[6] Reza Aslan, in *No God but God* concurs regarding the links between the three Abrahamic faiths: "All religions are inextricably bound to the social, spiritual and cultural milieux from which they arose and in which they developed...Prophets are, above all, reformers who redefine and reinterpret the existing beliefs and practices of their communities, providing fresh sets of symbols and metaphors with which succeeding generations can describe the nature of reality....Like so many prophets before him, Muhammed never claimed to have invented a new religion. By his own admission, Muhammed's message was an attempt to reform the existing religious beliefs and cultural practices of pre-Islamic Arabia so as to bring the God of the Jews and the Christians to the Arab peoples. '(God] has established for you (the Arabs) the same religion enjoined on Noah, on Abraham, on Moses, and on Jesus,' the Qur'an says. (42 :13)"

stories and legends come from the area extending from the Fertile Crescent, from Baghdad to Damascus to Jerusalem. The Bible and pre-Biblical stories unfold in the area—in the legend of the flood in Mesopotamia, the Ark ended up on Mt. Ararat, in Turkey, but the story originated in Iraq and is depicted on tablets in Ashurbanipal library.

The first Islamic prophets of the Holy Qur'an—Abraham, Moses and Jesus—are Jewish, and Muslims venerate them. "Most Arabs, particularly Jordanians, have nothing against Jews," Dr. Humam B. Ghassib, the Christian director of the Arab Thought Forum, explained. But he said that the politics of the Israeli state, in particular the persecution of the Palestinians, has caused so much suffering. The worst part of it is instilling in people the fear of extremism, a tool used by the Zionists to keep Palestinians in a colonial state, to perpetuate injustice. "Instead of having this siege mentality with the background history of Masada and the Nazi concentration camps," Ghassib asked, "why don't Israelis speak about the long tradition of tolerance when the Arab ruled Andalusia in Spain, from the 8th to the 12th centuries before the Catholics drove the Jews out? In *Ivanhoe* by Sir Walter Scott there is clear indication of this fact." Jordanians speak with reverence about Andalusia.

Ghassib, a professor of theoretical physics at the University of Jordan, attributed Jordan's stability to the exceptional wisdom of the Hashemite family—the whole dynasty beginning with Adbullah I saying there was nothing wrong with negotiating with your enemies. King Abdullah knew the Jews were backed by the superpowers of the day and he wanted to have a compromise. He realized that the Arabs could not have everything so why not decide on a partition—the Jews would have their state and the Arabs another. Abdullah I's brother, King Faisal, later King Faisal I of Iraq (a prominent figure who took Aqaba with T.E. Lawrence and corresponded with the British officials) thought of the Jews as an essential minority in the area, not (at first) as a political entity. They always sought to understand the world game of politics and never fell into the trap of demagoguery.

The religion of Oisifia, centrist Islam, enlightened moderation, is something HRH Prince Hassan, King Abdullah's uncle, has been writing about since the mid-1980s. "Even the Muslim Brotherhood are not extremists except a tiny minority which came from Afghanistan. The Hashemites base everything on consultations—on 'surra' in Islam—with tribal leaders and prominent figures, including the Muslim Brotherhood. There is dialogue, and when there is tension, it is always relative tension."

Then there's the issue of the caliphate. The Sunni-Shia schism was more political than religious, Ghassib told me. After the death of the prophet, there were currents and cross-currents. There came the great difference in opinion between those who wanted an Islamic state on the model of the Roman Empire or the Byzantine Empire (Sunni) and others, a traditional tribal state (Shia).[7] One wanted to be more contemporary and have more interaction with secular people (Sunni). Eventually great (Sunni) leaders succeeded in establishing the Umayyad dynasty in Damascus and Abbasid dynasty in Baghdad that were more worldly.

The Hashemite dynasty, the dynasty of the Sharif of Mecca, was built around a ruler who was at once imam, the religious leader, and the ruler of Mecca by Ottoman decree, and thus both a religious and world leader. "Under Ottoman rule, Jordan was the 'badlands' of the Empire whose nomadic tribes struck at will and could not be punished because no Ottoman army would follow or fight in the harsh desert conditions. They were left alone if they did not jeopardize their interests in Syria, Jerusalem or the Hejaz," according to the historian, Ghazi bin Muhammad. "Concerning the Arab revolt of WW I [as romanticized in *Lawrence of Arabia*] it was daring for one Muslim tribe [the Hashemites] to wage war against the [Ottoman] Empire."

---

[7] Thomas Friedman, in *From Beirut to Jerusalem*, gives a clear description of the difference between the Sunni and the Shia: "In the seventh century, shortly after the death of Islam's founder, the prophet Muhammad, a dispute arose over who should be his successor as spiritual and political leader, known as caliph. One group, the majority, argued that Muhammad's successor should be appointed through the process of election and consensus by the elders of the community, as was the tradition of the desert. Sunna in Arabic means tradition, and those who held this view became known as the Sunnis. A minority faction, however, argued that Muhammad's successors should come exclusively from his own family and their descendants. They insisted, therefore, that his first cousin and son-in-law—Ali—be appointed as leader of the community. Those who held this view became known in Arabic as the Shia, or 'partisans', of Ali. The Shiites were clearly influenced by the notion of the divine-right monarchy of pre-Islamic Persia (Iran)."

Jordan, an Islamic country with a constitutional monarchy, must nevertheless be under Sharia law in civil matters like marriage or there would be a revolt. The Hashemites have legitimacy because they can trace their lineage to the prophet through his daughter Fatima, wife of Ali, and their son, Hassan. Prince Hassan (and the entire Hashemite dynasty) follows the Sunni school and at the same time, he is descended from Ali, the Shia leader. It's indivisible. That is exactly why many Iraqis would like Prince Al Hassan to play a role because he is the only person who has Sunni as well as Shia within him.

The Wahhabi fundamentalist sect that came into being in the late 18th century has only recently begun to spread widely, injecting their puritanical element into politics with disastrous results. In the 1980s Osama Bin Laden, a Saudi Wahhabi, gave financial support and joined the Mujahideen in Afghanistan in fighting the Russians which later became the Al-Qaeda movement. But the current Al-Qaeda leader, Zawahiri, received his Wahhabi training in Egypt inspired by President Sadat's perceived betrayal of the Palestinian cause.

NASSER AND NOOR

WE HAVE COME TO LOVE so many Jordanians, including, of course, Nyla and her large family, Hana and Faazi, Katya, Katerina, Anton and Salwa. Nasser, of Turkish origin, and Noor, of Bosnian origin, have been living in London for twenty-five years but returned here the previous year and to our immense delight, we became close friends. In 1918, Nasser's Turkish grandfather was the station-master of the Istanbul-Mecca railroad who witnessed firsthand the rise of the Arab nationalists against the Ottoman Empire. The Turks under Ataturk wanted one language, one identity. With the Ottoman Empire dead, the French and British moved in to fill the void. Nasser's father studied at "Jebel Lebnon" in greater Syria (as Lebanon did not then exist) and taught in Damascus. An anti-colonial nationalist, he was arrested by the French in Syria and fled to Jordan where he met his wife and became a teacher in 1921-22. "We got rid of the British and the French, then the U.S.; now it's the Russians. Somebody loves us," Nasser joked.

Nasser's wife, Noor, is descended from Bosnian families who arrived in Ottoman Palestine in the late 19th and early 20th century due to sparring between the Austro-Hungarian and the Ottoman Empires. The Ottomans gave Noor's grandfather a significant parcel of land along the Mediterranean Sea in the ancient Roman village of Caesarea, south of Haifa. In February 1948, after the Haganah expelled Caesarea's non-Jewish inhabitants, and destroyed their homes and their mosques in what was known at the "Nakba" or "catastrophe," the area became an affluent suburb with homes owned by Prime Minister Netanyahu and Baron Benjamin de Rothschild.

In that same month, the family built a house on Mount Carmel in Haifa that had to be abandoned in May. Noor was born in June of that year. Her father, a doctor, could have gone to work in London but he felt deeply about the British betrayal of Palestine and so he packed up the family car and drove to Kuwait where the salaries were ten times those of other Arab countries; eventually, he was able to send all the children to British boarding schools.

In 1965, the family bought a huge tract of land in Sweileh overlooking the Jordan Valley but it wasn't until the '67 war on Palestine that the camps in Jordan's Baq'aa valley started filling up. Meanwhile, Noor graduated from the American University of Beirut and became one of Jordan's first female TV announcers. "We have all moved on," she said resignedly. Though a fierce advocate of the Palestinian cause, Noor, like the vast majority, just wanted to live in peace. "It's over," she said, meaning the two-state solution is the only solution. Another friend commented, "If the United States wants it this way, then we shall accept it." But this is not a universal Palestinian viewpoint and, of course, everyone at least expects compensation for their losses, a respectable fraction of the billions we give Israel annually.

WE HAVE TO BE LEFT ALONE

JORDAN DOES NOT HAVE a free press. Indeed, there are laws against the press speaking out against the government. "The *Jordan Times* is all fairy-tale stuff—happy man in happy land here in Jordan," Bob was saying. "The king has just received the president of the Republic of Ingushetia. Where is Ingushetia?" he asked. (Russian North Caucasus)

"Freedom is a difficult issue for Jordan," Dr. Humam Ghassib, the director of the Arab Thought Forum, told me. "Europeans and American have to realize that you don't have democracy in the absolute. It's not a full-fledged thing you can impose on a country. It has to come from within. He told me to look at the British system—how there was violence for a long time and it evolved very differently from France and the United States. "We have to be let alone to think it out and rise up gradually, step-by-step and pay our own price."

Many in the region are not free to write about certain aspects of religion and *everyone* is afraid of being ostracized if they go beyond their limit—religion, politics and sex. Social, not political, tolerance is the problem, he said. There was an Egyptian woman, then in her eighties, who was persecuted for her feminism, and a famous philosopher who was ordered to stop his work on mysticism. Author Naguib Mahfouz was almost ninety when someone attempted to assassinate him—stabbed him in the neck (!).

GOING TO CHURCH

FEAR IS OUR WORST ENEMY, the Bible tells us. At the Anglican Church of the Redeemer, near the first circle, nestled in the old part of town, Arab Christians celebrate in Arabic on Sunday (the first day of the Muslim week) but on Saturday nights, the services are in English. Reverend Malcolm White's sermon concerned Christ "going to the other side," referring to the passage in St. Mark when Christ is sleeping with his head on a cushion while the waters of the Sea of Galilee become stormy and of the disciples becoming afraid, waking up Christ who asks, "Where is your faith?" Reverend White spoke of the importance of fearlessness and going to the other side, literally or figuratively, with faith.

Afterwards, we met Jane Taylor, whose ready laugh, strength and beauty immediately drew us to her. After earning a degree in medieval history and moral philosophy at St. Andrew's University in Scotland, Jane, who came to Amman in 1978, has worked as a teacher, publisher, television producer, photographer and author of eight books. *Jordan: Images From The Air*, published in 1989, had royal financing and Jane became a minor celebrity when she managed to hang out of helicopters to take her image of, among other things, the fortress of Machaerus, home of Herodias. Herodias's sin was in marrying her living ex-husband's brother, Herod Antipas. It was against Jewish law to divorce her husband and then to marry his brother while her first husband was still living. After St. John the Baptist criticized their marriage, they beheaded him. Herodias had a daughter, Salomé, by her first husband, Herod II, but the historicity of Herodias pushing Salomé to dance and Salomé asking for the saint's head (according to the gospels of Mark and Matthew) is at best dubious. The ancient historian Josephus said Antipas put John the Baptist to death for political reasons because he feared his "seditious influence." The story of the evil seductress, Salomé, is a legend, an invention of the church.

Shortly before his death in 337 AD, Roman Emperor Constantine converted to Christianity; historians view it as a political act to undercut the old guard. "The Christians were the best organized group in the Byzantine Empire and Constantine realized that if he had the support of the Christians, he could do what he wanted so it was absolutely political. He continued to behave in a seriously unchristian way—disposing of a wife and a son—and it is said he was only baptized on his deathbed."

In 324, Constantine divided the Holy Roman Empire, into west (at Rome) and east (at Constantinople), creating the new (Greek) capital bearing his name. When Rome fell in 476, the Holy Roman Empire moved to Byzantium's Constantinople and that remained its center until Charlemagne was crowned in 800AD. In 1456 the Ottoman Turks defeated the Byzantines and ruled until the First World War. Jane and I spoke of the Ottoman Turks' influence over Jordan and the tolerance toward Christians ("Dhimmi") in the Ottoman Empire who were protected under Sharia law.

Jane's current project concerned the pilgrimage of a 4th century woman named Egeria from a coastal town in southern France to the Middle East ("some say she was a nun, but she could have been a rich independent woman"). We discussed the spirituality of Petra and her book *Petra and the Lost Kingdom of the Nabateans*. "Pagans have gotten a bad rap," she said, laughing. "Just as you think you've come to understand the Arabs, you realize you've been on the wrong track", and advised me to follow the path of the tribes.

THE TRIBES

AT A LARGE DINNER THE other night, Bob distressed a member of the Beni Sakhr tribe who headed one of large IT companies here (and was married to a beautiful French woman, and a member of the French group) by comparing his name to Benihana, the New York Japanese steak house. The man's prideful reaction inspired a more in-depth look at the tribes of the Hejaz.

All Jordanians of East Bank origin, ethnically Arab and either Muslim or Orthodox Christian, belong to a tribe—either settled, semi-nomadic, or nomadic, writes Ghazi bin Muhammad in *The Tribes of Jordan: At the Beginning of the Twenty-First Century.* These consist of: the "warlike" Beni Sakhr, the most powerful tribe with thirteen clans, the large northern tribe of Beni Khalid (mostly Syrian, Palestine and Kuwait), Beni Hassan, Beni Attiyah, Beni Hamidah; Ahl al Abal consisting of four large clans; the Huwaytat of the south consisting of twenty large clans; the Sardiyyah and Sirhan who used to rule modern Jordan but which is now ruled by the Hashemite clan of the Quraysh tribe. The 1986 Jordanian Election Law respects the essential nobility of the tribes who are members of Parliament and many Bedouins are members of the Jordanian army.

"Urban Jordanians including the oldest of the settled tribes regard Bedouins as 'natural brigands and uneducated, dirty cutthroats' whereas Bedouins and semi-nomadic tribesmen regard townsfolk as 'soft, effete and dilapidated peasants who eat too much, talk too much, sleep too much and hide behind trade to swindle them at every opportunity.'"

The tribes defend each other to survive and, in this ethos, a person views the world in concentric circles with himself at the center, then his family, extended family, tribe, country, nation, co-religionists, and finally humankind (a seemingly universal order of priorities). "It is this same mentality at the root of fractious individualism that has characterized Arabs as a people throughout history (with the brief exception of the period of early Islamic conquests) and that is in turn responsible for their having been historically and politically disunited and hence weak. Arabs have never achieved anything significant as a people except when united and they have never been truly united except under Islam."

From an Islamic perspective, he said, the world is seen as a kind of "temporary stage" where people can practice virtues and worship God through religion as revealed through the Holy Qur'an in order that the soul attain eternal felicity in the hereafter. Religion is infused into the very texture of daily life. The West's greatest sin for a Muslim is pride. Humility and patience are the most admired virtues. I am reminded of a line from T.S.

Eliot's *Four Quartets*: "The only wisdom is the wisdom of humility." When the Danes and the French published the cartoon that was seen as an insult to the prophet, the simplest solution, Majid told us, would have been to be humble and apologize. How you live, what you do and say, feels as if it carries with it a life or death sentence.

Majid told me he thought I had special healing powers. "Do you believe in a djinn?" (a spirit that can live in the body), Majid once asked me. I said I thought it was possible. Another asked if I could help a friend whose wife was sick with nightmares. Holy men had come and told the spirit to exit her body not by her mouth but by "the fingers of her legs" (her toes), not unlike the Chinese chi, the energy center in the ankle which with the appropriate pressure exits through the feet. This reminded me of an incident in *Come Tell Me How You Live*, when the women of the villages come to Agatha Christie for medical advice.

TOUCH WOOD

EARLY THIS MORNING I opened an account at the local HSBC. The account manager, Rania, a Christian Palestinian, said most Jordanians are dying to go to America and asked why we had decided to come to Jordan. I told her our families had been in America for three hundred years and that we needed a change (she smiled); also, I explained, having lived in Paris for twenty years, we wanted to see another part of the world. She said she hoped we would be happy in Jordan and then touched wood, asking if that was a custom in America as well. (A pre-Christian ritual to ward off bad luck by touching the spirits of sacred trees such as oak, ash, holly, or hawthorn; or, possibly, also a Christian practice relating to touching the cross.)

She asked me about the war in Iraq and what I thought about it and said that the rumor was that one million Americans had been killed (not 2500). I said that was nonsense, that both political parties voted in favor of going to war against a mass murderer who, bad intelligence told us, had WMDs. She said the Jordanian and American governments have an excellent relationship; she said her brother married an American and that for her, our two peoples are one. I agreed with her and mentioned a few people we knew in town—"Oh, she's Circassian and he's from Madaba," confirming what many have said about the importance of tribal affiliation. She told me she was a Christian from the north near Ajlun, where Saladin, the great Arab warrior, had his magnificent fortress. I asked her if it was true that the tribes are the key to understanding Jordan, as I had been told. She gave me a look. "There aren't many Muslims in America, are there?" she said. I said I thought many Muslims had emigrated there but few Americans have converted. I said there is one famous case—Cassius Clay became Muhammad Ali. She looked disapproving and quietly added, "Ours [Christianity] is a great religion."

Later that day, we dined with Anton at Nobile. His Christian family is from Karak, the site of a magnificent castle built by the Crusaders, who came to "Oultrejordain", old French for beyond the Jordan, in the 1100s (See Maps p. 303). Anton's family left Karak because one member wanted to marry a Muslim; so the clan packed up, and moved to Madaba—the city near Mt. Nebo where Moses looked over the Dead Sea towards the Promised Land—and became the leading Christian tribe of the region.

We were introduced to Ica, managing editor of the *Jordan Times* who told me she and everyone she knows used to look up to America. Now, because of human rights abuses, Guantanamo, and invasions of privacy at home and abroad after 9/11, she and everyone she knows no longer regard America as the home of the free.

Anton was also eager for us to meet Laetitia, a high-level businesswoman in the energy and security sectors, a Palestinian Muslim and a dark-haired "Ursula Andress" born in Jerusalem, who married a Frenchman and was a Washington socialite during the Reagan, Ford and Bush Sr. administrations. She spoke of growing up in Jerusalem in the '60s and how it never mattered whether you were Muslim, Christian or Jewish. She described peaceful childhood memories, emphasizing that the international city was not a dream. "It was a reality, a reality that has to do with the intense spirituality of Jerusalem."

"Is it true," I asked, as I had been told since my arrival, "that Jordanians 'hate' Israel?"

She answered, "Jordan doesn't hate Israel. Jordan does business with Israel, a country of supreme arrogance, who is nevertheless a neighbor. Israel uses Jordan as a buffer state to the extremist states. The reason why Jordan is stable is because Israel wants it to be so. A stable Jordan is important because of the long border we share."

As a child, it never occurred to her which religion her friends were and no one wore any headscarves. But then she noticed that a vivacious creative girl who worked for her was suddenly lured into wearing the hijab at the mosque she visited on Fridays; Laetitia asked her why she was clothed like a nun. After the funeral of a relative, fundamentalists came to the house of the bereaved to convert them and she asked them to leave. They read about the services in the newspaper and prey on the vulnerable.

When visiting Yemen in the '80s, she refused to wear the veil when negotiating a concession with the government because she wanted to be considered an equal. However, when she went shopping in the souq, she had no problem wearing one. "You know my father once asked me if I didn't feel safer putting it on in some countries and I told him, 'If I wore the veil, I would no longer be equal to the men in business.'" Laetitia is an advocate for renewable energy and building strong grid interconnections with countries around the Mediterranean where peak demand varies. "Regretfully," she said, "the political situation in some countries prevents the trading of electricity."

MARRIAGE AND DIVORCE

I HAD COFFEE WITH MARIA, a Palestinian, a striking widow in her early 60s whose husband was a high government official, and her friend, an attractive brunette in her 50s from one of Jordan's leading families. We discussed the importance of touch to the human race and how here the societal norms are reversed—men hug and kiss men but not women. They don't even shake her hand. "There is no dating here. Women are out of reach, although now many more go to university. Men can't touch them so they touch each other. But men like women," she said.

"Marriages are arranged and inter-marriage between cousins is common since that is the only permissible way for young people to see one another," Maria said. "Muslims and Christians don't marry outside the faith." She added that in Jordan, as recently as 1978, brides were not present at their wedding ceremonies. In the Qur'an the bride's witness—generally her father—and the groom hold hands and a white napkin is be placed over their hands as they consent three times to the union *without the presence of the bride*. In her memoir, *Leap of Faith*, Queen Noor wrote about being the first to ask if she could be present at her own wedding and to *herself* consent three times to marry. Today, of course, there are lavish weddings with brides in white gowns. "Everything is so focused on appearances," she said. "I can't go out in a track suit because it shows the body. I would like to spend more time in America."

"There's no divorce here, right?" I asked.

"They divorce like hotcakes here, what do you mean?" she answered.

"I mean women can't divorce here," I asked.

"Ah, I see what you mean, unless she has 'Hada' [translation: proof, something, perhaps a photo] in her hand, you mean. Normally, no," she said.

"Men can," I say.

"*Of course*," Maria bellowed, "Men can divorce in five seconds if they want to. He says *'You are divorced,'* and she has to leave the house. He has to think it over and if he wants her back, *she has to come back*. Women cannot say, 'You are divorced,' and the man will have to leave the house. *He has to say it to her.*"

"Three times, right?" I ask.

"Three times or once. I'll tell you something funny—if the man divorces the woman three times in five years or ten years, the first time he divorces her, he can bring her back. The second time he divorces her, he can bring her back. The third time he divorces her he can't bring her back unless she marries somebody else, divorces him and only then can he bring her back. Some men pay a man to act as a fake husband and tell him, 'Please marry my wife,' just for the night; and of course, officially he has to sleep with her but of course between them the real husband gives the fake one some money and tells him, 'Don't sleep with my wife; just marry her on paper and divorce her tomorrow.' Then they get married again. It teaches men a lesson not to divorce three times."

"HONOR" KILLINGS

HOW WE AMERICANS TAKE for granted our equal rights, free speech, and freedom to choose. Our neighborhood, one of the oldest in Amman, boasts sweet-smelling flowering bushes—orange blossoms, jasmine, bougainvillea— and an evening stroll in this gentle climate is a treat. One night, returning home, I noticed an elderly Arab was out for an evening stroll with his three wives, all of different ages, all wearing a headscarf, and all walking behind the old man in a dish-dash. I became conscious of four sets of eyes following me as I was driving alone and scarfless.

Arab women are the center, guardians of the honor and arbitrators of the family...and also targets for abuse. Women rule the roost and rarely leave the house. Traditionally, the woman is the storehouse of the family honor. There are few social welfare programs here because only 10% of women are "employed"; they are expected to take responsibility for the family. In a conservative country where women are covered, flesh excites, and if aberrations occur (like, insults, harassment, pedophilia) the score is settled within families. Our Arab-American friend remarked on an increase in child kidnappings in Atlanta and expressed amazement that Americans call the police.

We learned a lot through our Arabian nights, among other things, that dating can lead to death. Brothers or fathers murder sisters or daughters for having spoken to a man who is not related to her, on the smallest suspicion of sin; the murderers are rarely punished severely, if at all, and it is called an "honor killing."

We dined with a cosmopolitan Jordanian family as American as our own—the funny father, the mother who was the power behind the scene, the six happy children and nine cute grandchildren. One of the daughters lived in New York City with her Jordanian husband and two small children. She was thin and beautiful like the Arabian tree for which she was named. She said the Queen failed to stop the practice because Islamic extremists dominate the parliament, because it has its origins in misinterpretations of pre-Islamic Arab tribal codes and because the legal system also weighs heavily against women. (Bob hypothesized that it might have to do with getting rid of an annoying member of the family or with the division of the inheritance.)

Globally there are 5,000 cases of honor killings per year, overwhelmingly in Islamic cultures. Human Rights Watch reports a yearly rate of 25 and 30 "honor" killings in Jordan, making them the most common type of murder of women in the country and one of the highest per capita rates in the world. 95 percent of the women killed in Jordan for alleged violations of honor were later found to be innocent of immoral behavior (i.e. virgins.) Each year another 50 or 60 at-risk women are placed in administrative detention at the Jweideh Women's Correctional and Rehabilitational Centre for periods sometimes exceeding three years, imprisoned as a preventive measure because there are few protective services for women in Jordan.

Sentences for "honor" killers, a misdemeanor in Jordan, typically range from three months to two years, but average only six months, with time out on bail counted toward jail time. Although "honor" killings are against the tenets of Islam, violate seventeen international human rights conventions on which Jordan is a signatory, these malevolent articles (97, 98, and 340) of the Jordanian penal code are ferreted out to obtain lenient sentences. Every member of the monarchy has condemned these killings but no one has been able to change the codes.

In one survey, half of Jordanian Christians believed "The occurrence of 'honor killings' in Jordan is too high," whereas half of the Muslim respondents expressed some level of disagreement with this statement. To understand the issue of "honor" killings, I asked Dr. Ghassib why honor killings still exist. "The main thing is that it has nothing to do with religion. Nothing! Honor killings are committed by Christians as much as by Muslims [though the survey's results would seem to question this]. The tribal, traditional culture of close-knit villages is shameful but something the leadership can banish only by dialogue. I know a sad case of a girl who was killed by a Christian tribe that I belong to—a distant relative killed by her father. The mother tried to hide [it]. She ran away with a Muslim, lived with him for a little while and came back. There was shame all over. And the father and brothers could not get over that she lived with him in sin without being married. In fact, they did not have enough time to get married."

"Were they both killed?"

"No, that's the point. In honor killings, they concentrate on the poor woman though the man has as much to do with it. Usually they associate honor for some historical reason with, excuse me, virginity. The only legal way to date is marriage and not civil marriage but the traditional religious marriage."

That there are men who have multiple wives and girlfriends is of course hypocritical, he said, but the tribal mentality (which sanctions this) isn't as powerful as it used to be because of the challenges of outside factors—the international communications technology revolution, satellites, internet, travel abroad, cultural interaction.

Appearances are deceptive. "A Lebanese singer who exposes so much flesh may have a higher moral level than a girl wearing the veil. Once you are branded as this or that, it is terrible," he concluded. Poverty complicates the issue. The Muslim Brotherhood has the financial clout to pay women to be more Islamic in appearance, not appealing to the belief, rather to their needs. There is prostitution and "unusual behavior" in the Islamic world. "A religiously conservative journalist in the daily press pretended to pick up a girl, totally veiled and he told her, 'Do what you like but don't abuse the religious outfit.' With more females in university, many with the best grades, Jordan has moved far away from the day when girls were restricted from going to school. But the question of the role of women in society remains. Women are still persecuted. If one is objective, one couldn't possibly tolerate the trash one sees in the Western press [debasing women]. If you go to the Qur'an and the hadith, the Sunna, you find the highest respect for women— women took part in battles and there is great respect for mothers, not unlike the Jewish mother.

CHAPTER THREE
June

AT DINNER CHEZ Katerina, of Russian and Palestinian Christian extraction, and her husband Roland, a suave Frenchman who grew up in colonial Algeria, we were treated to French cheeses from Paris and, among other things, a large cooked ham, a rare sight in the Middle East (haram). We were happy to have been asked to what was Katerina's Sunday night tradition. With this select crowd—twelve, mostly Palestinian Christian couples—we began to discover the minefield of disgruntlement about the '48 and '67 wars, a constant rehashing of the events and replaying the history of colonialism from the Anglo-American policy toward Palestine/Israel.

In 1978, there were 50,000 illegal Israeli settlers, the Likud initiative to "make concrete the right to Eretz Israel." By 2006, it had grown tenfold, an estimated half a million illegal Israeli settlements in the West Bank and East Jerusalem. By 2015, that number grew to 700,000. Israel occupies territory deep in the West Bank and connects the settlements to each other with roads prohibited by the Palestinians from even crossing that road. Some describe this as apartheid since "the Wall" (or "barrier" as Israelis describe it) is designed to lock these settlements, roads and their surrounding lands into Israel. Hearing it for the first time was as nauseating to me as it was to hear of the Jewish ghetto stories of Warsaw.

There was one oval table of mostly women, and another large oval table of men. At first, it didn't occur to me that sitting with the men (and one other woman) was out of the ordinary. Gradually I began to feel that they really wanted me to know of their obsession about the loss of their land during the wars with Israel and the continued occupation of new Palestinian land. Our dinner partners fingered their worry beads and cast anxious looks in our direction. Not realizing the sensitivity of the issue, I asked why Hamas hadn't recognized the state of Israel, as had the Americans, the British and the entire international community. A simple response could have been, "Because Israel doesn't recognize the state of Palestine." But instead, one man began to dispute the Nazi death camps and said that perhaps it was 4.5 million instead of 6 million people who had been killed.

In those days, without knowing anything of the history of their suffering, to hate Israel to the point of reducing the number of people killed in the holocaust was nauseating to me and I left the table, joining the company of women inside. Meanwhile Bob stayed outside and told the assembled group of Palestinian men that his father, a Swiss doctor with the Red Cross and the son of a Calvinist clergyman, had personally treated survivors of the holocaust. Another American there, Dave, said his maternal grandfather was moved to donate money to the founding of the state of Israel after his son, a U.S. Air Force pilot, was shot down by the Nazis over Italy. At that point, *all the men got up* and left the party; Udo and Yolaine, the Brazilian Ambassador and his wife, stayed to try to calm everyone down. This was the first of two incidents in the course of the year that would strongly influence our life here.

A few days after Dave's remarks, Yolaine called asking me to come for coffee to discuss what had happened at Katerina's. She said she feared talking about it on the phone because of eavesdropping. I was grateful to be taken under her wing. She talked of how Dave's comment had spread like wildfire - a large rock thrown into a small pond—and said that we should be careful. She explained how, "They hate Israel—not so much Jews. People here can gossip and be very cruel, Emily. It is best not to discuss Israel."

Bob likes to play the devil's advocate, is mischievous by nature and enjoys creating controversy in conversation. I have given up guessing his political orientation. Bob's response to Dave's faux pas was amused indifference. "I am pro-Arab, pro-Israeli and anti-hypocrisy." Arabs are, by nature, kind, well-mannered and sentimental; they are also very angry. I felt then that I must evolve as an unofficial ambassador—someone eager to listen and make clearer who the Arabs are. I came to discover that the diaspora forced out of Palestine in the '48 and '67 wars is 6 million, exactly the same number as the number of Jews killed in the holocaust!

There is a direct link between this injustice and the helplessness that breeds terrorism. Indeed, the next day, we read in the *Jordan Times* that the Jordanian government had arrested another four Islamic Action Front MPs for paying condolences to Zarqawi's family, and for calling him a "martyr" and a "holy warrior." Hundreds marched to the Lower House to protest the MPs' actions. Many were relatives of the sixty killed in the November 9, 2005 bombing of the Hyatt, Radisson and Days Inn hotels. Addressing the marchers, Lower House Deputy Speaker Nayef Fayez said, "We respect your sentiments...we are against terrorist acts, their masterminds and those who carry out such acts. Our condemnation stems from our religion and reflects the country's stand towards terrorism."

A MUSLIM DINNER

A FEW WEEKS AFTER OUR arrival, Emad and Maram reciprocated our terrace invitation and we dined with the whole family—her father and young stepmother, her sister-in-law, and Emad's father and mother. Emad's father was an intensely religious man who had the keys to his mosque and opened it for the 4 am prayers. It turned out to be a cultural awakening. They were strictly religious Muslims, originally from Jaffa, south of Tel-Aviv. Sadly, Bob told me, they would never get their land back; that the subject was not even on the table.

On this occasion, I was nervous about what to wear and chose something to cover my arms and legs—a white linen pantsuit with a white linen shirt. I hoped that a large bouquet of white roses and lilies would be acceptable to our hostess. I had learned in France that every flower has a hidden meaning—chrysanthemums symbolize death for example, and yellow roses, jealousy. According to American (and French) custom and good manners, I stretched out my hand to Emad's father, making sure to maintain eye contact, as I was taught to do by my father during his race for the Senate when I was ten years old. The old man shook my hand but lowered his eyes and walked away, shaking his head. Afterwards, I learned that women here, particularly in religious families, do not shake hands with men. The custom is that men aren't supposed to really even look at women outside their family. It was odd but somewhat satisfying to be invisible, quietly observing everyone. That seemed acceptable. Everyone was happy, joking and laughing.

Maram came up behind me and asked if we liked "Jews". After our last experience, we became flustered and said, "Oh no." She then approached the others, pouring out glasses of freshly squeezed "jews", looking befuddled. Because they couldn't speak English well and we couldn't speak Arabic, the evening was awkward at first but my enthusiasm for Arab food warmed them a little.[8] Jordanian cuisine has been described as "Middle East international," a composite of Jordanian, Palestinian, Syrian and Lebanese. From Jordan comes *Mansaaf* (boiled lamb with a yoghurt sauce) and the delectable method of cooking stuffed lamb (*xaaruuf maHshi*), roast beef and chicken buried in the earth or sand or roasted on a spit. From Palestine come all the stews such as (my favorite) *Makloubeh*, upside-down meat and rice with eggplant. From Syria and Lebanon comes the world-renowned *mezzah*—twenty small dishes set out on round trays—served as a first course followed by grilled fish or meat.

Unlike in Western society, the men—Bob, Maram's father, Emad's father and Emad, our translator—were served first. Afterwards we went out to the terrace to eat our dessert of fresh melon. I was given the place of honor with Bob and the other men; and I thought how peculiar that none of the women were there. Maram's father, who had family in New Jersey, mentioned that he spent a lot of time trying to get a visitor's visa.

Finally, Maram, Emad's wife, came out and invited me to join the women. I told her I didn't speak Arabic. She said only one person didn't speak English, so I went in. Men and women separate after dinner here in the religious families (unlike Anton's family, although even then, the women tend to congregate with other women and the men with men.) The other women were inside, on the sofas, stretched out in comfort. They welcomed me with their eyes. An old Western was playing on television quietly and out

---

[8] Tiny green zucchini squash are stuffed with meat and spices, rice and meat wrapped in vine leaves, cucumber and tomato salad with lemon and the baba ganoush--bake three eggplants for one hour and peel an onion & tomato, combine with parsley and lemon.

of the corner of my eye, I found myself becoming involved in the plot, wondering what sort of Western appeals in the Arab world.

My hostesses were variously clothed: Emad's mother, who didn't speak English, wore a long black robe and white headscarf; Maram, a headscarf and Western clothes but with long sleeves and pants; and her sister was without a headscarf and in casual Western clothes. She asked whether I liked Jordan. I said Jordanians were most generous and welcoming. Then she asked why most Americans don't like Jordanians. I supposed she meant the common misperception that all Arabs are terrorists and America's love affair with Israel. Her comment surprised me and I wondered whether she was projecting, whether most Arabs don't like Americans. I said I wasn't sure that was true but if so, it was probably because Americans don't know the Arab world very well.

Our conversation seemed completely natural. But perhaps not wanting things to get too cozy, Maram's father suddenly *snapped his fingers* to signal to his wife it was time to leave. She rose on cue but hesitated long enough to maintain her good manners and to say goodbye in an unhurried way. I told her I hoped she would come to our house.

I noticed a picture of Maram with her hair long and free, and asked Emad when she decided to put on her headscarf. "About one and a half years ago," he said. "When she asked me if I thought she should, I told her she should do what she liked but if she 'puts it,' she could not take it off." Such is the power of husbands to set the rules for their wives. I am told this is true throughout the Arab world.

That night after the party, Bobby pointed out that it had been Katharine Graham who broke the tradition of separating men and women in America in the '60s, refusing to be segregated (though I doubt anyone snapped their fingers at her to obey). Women ran the show from behind the scenes, their femininity sometimes protected, and sometimes abused.

AISHA

VIRULENT FRIDAY AFTERNOON "sermons" concerning Islamic hadiths are broadcast throughout the city. The Qur'an does not interfere in political questions, but Sharia civil law, derived from the hadith, lays down very specific codes of conduct—how to wash, to dress, (the prophet's wives were veiled), what to eat (pork is forbidden), what to drink (no alcohol although some argue the Qur'an only forbids intoxication), how many wives a man can have—no more than four (although you can divorce the fourth in order to marry a fifth), and have, literally, thousands of girlfriends.

Unlike in the West, there are no equal rights since a man is equal to two women. In his book, *Jesus and Muhammad, Profound Differences and Surprising Similarities*, Mark A. Gabriel, PhD quotes the prophet as saying,

"Get witnesses out of your own men. And if there are not two men [available], then a man and two women, such as you agree for witnesses, so that if one of them [the two women] errs, the other can remind her." (Surah 2:282) and "Isn't the witness of a woman equal to half that of a man?"

One Arab scholar, Ahmed Youssef, the editor-in-chief of the Egyptian newspaper *Al Ahram*, and author of *Bonaparte et Mahomet*, told me that the Sunni-Shia split all comes down to an argument over a woman. Aisha, the prophet's twelve-year-old (second) wife, disappeared from the caravan one night and re-appeared the next morning in her shaded tent on top of her camel, being led by a very handsome youth of eighteen. The elderly prophet asked her where she had been. "She was at the end of the caravan," Ahmed began, "and had to relieve herself and while doing so, her necklace fell off and it took all night to find all the pieces, whereupon she gave up and waited for the morning light." So the prophet gathered three of his elders together, as he was democratically inclined, and asked them what they thought. Abu Bakr Bin Siddiq, Aisha's father, said, "Believe what your heart tells you." Umar Bin Khattab said, "You must trust your wife." Then the prophet asked Ali Ibne Abu Talib, his cousin and son-in-law, who said, "Stone her," and the other two threw themselves on Ali. Aisha never relinquished her anger toward Ali and later rode into battle against him." So the origin of the Islamic divide seems to be whether or not you trust your wife.

From this perspective, "Do not covet thy neighbor's wife," one of the Ten Commandments in the Bible could be interpreted to mean that a woman is chattel, along with the neighbor's house, ass and other animals. In the Qur'an, women are put in the same category as cattle or dogs. I asked Ahmed, "Are women thought to have a brain?"

He answered, "Men have in their imagination an image of the way they would like a woman to be."

"But," I asked, "did the prophet, did *he* think women had a brain?"

He shook his head and smiled. Women are referred to as a possession such as gold, silver, horse and cattle. In the *History of al-Tabari*, Volume IX, p. 113 comes this statement: "Treat women well, for they are [like] domestic animals [*awan*] with you and do not possess anything for themselves." Conversely, the prophet believed so highly in Aisha that she inherited the hadith, a set of thousands of laws interpreting what the prophet said, before the caliphs, the first being her father.

ISRAELI FANATICISM CREATED HAMAS, THE FRANKENSTEIN MONSTER

MODESTY IN WOMEN IS preferred and valued. I asked our foreman, Emad, if I should wear a headscarf as I noticed many young women who do. Although conservative, he dismissed the idea immediately: "There are many traditions in Jordan and all are acceptable—from those who wear mini-skirts and bikinis to those who wear headscarves." But he added, "anyway, you were wearing a scarf the other day." My Belgian cousin recently reminded me that only fifty years ago, her father would not have allowed her to leave the house without her hat or scarf.

I was walking the 400 yards between the French Embassy residence and our apartment, wearing a blue and green floral skirt below the knee and a long-sleeve light turquoise sweater, and had my first reality check on my appearance. My blonde hair was pulled back in a clip and I was wearing Hugo Boss sunglasses. A small truck passed and a young man stuck out his head, and with a contorted and angry face yelled something that felt like "Devil Woman!"—not that I understood his Arabic. Suddenly I felt vulnerable and I re-considered whether an unveiled Western woman who walks alone around Amman, dressed in a skirt, runs the risk of being insulted and harassed. Perhaps I would feel safer in loose long pants and a long-sleeved shirt. Because I prefer to dress as I like, I decided to drive everywhere from now on—between our house, the gym, the supermarket and even to the neighbors.

More and more women wear the headscarf, a friend told me, in order to get a husband, to prove they are chaste. One woman who works at the Save the Children office was told by her husband, "I'll only allow you to go to work if you cover up." She said it was a small price to pay for going to work. It can also be political.

Salwa, Anton's perspicacious wife, the university professor, is Jordanian—originally from Karak and Mt. Nebo. Always dressed fashionably, I was impressed by Salwa's command of issues but wary of her sharp tongue followed by the sweetest smile. Luckily I never felt the lash of the whip. You could easily see why one of her daughters was successful in media.

"A friend, full of life and energy and fun, showed up at work one day wearing a scarf. When asked by her boss, she said she was doing it because Arabs are being given such a bad reputation around the world—and Muslims in particular. She wanted to stand up and be counted as a Muslim. It was a political statement against the war on terror which has created a rebellion against Western perceptions," Salwa began.

"When I studied at the university in 1970, the headscarf didn't exist. Some village girls and old women in the West Bank—Muslim or Christian—would just put on the headscarf *in the peasant way* but none of this religious extremism existed. Now it's a matter of identity and 95 per cent of the girls at the university wear it or even the burqa with the face veil, though not the majority; it would be surprising to find a Muslim girl who is not covered and, by the way, the majority of the students at the University of Jordan are girls! It's an anti-West political statement, a form of rebellion," Salwa went on. "I heard that those girls are being paid by the Muslim Brotherhood to wear it. The money comes from somewhere else; the rumor is there are also rich girls taking money. Many of the teachers are covered. When I first joined the department in 2000 there weren't many covered; we even have an American married to a Muslim and now she is covered."

"Is it partly because they are being harassed?" I asked. "It has nothing to do with harassment; it's for identity and religious reasons."

"Does it frighten you?" I asked.

"No," she said, "but I'm not comfortable with the situation because this is fanaticism and I don't like to live in such a society. The headscarf has become a fashion, a matter of identity and defiance. Men grow their beards and women cover themselves to show we are Muslims—that we exist. It is anti-West sentiment. To assert themselves for their identity, to defy the West and America."

"When did this start, this anti-Americanism?" I asked Salwa.

"It has always existed but it became so apparent because of the hypocrisy of America. It all started in the 1990s with the invasion of Kuwait. The U.S. said we have to free Kuwait," she declared with some emotion. "We are in the 20th century and no country should be occupied but Palestine is occupied by the Israelis. Why doesn't America do anything about Israel? The U.S. is always measuring things on different scales. It has always existed but not so obviously up until 1990. Now, the nuclear debate—we are not pro-Iran; we all hate Iran in this part of the world. Iran has always been the traditional enemy of the Arab since the beginning of Islam. Israel has a nuclear program; why doesn't the U.S. say anything? The Israelis continue to dig deeper into Palestinian territories. Why doesn't America say anything?" she demanded.

"What do you think the solution is to the peaceful coexistence of the Arabs and the Jews?" I asked her.

"It could happen if America were not so biased. We are not against Israel's right to exist. We acknowledged that the UN has approved the State of Israel. We are not asking for the destruction of Israel. We just want to live in peace. But Israeli fanaticism created Hamas, the Frankenstein monster that they cannot get rid of."

"You Jordanians want the two-state solution?" I asked.

"*Of course we want the two-state solution.* It can only happen if Israel helps the Palestinians to create their own state. They are not working hard enough. Whenever anything happens, America sides with Israel. This does not solve the problem. It would be better if America looked at the problem in a more objective, moderate way—to try to back up the Palestinians.

"America is asking for democracy. Look what democracy has left in control: Hamas in Palestine and a mess in Iraq. They could have defended Saddam as they did before. Democracy is still premature in this part of the world, I'm sorry to say. Even my 12-year old-son expressed incredulity that the Americans could be so naïve, and saw that sectional infighting called for a dictator there. The biggest mistake in the history of the world was the invasion of Iraq because now Iraq has become the center for terrorism."

ONE OF THE WORST TYRANTS OF THE 20TH CENTURY

THERE ARE SOME WHO do not believe intervening in Iraq was a mistake. I interviewed (the late) French Ambassador Bernard Dorin, "un conseiller d'État", who specializes in conflict in the Middle East, in Paris on one of my trips home. "The Americans have done a great service to humanity by getting rid of one of the worst tyrants of the 20th century after Stalin and Pol Pot for his massacres of the Shiites and the Kurds," Dorin said.

"The U.S. Congress and the journalists are wrong to say we must stop the intervention in Iraq; this can only lead to disaster. They claim a parallel to the Vietnam War. In Iraq, the U.S. is trying to prevent a full-scale civil war [one that they started. Before the Sunnis and Shia got along fine, according to my Iraqi friends.] Until the downfall of Saddam, the Sunnis, one-fourth of the population, controlled Iraq. The Sunnis, allied with former Baathists and Al-Qaeda, are in a real power struggle with the Shiites who comprise 60 percent of the population and who dominate Iraq's one-man, one-vote parliament. There is also the threat of 200,000 Turkish armed troops amassed on the Kurdish border and ready to attack were the U.S. to withdraw, fulfilling their longstanding dream of destroying the Kurds. The U.S. must stay another eighteen months to three years [until 2009] in Iraq and Afghanistan or risk open civil war and total chaos.

"Who is the enemy?" Ambassador Dorin asked rhetorically. "Al-Qaeda is an Islamic extremist organization born of frustration toward those they call the near and the far enemy, the Shia being the near enemy. The civil war between Sunnis and Shia is 'une haine historique', hatred that goes back through history to the time of the 4th caliph, Ali, the husband of the prophet's daughter, Fatima. Shia which means 'cassure' [*break-up*] stems from a battle at Kerbala in the 7th century, the first war between the two sects, when women and children were massacred. In addition, [Sunni] Al-Qaeda is a reaction to the failure of the Arab conquest of Western Europe and India, from the 8th to the 16th centuries and also when Islam was overtaken in the 19th and 20th centuries by the British, French, Italians and Russians and the dream of a free Islam was effaced by both countries and corporations. Americans should know just who they are dealing with—a small radical anti-colonial, anti-corporate, terrorist organization."

THE SUCCESS AND FAILURE OF THE ARAB CONQUESTS

DORIN IS REFERRING TO the extraordinary success of the Umayyad (661-750) and Abbasid (750-1258) dynasties. Andalusia is laced through Arabic music, with a surprisingly strong element of nostalgia, harking back to a time when they owned Alhambra and the Spanish region around it for hundreds of years. The Islamic monarchies drew on the knowledge and *savoir faire* of Greece and Persia, the fabrication of paper from the Chinese and the decimal system from India. From the 6th century, Mecca was an important commercial crossroads and the prophet Muhammad (530-632AD) was himself a merchant. With the tradition of the pilgrimage to Mecca also came the free exchange of ideas as far as Asia with the result of significant numbers of Muslims in China, India and Southeast Asia.

Walid I, the Umayyad caliph (who, with his father, Abd al Malik, built the Dome of the Rock in Jerusalem and), insisted on creating the Great Mosque in Damascus and went on to conquer all of North Africa and Spain (705-715AD); he also built one of the most beautiful desert castles in Jordan. Qusayr Amra, an early 8th century AD spa and hunting palace, the world's sole example of Umayyad art. Fifty miles east of Amman, a wall painting, dating from the early 8th century, depicts him receiving tribute from six leaders of the other continents, named in Greek and Arabic script: Caesar, the Byzantine emperor; Roderic, the last Visigoth king of Spain, defeated by the Arabs in 711; Chosroes, the Persian emperor; and the Negus of Ethiopia. The two (defaced) remaining figures, perhaps the Chinese emperor and a Turkish or Indian prince, are shown as subordinate rulers offering homage.[9]

---

[9] In the first centuries of Islam such representations were forbidden in sacred places like mosques, but not in private houses. The frescoes, in remarkably good condition, are unusual for their depiction of human life; besides the emperors of six continents paying him homage, there are dancing women and musicians, women and children bathing, lions and gazelles, hunting scenes of wild donkeys in a tradition dating to the Neolithic Age, a reclining figure reminiscent of William Blake, monkeys, bears holding mandolins, birds in a trellis, artisans at each phase of the building's construction, and the most remarkable, a little dome of the *calidarium*—the earliest known representation of the night sky in the round. "Christian communities continued to thrive and it is possible that Christian artists and artisans may have worked for the caliph or his family to decorate this and other palaces," Dr. Gaetano Palumbo, director, World Monuments Fund for North Africa, the Middle East and Central Asia, commented, (currently partnering with the Jordanian Department of Antiquities and the Italian Institute for Conservation (ISCR) to restore the palace.)

In 732 AD the Frankish ruler and grandfather of Charlemagne, Charles Martel, stopped the Umayyad advance at Tours where they managed to kill the caliph and won the battle. Baghdad - meaning gift (*dad*) of God (*Bagh*), was founded in 762 by Al Mansur (754-775), of the Abbasid dynasty—a Central Asian Iranian descended from a Buddhist priest—who moved the capital from Syria where the Umayyads had ruled for a century to Iraq, at the intersection of the trade routes. After 762, Baghdad, a city of museums, hospitals, libraries and mosques, became the center of education and culture. The Greek ideas that inspired the Renaissance were recovered in the East, inspiring the Arab golden age and then much later repatriated to the West in translation from Arabic. The scholars of the Muslim world not only translated Greek, notably Plato and Aristotle, but also Hindu texts into Arabic and made important contributions to medicine, mathematics, astronomy, chemistry and literature. One of the most famous centers of learning was Beit al Hikmah (*the House of Wisdom*) attracting scholars from all over the world. The most famous mathematician of the time was Al-Khawariszmi, author of *Kitab al-Jabr*, is the father of algebra and the source of the word algorithm.

The reign of Harun al Rashid (786-809) is considered the apogee of Abbasid power.[10] Julius Köckert painted the scene of Harun receiving a delegation from Charlemagne at a time when Europe had little to offer the far more sophisticated Islamic societies. In 802 Harun sent Charlemagne presents unknown to Western Europe then in the Dark Ages—silks, brass candlesticks, perfume, slaves, ivory chessmen, balsam, an elephant, and as mentioned earlier, a water clock that marked the hours by dropping brass balls into a bowl as mechanical knights, one for each hour, emerged from little doors which shut behind them. Islamic thinkers and scientists contributed to making Aristotle known in Christian Europe as well as Alexandrian mathematics, geometry and the astronomy of Euclides and Claudius Ptolemy. There were eight hundred doctors in 9th century Baghdad and Ibn Sina (known as Avicenna in the West) is often considered the father of modern medicine.

Likewise, in literature, Islamic societies were far ahead. In the 9th-10th

---

[10] Bernard Lewis, *The Middle East: 2000 Years of History from The Rise of Christianity to the Present Day*. Phoenix: 1995 p. 77

century, *One Thousand and One Nights*, (*Kitab Hadith Alf Layla*) was published, unknown in Europe until the French translated it in 1704; this collection of stories including Ali Baba, Sinbad, Aladdin, and Scheherazade, (both character and storyteller), inspired by the heroes of the pre-Islamic Sassanid Kings (224-636 AD), remains one of the great classics of all time. According to the story, Shahryar (king) found out his wife was unfaithful to him and married a new virgin every day, beheading the previous day's wife so she would not have the chance to be unfaithful. He had had one thousand wives by the time he was introduced to Scheherazade, the vizier's daughter.[11]

After Harun, the Moorish capitals in Spain and North Africa became independent with their own emirs and in 868 Egypt fell away and merged with Syria. Civil war between the Arabs and the Persians broke out in Baghdad ending in a Persian victory. Although Baghdad still had control of

---

[11] In Sir Richard Burton's translation of *The Nights*, she was described in this way: "Scheherazade had perused the books, annals and legends of preceding Kings, and the stories, examples and instances of bygone men and things; indeed it was said that she had collected a thousand books of histories relating to antique races and departed rulers. She had perused the works of the poets and knew them by heart; she had studied philosophy and the sciences, arts and accomplishments; and she was pleasant and polite, wise and witty, well read and well bred. Against her father's wishes, Scheherazade volunteered to spend one night with the king. Once in the king's chambers, Scheherazade asked if she might bid one last farewell to her beloved sister, Dunyazade (دنيازاد *Donyāzād*), who had secretly been prepared to ask Scheherazade to tell a story during the long night. The king lay awake and listened with awe as Scheherazade told her first story. The night passed by, and Scheherazade stopped in the middle. The king asked her to finish, but Scheherazade said there was no time, as dawn was breaking. So, the king spared her life for one day to finish the story the next night. The following night, Scheherazade finished the story and then began a second, even more exciting tale, which she again stopped halfway through at dawn. Again, the king spared her life for one more day so she could finish the second story. And so the king kept Scheherazade alive day by day, as he eagerly anticipated the finishing of the previous night's story. At the end of 1,001 nights, and 1,000 stories, Scheherazade told the king that she had no more tales to tell him. During these 1,001 nights, the king had fallen in love with Scheherazade. He spared her life, and made her his queen."

the trade routes, the dynasty declined because of overspending combined with a diminishing supply of metals, gold and silver, with their loss to invaders and because of a bloated bureaucracy (like the graft and cronyism in Iran's banks today). In the 10th century, when religious traditions began to interfere with creative energy, free arbitration, and advancement on the basis of merit, caliphal power broke down.

The Crusades in the 11th and 12th centuries followed by the Mongols—Genghis Khan in 1206—who conquered a great part of Euroasia and also destroyed Baghdad in 1258—ended the golden age. According to Ibn Khaldoun, who wrote *Al Muqaddimah*, the invasions ruined the Arab caliphates, their libraries and schools, as did piracy along Arab commercial routes. This famous historian of the Islamic medieval period, whom some consider the father of sociology, invented the theory that the social cohesion that can result from tribes, enhanced through religion, can also lead to a society's downfall. He believed in the cyclical nature of civilization. He was also the first to hypothesize on "value-added"—labor, skill, techniques, etc.—in political economy,

"In the high Middle Ages, the commerce of the Islamic Middle East was in every way **ahead** of that of Europe—richer, larger, better organized, with more commodities to sell and more money to buy and a vastly more sophisticated network of trading relations. By the end of the Middle Ages, these roles were reversed…[although Middle East trade] continued for more than a century after Vasco da Gama arrived in India…[Portuguese domination in the East was remarkable]…It is even more remarkable that the great Middle East powers—Mamluk Egypt, Ottoman Turkey and Safavid Iran—were unable to muster either the economic strength to compete with them or the naval strength to defeat them." Military aristocracies dominated at the expense of commerce and production just when the sea trade was taken over first by Italian, later by northwestern European cities with more effective methods. [12]

The Ottoman Empire, from the 14th to 17th centuries, was at its height under Suleiman the Magnificent, an admirer of Alexander the Great. The 16th century Ottoman monarch oversaw the golden age of its legislative, artistic, literary and cultural development. His empire extended from the

---

[12] Lewis, Ibid., p. 177-178

entire Arabian continent to the Balkans all the way to Vienna, thanks in part to Suleiman's alliance with François 1 against the Hapsburgs. Their decline came when they no longer respected and assimilated populations under their control (that had once reached 37 million), when they allowed religion to interfere with the stimulation of ideas, and when Western Europe's commercial markets began to dominate trade between Europe and the East.

ONE JORDANIAN-PALESTINIAN DINNER

OUR NEIGHBORS—NORA, A Palestinian Christian from Bethlehem, and Riad, a Jordanian—invited us for dinner. They met in Libya while he was working for a Jordanian trading company importing steel from Libya and she for Occidental Oil. At about eight we went over and there was no one at home. About eight thirty, Nora called at our front door and asked, "Where are you?"

I said, "We came but there was no one there."

She said, "Well, come now."

Now I understand Spain, ruled by the Arabs for centuries, and my Spanish friends' custom of eating late and their lax punctuality.

Conversations always come back to the same central topic, in this case, the horrors along the border in '67-'70 that have almost a biblical ring to them. "I was having my baby in 1970, so I wanted to go home to Bethlehem in order that the child would have papers and be registered accordingly. It was three years after the 1967 war and the Israelis had taken away my residency papers when I left, knowing that the only way that me or my son could return definitively would be with these papers or by the invitation of someone there. So I went to Bethlehem and had my baby and with my Jordanian passport and the twenty-day-old child, I went to the border but the Jordanian authorities were not allowing any more Palestinians into its territories. So I cried and cried for two hours and the baby was turning red and blue from crying. Finally, because I was working for Occidental Oil in Libya, I remembered I had a Libyan residency card and so I lied and told them I was in transit and was boarding a plane that night. In fact, I was going to see Riad's parents. But anyway, they let me through." Nora added rather desperately, "We were happy under the rule of Jordan [in the '48-'67 years when the entire West Bank, which includes Bethlehem and East

Jerusalem, was open]."

We returned the invitation for dinner one night at sunset when the view of all Amman from our penthouse terrace is breathtaking. Nora, a Coptic Christian, murmured, "Masha' Allah"—("*May God protect me from envy*" and also "*Bless this House,*" or "*Peace be to your house.*") We asked them why they were clearing the lush empty land next to our lot that had turned green from spring rains. They told us it was to keep away the scorpions and the snakes. "The what?" I asked? "What kind of snakes?" (There had been several large red ants on the terrace near the water tank and a huge June bug basking on the terrace in the morning heat.)

Nora was wearing spaghetti straps on this hot summer night. Mother of two marriageable daughters, she told us she would rather her daughters die than marry Muslims, to be required to become Muslim and be clothed to the wrists and ankles. Christian men who marry Muslim women must convert to Islam; the children will be Muslim, as in the Jewish faith. As Christians, women are free to choose whatever dress they want. How sad to see the woman's body as an object to be covered. Nora and Riad told us that American men come here to find subservient wives but I never met any; others, it is said, convert to Islam in order to have many wives. [13]

A group of American businessmen working in the Middle East also

---

[13] One of the prophet's wives, Maria, also a Coptic Christian like Nora, was so beautiful that the prophet Muhammad asked her to cover herself so as not to tempt men. But there is nothing written in the Qur'an instructing the faithful about women's dress. Reza Aslan, in *No God but God* explains, "Although long seen as the most distinctive emblem of Islam, the veil is, surprisingly, not enjoined upon Muslim women anywhere in the Qur'an. The tradition of veiling and seclusion (known together as hijab) was introduced into Arabia long before Muhammad, primarily through Arab contacts with Syria and Iran, where the hijab was a sign of social status. After all, only a woman who need not work in the fields could afford to remain secluded and veiled. In the Ummah, there was no tradition of veiling until around 627 BCE, when the so-called "verse of hijab" suddenly descended upon the community. That verse, however, was addressed not to women in general, but exclusively to Muhammad's wives: "Believers, do not enter the Prophet's house...unless asked. And if you are invited...do not linger. And when you ask something from the Prophet's wives, do so from behind a hijab. This will assure the purity of your hearts as well as theirs." (33:53)

came. One said that this is a civilization that has never had a renaissance (presumably he knew of the golden age and was hoping for the sequel): it is still coming out of the Middle Ages—he gave it a date of about 1600—where Bedouin men veiled their women to protect them from rape and the covetous eyes of other men. Originally, it was a loving gesture, not a restraining one.

It's not just that half the population is invisible. "It's worse than that," said another. "There is a joke going around Saudi Arabia: 'Women are like Persian carpets; the more you beat them, the more comfortable they get.' And they really laugh,'" this father of two girls said. "If you read in a government-censored Saudi newspaper," the businessman continued, "that 90 per cent of all women over the age of thirteen are beaten either by their fathers or their husbands, you know that it is becoming a big problem." At the Four Seasons, I watched small girls getting out of the swimming pool being berated while the boys were praised.

A ROYAL INVITATION

JORDANIANS DO NOT GENERALLY invite Americans to their houses. We were told we were a certain type of American because we were fluent in French. Our reception varied from warmth to outrage. I wondered if I was an insider or a bystander to society here. Another European friend reminded me, "Truth is private. It's a civilization of appearances. Everyone knows it. Everything is in code. That's the Orient."

"When you are new to the country," a European friend here told me, "people want to look after you. If they feel they don't have much in common with you, once they've been seen to do the right thing, they can move on, having made sure their honor is safe; and then you just see them occasionally, so it works quite well. Actually it makes things easier to navigate because it avoids a lot of awkwardness." When our Jordanian royals, Hana and Faazi, invited us to dinner, I was overjoyed; in later months when they let me go as a friend, I realized the truth of my friend's comment, a bitter disappointment.

At their beautiful house in the splendid development next to King Abdullah's palace adjacent to the new gigantic mosque, perched on a mountaintop, the garden, with its large leafy trees swaying in the gentle evening breeze and numerous species of palms, lit from below, revealed a carpet of bougainvillea. Further down, a manicured lawn and arbors of red roses surrounded an illuminated swimming pool. Waiters served cocktails and canapés, and conversation was a constant mix of French, English and Arabic. A large buffet supper of steamed lamb with almonds and rice and other delights had been set out on two round tables for twenty guests. The seating was open.

On my left at my table was a kindly heart surgeon who had referred one of his students to be doctor to the king, and on my right was the editor of the leading Arabic newspaper as well as one of the best English language papers in the region—the *Daily Star*. When he discovered I was a journalist by background, he told me his lead for the paper the next day—Bush had said that the war in Iraq was unwinnable. There was no conclusion to draw, he said, other than that Iran and the U.S. had made a deal over nuclear energy—as long as Iran would help to keep the peace in Iraq. (It was an interesting thought but we discovered the next day that this was not in fact his lead.) If Iran were given a freer hand in Iraq, I said, it would jeopardize the lives of Iraqi women, among the most educated in the Middle East— since they would come under the influence of fundamentalism. I told him of my conversation with Mrs. Khoury and that her answer had been that to combat fundamentalism, democracy must exist and, therefore, I asked her whether what Bush was doing correct—encouraging democracy from within Iraq.

People can't understand why Iran, which has called for the destruction of Israel, is so vilified for wanting nuclear energy. "They cannot understand," she said, "why the U.S. would not speak to Iran when they speak to England and France who also have nuclear energy. Obviously," she said, "because Iran has publicly stated that it was in favor of the destruction of Israel."

A learned Arab sociologist with a PhD from an Ivy League university, sitting next to the editor, began wringing his hands and fingering his worry beads, leaning closer to the editor, who, red in the face, exclaimed, "It is not what Bush is doing in Iraq that we are against so much as the failure to pressure Israel into going back to the '67 borders."

I agreed with him and raised the ante a little by saying it was too bad there couldn't be a one-state solution where everyone shares the land. But this did not go over well. I asked why the Palestinians had refused to accept the 2000 peace accords. "That," the editor explained, "was because the extremists had come to power and the Israelis were refusing to give way. Under Clinton, Barak came closest to a peaceful solution." Then the two stood to get their dessert, happy to remove themselves from the table, leaving me shaking, as the kindly doctor attempted to converse with me.

What many want, an American friend told me the next day, is for the Jews to return to Germany or Russia or wherever they came from, however impossible that is, given that international law recognizes the state of Israel. President Bush's strongly pro-Israeli foreign policy reduced everyone here to utter mania. However much they love our people and our universities, our foreign policy is universally hated in the region. It is the failure to consult, to find a common solution, to reach out to the region that galls and humiliates them.

The tension in the air was thick when the editor and the sociologist returned to the table and no one spoke. I then realized I had the floor, so I changed the subject and asked the other people at the table why the Arab nations had abandoned Iraq? Secondly, why, as Prince Hassan had said, didn't the rich nations of the Middle East help the poor nations—Jordan and Palestine? The Gulf States have $500 million a day in revenues. "They could eradicate poverty in the region," I said. The other people at the table froze, perhaps unused, in these circles, to anyone, especially a woman, asking such questions.

"Between 500,000 and 1,000,000 Iraqis—a quarter of the Jordanian population—have come to Jordan and will keep coming if something isn't done. What is the Jordanian government doing to help and, if nothing, why not?"

(Pause)

Finally, one man offered, "Because there are millions of miles of land mines."

"Who put them there?" I asked.

(Silence)

"Who put them there?" he murmured to his neighbor, pensively.

"The Iran-Iraq war has left its scars," they finally said.

Then I asked, "How is the water situation in this country?"

"Bad," they said.

"What is being done?" (Silence).

I thought to myself that if Bush would only express more concern about water, it would help the U.S. in the region. If only Prince Hassan's supranational Jordanian-Palestinian-Israeli-Lebanese-Syrian-Turkish "Mediterranean Union" existed to deal with the regional water problem (especially since the Israeli occupation of the Sheba'a Farms of Lebanon.) Then Hana—chic, kind, and calm—came over to say a welcoming hello and sat next to me. There was utter silence.

Every night, the national obsession about Palestine reared its head with the deep conviction that Israel, backed by America, would never change, that justice would never prevail. Perhaps imbedded in the reason for their distress was the hope that one American writer could awaken the world to the injustice toward the Palestinians. The freeze after the fire at the dinner table could have been cultural—not only was a woman leading a political discussion rare, but religion, politics and sex are taboo. And, as mentioned, the lead in the *Daily Star* the next day was not about Bush declaring the war un-winnable but was quite the opposite—that Iraq had its greatest chance ever to succeed as a country.

CHAPTER FOUR
July

" A MERICANS LIVE TO WORK, the French work to live and the
Jordanians live," one friend told me, motioning to the banquet
before him, surrounded by family and friends. When I first moved to Paris
thirty years ago, the service economy seemed decades behind New York but
Amman introduces a whole new definition of time. In Jordan, a civil
servant's salary is so low, you work from 9 to 2, then you visit your family
and friends.

THE ECONOMY
The riches that war brought

UNTIL THE END OF the '70s Jordan was, as I have said, a small country, with
few resources and a weak economy. During the Iraqi-Iran war in 1980
Jordan became the only access for Iraq to the outside world and it began to
grow. All the war arms and machinery came through port of Aqaba—Iraqi's
food, medications, and equipment—so Jordan was the beneficiary through
the entire Iraq-Iran war, then the first Gulf war, then thirteen years of
sanctions. Now a huge part of the Jordanian economy comes from the
investments and expenditures of the 700,000 Iraqis who fled Iraq during the
period from April 2003 until today. More revenue comes from conferences
and meetings organized for reconstructing Iraq.

Michael Jansen, in an op-ed piece, spoke of the emergence of a new economic dependence between the new Iraq and Iran because (thanks to President Bush) both are now Shia-dominated: "During the Iran-Iraq war (1980-88) Iraq used Jordanian ports to bring in the goods Baghdad required and relied on Jordan as a transit state for Iraqis travelling abroad. Today Iran and Syria provide Iraq with the produce and consumer goods it needs to provide for the populace. Iran is also offering Iraq desperately needed electricity and other essentials."

An oasis of stability in the middle of a tumultuous region, Jordan has also benefited from the U.S.'s, Saudi Arabia's and Qatar's commitment of millions in foreign aid. Between 2006 and 2015, Jordan's per capita GDP tripled from $4,900 to $12,397, in 2015, pulling itself into the middle ranks of world global finance. French investments had reached 800 million euros over the previous five years, mainly in the banking, hotel and telecommunications sectors. China was the third largest foreign trading partner behind Kuwait and France, with commercial exchange between the two countries reaching one billion dollars the previous year. In the south, the Qualified Industrial Zone, the Gap and Ralph Lauren Polo and other U.S., E.U. and UAE garment factories, had long been a source of jobs and income. China was running 22 garment factories in Jordan's QIZ employing 22,000 people, half of whom were Jordanian. The king had visited China seven times since his accession to the throne and China's ambassador to Jordan, Gong Xi-aosheng, said his country was committed to supporting the Kingdom's development process with major investment initiatives in 2007.

Birthrates were now also in the middle range. It was among the countries with the highest military spending in the world as a percent of GDP, and one of the lowest death (including suicide) rates in the world. Most of what was imported here came by boat, including our personal belongings from Paris which made their way through the Mediterranean, into the Red Sea and finally into the port of Aqaba. The narrow Gulf gives Jordan access to the oceans. A coastline of 40 kilometers (25 miles), bordered with coral reefs, with the (Israeli) mountains of Judaea and Samaria in the distance, is important to the economy.

In the previous two years, Jordan had improved the port facilities but at a terrible price. The beautiful coral reefs on which the plentiful fish supply depends were being destroyed in order to build a new port near the Saudi border. So if you're a fish lover like me, and oil for transport is no longer available, you might find yourself with a new steel port but nothing to eat. Years ago, Jordan was self-sufficient in wheat, grown all along the airport road into Amman. In an ironic reversal of roles since agrarian life began here thousands of years ago, only American wheat was shipped into Aqaba, potentially disastrous should the port be endangered. Jordan exports potash (from the Dead Sea) but apparel exports comprised almost 90% of Jordan's total exports. Agricultural products—vegetables, mainly tomatoes, were shipped throughout the Middle East as were high quality olive oil, nuts, dates, figs, citrus fruits and recently, flowers, including roses. Young boys hawked white and red roses to drivers stopped at intersections for next to nothing.

There was also a huge growing industry in health tourism—high-quality surgery for less than in the West—including surgery for heart disease, head injuries, plastic surgery, dentistry and ophthalmology. Americans were coming to Jordan because surgery here was so cheap compared to the U.S. and more than made the airfare worthwhile. Indeed, Jordan had become a medical hotspot in the Middle East, not only for cures but for surgery—56 private hospitals offer neurological, heart, orthopedic and kidney surgeries, bringing an influx of $700 million annually, and the "medical tourism" was growing by 20 percent every year because the price for such operations was one third of what it was in the West.

In the pre-ISIS years, tourism was big business—in a slow month, 25,000 visitors to Petra alone, generating 544,000JD in revenues ($800,000). Petra, the rose city, known among other things, as the backdrop for *Indiana Jones and The Last Crusade*, is breathtaking on Thursday nights. The siqq (where the scene with the cascading boulder took place) is lit with candles, and the ancient nai, a flute-like instrument made from bamboo, open at the tip, calls to visitors through caverns to the source—a turbaned man in a white robe near the "treasury" building. There are kilometers to explore once one is inside the vast site of multi-colored stone—a huge amphitheater, monasteries, a Roman colonnade and plenty of camels and donkeys to carry the weary.

130,000 Hungarians visited Jordan in 2007, mainly religious tourists. On our first trip to Jordan in the spring of 2005, we stayed at the Mövenpick on the Dead Sea next to Christ's baptism site, a low-lying copy of an ancient village whose architecture and landscaping is delightfully in harmony with the environment—close to nature and full of flowering plants. Our bedroom, with ceramic-tiled accents, featured a private veranda and outdoor jacuzzi. We enjoyed an elegant buffet on a screened-in terrace, fragrant with the bushes just outside, and full of candles and romance.

Tourists are also fascinated by the castle at Karak, a city at the crossroads of Jordan, on the top of a mountain, that has been inhabited by centuries of different tribes—Moabites, Nabateans, and famously, the Crusaders—who left their mark so decisively that it remains thrillingly intact—giant halls for horses, rooms for master, slave, and prisoner, as well as remnants of kitchens and water systems. My husband and I instinctively knew when we were in the chapel and posed for our 25th wedding anniversary photo.

Jordan relies on heavy import duties for revenues but it didn't occur to me that a box of Italian clothes from Artigiano that had arrived in Paris would cost me 100% duty. Bob, Majid and I went to the customs house and argued with the officials to reduce it to their usual exorbitant duty for luxury goods but I noticed that Majid had to slip the man handling the thing a huge wad of bills as a bribe. Limited supplies of German merchandise (the most sought after)—like extractor fans—carry heavy duties. At the local Villeroy and Boch store, Bob noticed a champagne-colored faucet for the guest bathroom and asked the price. $800. "And, for that price, does champagne pour from it as well?" he asked. "No sir, this is the famous designer Philip Starck," the salesman answered.

SIGHTSEEING

EVERY FRIDAY, THE DAY of rest and prayer, we took a drive to discover something new. We started out for Salt, a northwestern suburb of Amman where Job is buried, but took the wrong road and ended up miles north at Umm Qays, which means *mother of all crossroads*. Overlooking the Sea of Galilee, this is where Jesus walked on water and multiplied the yield of fish and bread to feed thousands of his followers; and where Christ drove the derangement out of madmen and transferred their troubled spirits into a herd of pigs who ran into the sea. (Mark 5:1-18)

At night at this beautiful Roman site, with the darkened hills of the

Golan Heights in front of us and the Sea of Galilee with the lights on the Israeli side twinkling in the distance, the only thing I could think of was the hope that children of all races and creeds could run freely on these hills. The collective yearning to go home made me wonder again whether it was possible for one state to exist—whether it would ever be possible to at least have the choice of going home.

Slightly to the southwest of Amman lies Iraq al Amir, a castle built in the 2nd century BC by a Jewish family named Tobiad. At that time the palace was surrounded by water and populated with exotic wildlife. Neighbors were encroaching around the site with no one to protect it—chickens ran through a former ancient gate. Some say the monarchy does not protect the site because of its controversial origins; others say it's the local mafia.

Afterwards, we lunched at a local restaurant where the other customers, men and women in headscarves, were eating at separate tables, while their children played in the stream. Ten-year-old girls came shyly and sweetly up to me, told me their names and asked me mine. Waiters chose us a carp from the stream and then barbecued it for us and served it to us with cucumbers and tomatoes in a hot sauce with bread. Our peaceful lunch under the trees beside the stream was interrupted by a brawl among the men watching the World Cup.

The historic heart of Amman is the Citadel with its small archaeological museum housing some of the famous Dead Sea Scrolls dating from 100 BC to 100 AD, some in Aramaic and a few in Koine Greek. Discovered between 1947 and 1956 in eleven caves in Wadi Qumran on the Jordanian side of the Dead Sea's northwest shore, some of the 800 documents from the Hebrew Bible are of great religious and historical significance, as they are practically the only known surviving Biblical documents written before 100 AD.

The Nash Papyrus from Egypt, containing a copy of the Ten Commandments, is the only other Hebrew document of comparable antiquity. Some scrolls are written. The biblical texts cited most often in the Dead Sea Scrolls are the Psalms, followed by the Book of Isaiah and the Book of Deuteronomy. Other important texts include the Isaiah Scroll, a Commentary on the Habakkuk, the so-called Manual of Discipline (Community Rule), which gives much information on the structure and theology of a sect, and the earliest version of the Damascus Document. The so-called Copper Scroll, which lists valuable hidden caches of gold, scrolls, and weapons, is probably the most notorious. Gold, silver and copper were mined in the Middle East in prehistoric times and bronze was made in east Mesopotamia in the third millennium BCE.[14]

For perspective on the archaeological riches of Jordan, I asked Jane Taylor to The Wild Jordan Nature Center (dedicated to helping to save the wild parts of Jordan) overlooking the Citadel, one of the earliest fortifications known to man. The Citadel in Amman goes back to the Neolithic period. Some of the walls were built in the Middle Bronze Age, 2nd millennium BC, and the Iron Age, 8th century BC, as well as during the Hellenistic era, 2nd century BC and the late Roman to early Islamic Ages. "It was capital of the kingdom of Ammon, where King David sent Uriah, the Hittite, into the front lines of attack so that he (David) could have Bathsheba. *Things were very much going on* before Alexander [the Great} came through. For two centuries before Alexander, Jordan had been under Persian control but the Persians exercised a very light hand. Before that, it was ruled by Babylon and earlier still by the Assyrians. The local kingdoms such as Edom (southern Jordan), Moab (middle Jordan), Ammon (the Amman area), operated relatively independently and paid tribute to whomsoever was their overlord at the time.

After the death of Alexander (323 BC), his generals Seleucus and Antigonus carved up of the Greek Empire in Mesopotamia, the northern part of Syria, and a chunk of Asia Minor, while Ptolemy, Antigonus's nephew took over in Egypt, Jordan and southern Syria. The brilliant general Pompey defeated the Seleucid Kingdom in 64 AD and made West Asia, including Syria, provinces of the Roman Empire. (Romans spoke Greek but Latin was their written language.)

After Rabbat Ammon passed from the Seleucids to Ptolemy II, it was renamed, the Greek *Philadelphia* meaning brotherly love (phil=love, delphus=brother), because his nickname was Philadelphus. Amman is part of the Roman Decapolis, (ten cities), which is somewhat of a puzzle for modern scholars because different texts name different cities as members of the Decapolis. In fact the ten cities in the Decapolis fluctuated depending on the

---

[14] Bernard Lewis, *The Middle East: 2000 years of History from the Rise of Christianity to the Present Day*. Phoenix: 1995, p. 168

fortunes of cities' rise and fall. So, it has been variously and generally described as a league of ten cities, a geographical area in which ten cities dominated but not always the same ones. They were given semi-autonomous status under the Seleucids and the Romans.

In general they agree that Damascus, Hippos, Canatha, Dium and Raphana (all in modern Syria) were part of the Decapolis confederation. The Gospels of St. Mark identified Scythopolis, west of the Jordan River, as the largest city and capitol of the Decapolis. The city-states in present day Jordan include Rabbat Ammon or Philadelphia (Amman), Gedara (Umm Qays), Gerasa (Jerash) and Pella (Tabaqat Fahl); also Abila (Tel Abil), Capitolias (Beit Ras) and Dion.

"In this Hellenistic, post-Alexander period, there was a lot of Greek influence, but local people had already made their own temples. With something as strong as Greek architecture, it is quite dominant, but if you take a place like Petra, they used all these design ideas and made something that was completely individual so that you can recognize elements from Egypt, from the Greek world, and from the Roman world," Jane explained.

I was interested in whether the architecture of Jerash was influenced by the Greeks and how closely linked the temples were to the designs of Vitruvius—the celebrated Roman writer and architect (80-15 BC)—who wrote the definitive book on how to build a temple, a theater, and the measurements for good acoustics among other notable achievements.

"An awful lot about the temples in Jerash was not Roman; there is a strong oriental element to them," Jane commented. When they were working on the Temple of Zeus in the 1960s, they were convinced that the temples were based on Vitruvius's design principles and they re-erected three columns with the measurements that would have been appropriate for a Vitruvian-style temple. Instead, they found that the measurements for the Zeus temple were based on Oriental design principles—on the design of local architects, indicating the sharing of ideas.

"Herod was tremendously eclectic in the design of buildings. He loved lots of pools of water in the desert castles and theaters so they borrowed Roman principles—the one in Petra is too—it's pure Vitruvius, apart from the fact that it's cut from the rock instead of being built up from the ground. Local people took what they knew about Greek and Roman architecture and then they added their own ingenuity, Arab knowledge of local materials being superior."

The Nabataean treasury in Petra is an Egyptian take on a Roman design. Craftsmen from Alexandria came in the 1ˢᵗ and 2ⁿᵈ centuries BC. Nabataeans could employ whoever they wanted even in the 1ˢᵗ century BC and although the caves are gorgeous, they lived in houses. Rome wasn't able to take Petra from the Nabataeans until 106 AD. The last king ruled for a long time, from 70 AD to 106 AD. There doesn't seem to have been a war—the Romans just took over.

Interestingly, there are very few archaeologists who believe that Moses took the trip from Egypt to Mt. Nebo (13ᵗʰ century BC), and scholars refute Israelis' ancestral, Biblical claims to the land. The only evidence for the Exodus is in the books of the Old Testament. They were forty years in the desert and in the whole Kadesh Barnea area between Egypt and Israel where they were for decades they haven't found a single cemetery. As Edom is described in the Exodus, Moses goes to the king of Edom and asks to be allowed to travel along the King's Highway, promising not to touch their water, their women, their corn, and to behave impeccably; then the Bible goes on to say that the king of Edom sent out the army to make sure that they pushed off.

"Those early books of the Bible were written about 600 years *after* the Exodus, and at that time Edom did have a central government and a king. It seems that they [the Jews] may have conflated their story with the earlier exodus of the Hyksos, a group of Canaanites—probably in the 17ᵗʰ century BC. They went along the Gaza coastal area and there is much more archaeological evidence of that exodus than there is of the Moses-led one 300 years later. But the Hyksos are not invested with the same tale of origin. The Jews and the others were all Canaanite tribes and they attacked fortresses on their way through."

DARAT AL FUNUN

DARAT AL FUNUN IS NOT just a gallery to promote a renaissance of Arab culture, but a symbol of the multifaceted nature of Jordan. Perched on a green hillside overlooking the oldest part of Amman, the early 20th century buildings of the Khalid Shoman Foundation made from local stone stand alongside a Roman temple dedicated to Hercules; in the 6ᵗʰ century, the temple became a Byzantine church to honor St. George, (Isham Khader in Arabic) and today provides a majestic backdrop to musical events in summertime. In the 7th century, Muslim holy men also came here to pray and their prayers, alongside those of their predecessors, are inscribed in stone.

British explorer Major C.R. Condor, who first identified the site in 1881, speculated that it was sacred, "a tomb or cave-dwelling of some saint." One of the three houses was built by the Circassians of Russia's northern steppes who came to Jordan in the late 19th century. The main building is in the Venetian style, characteristic of the Mediterranean architecture that was in fashion in Beirut, Haifa, and Jaffa in the 1920s. The place, cut into the steep rock, is reached on what must have once been a goat path not far from to the Citadel that is reputed to have been the site of where David sent Uriah the Hittite into battle so he could have his widow, Bathsheba, who, later, gave birth to Solomon. It was an area of passage between the great Pharaonic, Mesopotamian, Greco-Roman, Ottoman, and Persian empires. Many Jordanians, like the Lebanese Arabs who were Phoenician, can trace their origins to the ancient Canaanites.

Suha Shoman, founder of Darat Al Funun, named the Khalid Shoman Foundation after her late husband, formerly deputy chairman and president of the Arab Bank. Khalid Shoman's father, Abdul Hameed Shoman, founded the Arab Bank in 1930 when Jerusalem was part of Palestine. (The bank's founder's grandson, also named Abdul Hameed, is the current CEO and chairman of the Arab Bank.) The site was bought in 1991, and since then has sponsored numerous exhibits in its gallery and played host to scholars who study in its extensive art library. Suha and Khalid believed that the private sector could play a role in nurturing Arab culture, to spread ways of thought to "promote the renaissance of the Arab nation."

Standing outside, mid-way between a Roman head and a modern Iraqi sculpture, Suha Shoman, the founder-chairman of Darat Al Funun and the Foundation, asks rhetorically, "What does this imply about our origins? Here there is an unbroken link to our past. The Mediterranean basin was always home to Arab Christians, Jews and Muslims. To use the historical myths surrounding the Judaic kingdom as a justification for aggression is to distort history. This place is a symbol of tolerance and the continuity of our past. We believe in Abraham and have no hatred for the Jewish tradition. But we are anti-Zionist, those who want to declare that Palestine is the exclusive state of the Jewish people; we Palestinian Arabs want the right of return to our homeland without any impediment."

On the half-moon terrace with Roman columns overlooking the Byzantine church, one can almost hear the faint tinkling of glasses and polite chatter. Winston Churchill made sure Jordan was never part of the British mandate set up after World War I in Palestine. It was created as an emirate but Peak "Pasha" followed by Glubb "Pasha" were the British heads of the Arab Legion between 1921 and 1957 at the request of Emir Abdullah I and the first floor of the Darat site was their official headquarters and officers' club. In 1956, King Hussein replaced Glubb with mostly Jordanian Bedouin officers.

"King Hussein got the British out," said Suha whose grandfather, a Palestinian from Jerusalem, was part of the Great Arab Revolt with King Faisal in Damascus. King Hussein ordered that her grandfather be interred next to the King's great grandfather, Sherif Hussein, Abdullah I, at the Dome of the Rock in Jerusalem. "The region of the Fertile Crescent was one nation, Syria, and it was divided by the British and the French," Suha asserted.

Suha was born in Jerusalem in 1944, grew up in Egypt from 1948 to 1961, and studied in Beirut and Paris for her doctorate in law. Jordan has become her new home and a home to many artists. "My work is a tribute to my love for Jordan. I am doing here what I was not able to do in my own homeland. This is a home for Arab artists. Many have come to us in times of great difficulty."

During the first Gulf War, in 1991, artists like Nedim Kufi, currently a resident in Holland, had nowhere to go and the Darat gave them refuge, assisted them and showcased their work. "We supported Arab artists before it was the fashion to do so. We show the art of the Arab world, not of the Islamic world, not of the Middle East for that would exclude North Africa— Morocco, Tunisia and Algeria. We bring together all Arab artists regardless of national boundaries and religion."

In October 2008 for the 60th anniversary of the "Nakba," a term Palestinians use for the forced exodus of three-quarters of a million Palestinians from their land in 1948, the gallery chose Scottish artist Jane Frere's *Return of the Soul*. First moved by her visits to a concentration camp in Poland to explore the Jewish narrative and the brutal consequences of the

Holocaust, she later came to understand the ethnic cleansing policy used by Israel "to drive Palestinians into exile through massacre, rape and both violent and psychological warfare." Thousands of tiny wax figures are suspended in air. "If land is pulled from under your feet," the artist explained, "severing the roots that have maintained you over centuries, your unbound spirit has nowhere to go, [and] remains trapped in limbo."

Each is an individual tale of a people who still suffer from injustice. The final product depicts a calamity. The current photography exhibit by Ahlam Shibli showed life in Arab Al Sbaih, a village in the Lower Galilee where the grandparents of the Palestinians used to hide from Israeli artillery in 1948 and which in 1967 became Israeli. The grandchildren of those who fled to these hills were only able to build houses on their neighbors' ancestral land, never their own, causing trouble within the Jordanian refugee camps where the rest of the families reside. Moreover, in order to build a house, you had to give up your Palestinian identity and become Israeli, join the Israeli army, and fight against your own people. The photographer was contrasting life in the Galilee with life in two of Jordan's ten Palestinian refugee camps—Baq'a and Irbid. It showed how communities never moved on but continued to name their shops after places in Palestine: "Cafeteria Palestine," "Jerusalem Center for Frozen Fish and Market."

"In the camps, you have a home but no houses of your own," Noura Al Khasawneh, assistant director, explained. "In the Galilee you have a house but you don't have a home. The dilemma is you either have a house or a home but you can never have both."

CULTURE AND THE ARTS

HAVING SUNG FOR MANY years with the Paris Choral Society, I hoped to continue my vocal training, and discovered the Noor-Hussein Foundation's Jordan Conservatory of Music was close to my house. When the Jordan Conservatory director eyed me and asked if the enrollment was for me *or my children*, I realized it was a children's school. I noticed that my name on my voice teacher's attendance sheet was Emily George meaning Emily bint (daughter of) George. My whole name is Emily George Cabot Lodge because they require the first name of my grandfather (Cabot). Bob joked if you were Ms. That, and Thayer's (his lawyer's) daughter and if our friend

David Dunn was Thayer's grandfather, you would be called, "Bin [sic] Thayer Dunn That."

Last night, we drove around in circles trying to find the Royal Cultural Center, to attend an opera, the first ever performed in Amman, organized by the French Embassy for the restoration of Petra. Bobby kindly passed me a tranquilizer from his wallet and congratulated me for keeping calm.

The works of thirteen Kuwaiti artists, Egyptian artist Amal Kenaway and German artist Antje Majewski were featured in the lobby. *Abu Hassan*, an operetta by Carl Von Weber, based on a *One Thousand and One Nights* tale is a story of a husband and wife and their ruses for paying their debts.

First, the husband suggests his wife seduce Omar, the caliph's treasurer, since he knows Omar lusts after her. She refuses and locks Omar in a closet where he stays for the rest of the opera; then the husband and wife play dead to elicit the sympathy of the caliph, but when they see how they have aggrieved him, they reveal their trickery; then they publicly accuse Omar, the treasurer, of seduction and open the closet door. At this turning point of the opera, the caliph agrees to forgive their debts. The moral of course involves the power of seduction and how it weighs in the balance of choices open to wives—a good subject all too frequently twisted in Arab society but in this context, successfully transformed into comedy.

A lavish party at the French ambassador's house followed the opera; our hostess, Donatella, a loquacious Italian countess, wore a long dress made of pale purple silk from India. There was roasted lamb hand-cut from a spit and placed in small pitta envelopes and a large assortment of hors d'oeuvres.

POVERTY

THE POVERTY IN THIS country was overwhelming and too much food was wasted on special occasions, especially weddings. Small boys would sit by the highways with their heads in their hands and occasionally get up the courage to sell something to the people stopped at the light—chewing gum, flowers, flags, or delicious fresh figs. For a few days I'd been trying out a new maid, who asked me, "Rich people don't pray. Do you pray, Madame?" I answered, "Of course I do," and wondered at the enormity of her statement.

The British ambassador here had just spoken at a lunch about the 14 per cent income gap between Protestants and Catholics as the cause for the civil war in Ireland. "Imagine," he said, "if one side was seven per cent and the other 93 per cent, as is the case in the Palestinian-Israeli ratio." The British and the Americans must be aware that poverty is the root of the problem. At that moment, Israel was taking the opposite occupation strategy as the U.S. did after WW II toward the Japanese. If they were to build the society up instead of tearing it down, there would be peace.

THE LANGUAGE KEY

THE ARAB LANGUAGE WAS beginning to seep into me. Allah is the name employed for God in all three Abrahamic faiths here. Our God, I discovered, is their God. I recognized words and common in conversations. May God give you health and strength—one of the most repeated expressions in the Islamic faith—"Allah yatik el afyeh." "*IftaH* means to open, *FataH* is the past tense, opened, and *FateH*, meaning '*opening*,' is also the name for the PLO party founded by Arafat. The Islamic armies that conquered most of the Middle East in the 7th and 8th centuries are called the '*FaateHeen*' because they opened the countries to the Muslim faith," Nyla told us.

The proverbs taught us how much we have in common with the Arabs.: "Illa faat, maat" means literally *what has passed, has died* or *let bygones be bygones*. Another is "Illi byrob el bab, byisma9 il joab" meaning *he who knocks on the door shall find the answer*, or the Biblical, "*seek and ye shall find.*" Another is "iza fi Iradia, fi tariq"—or "*where there is a will, there's a way.*"

"We have a proverb," Nyla told us, "for when you say, 'I wish.' 'A wish never built a house.' (Kilmet yareit, homorha ma amarat beit.) Another proverb I like more… 'If you plant the word, lau, (meaning 'if'), 'I wish' will come up: (Iza tizrah kilmet lau, yareit) in other words, with wishful thinking, you get nothing."

OLD AMMAN

THE NEWLY RENOVATED GALLERY named "Lines" is in an old house in Wild Jordan, deep into the wadi, and still has a courtyard full of eight lovely orange trees. Zara, the wife of a former director of the Central Bank, an artist and philanthropist, had invited us to the previous night's opening of her art center and school with an exhibition by Hind Nasser, which reminded me a little of Georgia O'Keeffe's work and an early period of Kandinsky's. In the old part of Amman, the architecture of the "first circle" has a Bauhausian feel. There are also some small villas with Palladian windows, tucked away on the narrow streets off Rainbow Street. "Tout Amman" was there and the air was filled with the cheerful sound of the members of a small world greeting one another. "There is nothing more heavenly than an 'orangerie' in bloom," Ghada, my Syrian friend from Damascus, was saying. All the women wore calf-length dresses or trousers, making me self-conscious in my knee-length sleeveless pink and orange print.

In the 1950s and '60s, the Turkish Princess Fahrelnissa, a prominent artist whose work is part of the Istanbul museum collection, befriended young artists like Hind Nasser. The princess is the mother of Prince Ra'ad whose father, Zeid, was the brother of King Faisal I of Iraq prior to the bloody revolution that eventually brought Saddam Hussein to power. Hind is a lively member of the arts community here though Mohanna Durra is the most famous Jordanian artist today.

There isn't a tradition of free speech here to give voice to the arts. At lunch at Centro, a hopping local restaurant, I spoke with a friend of Hana's from Beirut who had just seen *The Vagina Monologues* which addresses PMS, menopause, sexual abuse, rape and adultery. This play could never be performed in conservative Amman, which has only nine nightclubs.

Anton and Salwa hosted a dinner that night that also included Katya, our Circassian friend. Their 1950s restaurant, Nobile, has the look of a Tuscan villa, constructed in amber stone, built into the side of a jabal (mountain) overlooking a wadi (valley) and with a large court, big enough to host sixty people for dinner. Everyone was smoking hookahs outside and drinking a delicious mint-with-vodka concoction. Every night from May to October is beautiful—dry and cool but warm enough for a sleeveless dress. Anton believes in tolerance above all else, that faith and fashion have nothing to do with one another. At Nobile there was always a plentiful supply of bosomy women in tight jeans.

Rotary Wednesday

At a Rotary Club lunch, we met Anne, a gregarious Texan whose business was selling textbooks about English as a foreign language in the Middle East. She noticed that Bob had been climbing down the wadi from our house and up the jabal to the Radisson Hotel. Being new to Amman at that time, he had thought he could walk to the hotel since it looked so close. Anne, whose unceasing laughter stood out here, quipped, "Who do you think you are, Moses!?"

Katya announced that the Gift of Life program had raised $13,529 to treat Jordanian and Iraqi children with severe heart trouble. Seated next to me at lunch was Nadia, of the National Society for the Enhancement of Freedom and Democracy (JUND), a tall, good-looking freelance journalist, who had recently entered political life. Some Muslims say Islam is more democratic than democracy because it is founded on compassion toward the less advantaged but she told me this does not translate into democracy in government.

"The whole problem is the election law," Nadia said. "Under the 1989 law, there was a multi-vote system according to constituency. For the big cities, like Amman, three to four names were allowed. In 1993, this was changed to one man, one vote. What this means, practically speaking, is that the tribes in parliament rule the country and their terms are four years. People will vote in the Parliament for their tribe (which means minorities won't be represented). They don't want to change the system, first, because the system is patriarchal. They don't want women to improve the personal status laws—the divorce laws and the laws against honor killings. [Women only got the vote in Jordan in 1974; in the U.S. it was 1920]. Their interest lies in keeping women weak so that they do not have their own financial resources. Secondly, the Muslim Brotherhood is very well organized and they do not want them to take over."

Water is the probably the single most important issue in a desert country like Jordan and yet there was no major centralized body to deal with it. Over the years, many dams collected water from streams that depended on rainwater but without any unified government system. Where it was caught, the water was directed into the bigger streams and those were cleaned. The government was encouraging "desert dams" for cattle growing—or "sand dams"—which was nothing more than digging big holes, lining them to receive winter rainwater, then using it during the summer. The Rotary started a project to save rainwater in Karak. In the winter, the plentiful rain fills the dams but without a system for catching the run-off. On a local level, clans within tribes feud over land and look after their own land-holdings, not beyond. Although the problems are regional, there are scattered projects here and there.

"There is no community mentality to try to make things better," said one member. One tribal leader, who spent $75,000 to build a dam to collect rainwater, sells it throughout the year and he's already turning a profit. Although from a traditional background, he was educated abroad and quite forward-thinking whereas most tribal leaders don't necessarily want to get their hands dirty."

Nevertheless, such an approach would have royal backing for Prince Hassan has said, "Let's tackle these areas on a regional, multilateral level and involve Syria, Egypt, Palestine, Israel and Saudi Arabia which all border the Jordan Valley in a small area." The Royal Scientific Society, founded in 1980 by Prince Hassan, had an environmental sciences arm dedicated to water and alternative energy research projects but it was a research body with no actual power.

THE GUTSY PRINCESS

AS A YOUNG PRINCESS, Aisha lied to her father, King Hussein, who had forbidden her to join the army, and then parachuted down in front of him during a ceremony. Due to a diplomatic emergency, she was unable to give the Rotary talk and her replacement that day was Ola, the creator of Global Village, modeled after the commercial success of Dubai, who gave a presentation about the Village set to open in Jordan in July. Once a year, dealers from all over the world come and offer their wares tax-free. As the taxes on goods here are sometimes between 20 and 40 percent, that is a big saving and friends told me later that they found everything from pearls to rugs at the Global Village. I happened to be seated next to Ola at lunch prior to her presentation. A leading Jordanian businesswoman, she was one of the richest and also one of the most voluptuous woman in Jordan. She spoke to me privately of the beauty of the female form. I asked her whether girls here grow up being ashamed of their sex, as is often the case elsewhere. She was shocked: "When God created woman, He created a work of art. Women must recognize and revel in their beauty. Think of her lips, her breasts, her waist and hips, all for the function of giving birth. Men, on the other hand, are not works of art; they are created to be athletes."

THE UNFORTUNATE AMERICAN

ANOTHER ROTARY CLUB LUNCHEON featured a student leader from the University of Wisconsin, here on a State Department grant to foster understanding between Islam and the West. He failed.

I was chatting with him, saying how Jordan really is Palestine, historically and many other ways—how Palestinians contribute so much to this country, and how hated Israel is for the illegal occupation of their land. It had a bad effect on him and he launched into a diatribe saying Amman was a mere transit point between Baghdad and Damascus, Jerash and Petra. He went on to point out that when the Circassians were "kicked out" of the Russian steppe and made their way to the Jordan Valley in the late 19th century, it was such a primitive place that a railway car served as their palace. He even made a vague reference to extremist Israelis' ancient claims to this land. He also said that when he told his Jewish tailor he was going to Amman, he said, "Oh you mean Rabbath Ammon," the Old Testament name. Finally, he said, it was the Palestinians who had made Jordan a success, knowing that Jordan had once had a short civil war with the Palestinians; in spite of Jordan's beautiful and talented Palestinian Queen, tensions between the Jordanian minority and the Palestinians still exist.

Furious Rotary members stood up and asked, "Who are you to tell us our history? You should know that Jordanians are welcoming and kind but when we are angry, we fight back." I was embarrassed that he was American and thought how sad for him to have sabotaged his own future in Jordan.

THE WELCOME RULE

JORDANIANS ALWAYS SAY THEY have problems with U.S. foreign policy but not with Americans. They almost prefer people from the outside. They prefer Westerners to Syrians or Iraqis because of the inter-Arab rivalries.

Europeans have had the same sorts of rivalries. Perhaps living in the desert fosters the tradition of befriending the next interesting person that comes along. Arabs are aware of their image as either oil sheiks or terrorists, they know they have something to prove, are quite eager to rectify it, and go out of their way to do so.

At a Rotary gathering, a social studies teacher told me the curriculum teaches the children the positives and negatives of Jordanian history. The Bedouin tribal tradition of inordinate hospitality comes from the legend of Hatem: without any sheep, he killed his horse in order to provide food for his visitors, foregoing his mode of transportation and risking his life. The evil side of Jordanian culture, conversely, she said, is the mistreatment of women—in some tribes, if more than one baby girl was born, she was buried alive in the sand. Although the prophet is said to have had thirteen wives—some for personal reasons and others for diplomatic reasons—he attempted to limit the number of wives to four to protect them and strengthen their power. After the prophet, the sultans took four wives but increased the number of slave girls to the hundreds.

Her husband, Daoud, CEO of United Technology Solutions, (in partnership with Oracle, a competitor of Microsoft in database software) was the treasurer of Rotary Amman. Contrary to what is generally reported in the Western press, USAID helps young Jordanian people to make information technology their focus. But Daoud was not interested in this type of CV and would rather have seen one with a liberal arts background, echoing the opinion of a friend and top U.S. IBM executive.

My first question is always, will there be peace in the Middle East? Will Hamas ever recognize the state of Israel? The answer: Will Israel recognize the state of Palestine and Hamas, one of its democratically elected parties? Bob interjected, "Impossible because they have vowed to destroy the state of Israel." This little conversation was the whole problem in microcosm: neither side was willing to extend the working hand—not even in this assiduously generous and hospitable country—and Nasrallah, Hezbollah's leader, had become a hero.

NABA

THE HORROR IN IRAQ continued day after day and still no interior or defense minister had been appointed. The number of American soldiers killed in Iraq had reached 2500; the amount spent on the war was $350 billion—sobering for what was intended to be quick. Bobby commented, "After a year, the U.S. will have to withdraw, then it will be very Hobbesian, like Rwanda. Everyone will be at war with everyone."

The day before we had read that one Iraqi woman lost her husband, age fifty, and all her sons, two of whom were the same ages as ours—25 and 21. I burst into uncontrollable tears.

Bob asked, "What is the matter with you?"

"I grieve with that woman. Her sons were exactly the same age as our own."

The next day, a new horror: in Baghdad, twenty-four teenage students, on their way to take their college exams, were dragged from their school buses and shot, one by one, in the head by rogue militia dressed as police. That day twenty-one Shiite college students were murdered on their way to take their exams, north of Baghdad (four Sunni students were released). Then came the gruesome discovery of seventeen severed heads in a melon crate. Death was always around us—from Baghdad to the Gaza Strip.

Everyone was conflicted about Iraq. Some felt guilty for abandoning them and they wanted the Americans to solve the problem…with good reason. But the Americans committed some serious errors—*erreurs de comportement*, as the French say, *inviting* a terrorist response. They went house to house with dogs, an animal that is considered repugnant in the Middle East. Secondly, they searched women in their houses which is absolutely forbidden by Islamic law for a man who is not a woman's husband.

On a flight from Amman to Paris, the men and women were being processed in separate lines at security while Gulf princes were whisked through. Flustered, I found myself seated next to a serene woman from Baghdad who told me she didn't mind the separate lines, she was happy just to get on the plane. Naba, a University professor, was full of dignity and love in an environment in which many were deprived of basic human rights. She was a Shia who had been nominated by Adnan Pachachi to be Deputy Education Minister. She spoke of her NGO, New Horizons for Women and Youth and her speaking tour to Northwestern University, the University of Chicago, Georgetown University and on National Public Radio, as well as her appointment as Iraq's Deputy Education Minister by Adnan Pachachi.

At lunch in the Four Seasons' Square Bar, she spied many Iraqis, whom she could identify by their accents—one-third of the population here, she said, five hundred thousand people. "The entire Iraqi government is here—the director of the Central Bank, there's…" her friend said, her voice trailing off. "You know, Jordan is made up of Bedouin tribes. Baghdad has a long history. Baghdad is Baghdad."

We dined with some Palestinian friends of Naba's—one from Jerusalem, the director of an Arab women journalists group, the other from Hebron. Her brigadier commander husband said, "Americans here in Jordan are not safe even for two hours—that's how dangerous it is." He also said America should stay in Iraq.

"Why?" I asked.

"To win!" he exclaimed. Regarding Palestine, he told the story of attending a conference where he asked to be seated next to a member of the Likud. Pretending he was Israeli, he suggested purifying the West Bank by killing 4,000 Palestinians a day for fifteen years; his Likud dinner partner was shocked at this idea. There is always the subtle and not so subtle correlation made that Americans are Zionists. As if we didn't know, he added, "God loves all of us, all the time."

On parting, Bob called to him, "Get more opinionated. Stop being so wishy-washy."

He laughed nervously as if he didn't understand.

In the car going home, Naba slowly removed the necklace and earrings she was wearing—a turquoise with diamonds surrounding it—and gave them to me. I had admired them earlier in the day and she said she had been thinking what she was going to give me. You have to be very careful in this part of the world because if you admire something, people will give it to you; the convention is you must refuse to take it three times, and if, after that, the giver still insists then it is rude not to take it.

I later received this letter from Naba, describing a video:

(the text of the video) "My Name is Baghdad [call to prayer sounds]… I have lived so happily in palaces of black gold and precious stones. The Tigris flowed on crystal paved roads. A thousand caliphs jostled to dance with me. [The beauties of Baghdad are shown in photographs and paintings.] They called me the city full of grace. God, how time passes. They called me the capital of enlightenment. God, how everything is lost. My name is Baghdad and I have fallen under the fire of armored tanks. [CNN footage of "Shock and Awe".] My name is Baghdad, a disfigured princess. Scheherazade has forgotten me. I live on my land like a poor beggar under the bulldozers. A spirit haunts me. I mourn my ravaged beauty over the smoldering stones. It is my soul they are assassinating... God, how everything is lost... My tales of one thousand and one nights no longer interest anyone. [The screen goes black.] Can we do something ?"

VISITORS

MY SPANISH FRIEND, Irene, had come from Paris. Her outstanding feature is her hair that stands out like topiary and her abhorrence of brashness in people and things. She spent hours putting paper covers around the bright lights on the terrace to soften the glare. Her subtle characterization of Bob as "the master of deflection" fits just right. I often ponder the wisdom of her humor concerning a friend in Paris, "The combination of being extroverted and not very clever doesn't go over well with the French."

Irene brought our younger son, George, 21. He has the tall, thin body of a cyclist, with blond hair, piercing blue eyes and a noble Gallic nose. His brother, Maxwell, once described his younger brother as being "the milk of human kindness." When I held him as a baby, he had the look of an owl, a quiet, wise observer. Every so often, he comes out with some incisive, razor sharp remark but said with the greatest tenderness, as if an invisible knife had pierced the air. He told us he doesn't like to impose his presence in places where he feels Americans aren't welcome. Hana remarked, "Sensitive boy."

I was trying to repay the multiple kindnesses of our Jordanian hosts by inviting our closest friends to a dinner on our terrace—Anton and Salwa, Katya, Hana and Faazi, Yolaine and Udo, Roland and Katerina. We were thirteen and the table was set outside with white linen and silver candlesticks. I made a lamb salad on a bed of spinach. Anton asked how dare I cook their national dish—only half-kidding—and said, "Lamb should always be served hot," reminding me of the surprise of a Frenchman when I served "lapin à la moutarde."

GERASA, THE DEAD SEA AND PETRA

ONE OF THE GREAT bonuses of living here are the outstanding archeological sites. Bob, George, Irene, and I drove to the largely intact Greco-Roman city of Jerash, 45 km north of Amman—as well-preserved as Ephesus. Perched on the top of a fertile valley with a good stream, the site has been settled since Neolithic times. Its early Semitic name was Garshu. Either it was re-founded by Alexander the Great or by his general, Perdiccas, for the purpose of settling Macedonian veterans or, more likely, later, by the Seleucid King Antiochus IV (175-164 BC). Little remains of the Hellenistic era because the Roman city of Gerasa entered into Pax Romana—a period of prosperity as one of the ten cities of the "Decapolis" mentioned earlier. The 1st century AD town plan featured two major colonnaded crossroads, north-south, and east-west. Chariot wheels mark the stone. The lovely Oval Piazza served as the gathering place for worship at the temple of Zeus and also as a marketplace. Although the temple of Zeus is largest, the precinct surrounding the temple to Artemis, the Greek equivalent of the Roman goddess Diana, perched in the middle of the settlement, is larger.

One of the mysteries of architecture is that the Artemis temple's columns move slightly and guides enjoy amusing visitors by placing wooden matches in the spaces where the stones meet to show how they lift—the wonder of ancient architecture built to withstand earthquakes. Down the hill are the market arcades and the sculptured grape leaves engraved at the nymphaeum, so named after the statues of water nymphs—it was the collection point for water, and a city's status was to a large extent judged on how much water they could get flowing through the nymphaeum—the more water the higher the status!

Although it was still swelteringly hot, I was eager to show our guests the Dead Sea, only 45 minutes south of Amman and then on to Petra. This lowest point on earth, 394 meters (1,293 feet) below sea level, is a kind of hell (in July) and heaven on earth. The Mövenpick Hotel was built in the low-lying bungalows in the style of an ancient village (I love it for the pretty flowering bushes and birds but George compared it to Disneyland).

George—who had bicycled from Paris to Berlin to see the World Cup games—arose late and was enjoying the total spa experience—one that is recommended for athletes in recovery. An endurance freak, he loves any and all seas, and took off for the "beach." At sunset, the approach to the beach was difficult. The air moved in a wavy pattern, as in the desert scenes in David Lean's *Lawrence of Arabia*; beyond the sea and the wavy air, one could make out the hazy pink hills of Jericho. We experienced the odd sensation of so stiffly floating that swimming is impossible except for vertical bicycling. With light-sensitive eyes and contact lenses melting, I returned to the room on George's arm. Meanwhile Irene, in her yellow bikini with white dandelions, happily installed herself on the beach, chatting with an eager Jordanian. By the time I took a cold shower and returned to the beach, it was almost dark. The hotel personnel sent us home for safety reasons, they told us. We enjoyed a delicious buffet supper on the screened-in terrace.

On the day of our departure from the hotel the next morning, Irene and I arose at six to float in the sea, when the last of the evening air had left the slightest layer of coolness. It was clear enough to see the mountains of Jericho, now occupied by extremist Israelis, looming from across the sea. An Arab woman in a billowing black silk burqa was attempting to enter the sea, fully clothed.

We considered going a little farther south to see Lot's cave, Deir 'Ain 'Abata. After leaving Zoar as fire and brimstone rained on the Cities of the Plain, Lot and his daughters settled in a cave in the mountains. Legend has it that since they were the last people on earth, the girls, worried about perpetuating the race, decided to get their father drunk and have intercourse with him, or so the guidebooks say. Both became pregnant and gave birth to sons whom they named Moab and Ben-Ammi (Genesis 19 :30-38). Thus, the Bible explains the origins of the Moabite and Ammonite peoples. Lot's cave, where the family traditionally took shelter, was a holy site from the Byzantine to early Abbasid periods, (5 BC - 8 BC), and there is evidence for earlier occupation going back to the Bronze Age.

At Karak, at the crossroads of the central axis of Jordan, we stopped at the Crusader castle. Taking the King's Highway south, one comes upon the Dana Reserve, with the blue mountain range—gigantic and barren like a scene from *Star Wars*. At Petra, the *siiq*—the cavernous narrow entrance to the ancient rose city deep inside the towering rocks—is a kilometer long. There are pagan and Christian sacred sites in little nitches in the siiq as well as at the tops of mountains with astonishing gradations of blue, pink, and yellow; centuries of pilgrims have climbed steps in the rock. One lone 450-

year-old pistachio tree stands in the sand at a place that used to have a fountain—the watering hole and central gathering place of the ancient city—and the biblical importance of the shade of trees instantly became clear.

At the end of the Roman colonnade, where camel and donkey riders vie for clients, there are two or three large berry-bearing trees providing shade for a restaurant offering a large buffet of home style cooking—grilled chicken and lamb, hummous and salads. The climb to the Al-Deir monastery, hair-raising as it is, has fantastic views of the valleys of Little Petra, Wadi Jarasa, Bedaf Wadi Arabe and Feinan. Walking twenty kilometers through this city that was once inhabited by more than 30,000 people, makes the return to the Mövenpick Hotel at the end of the day, like returning to an oasis after the brutality of the desert.

Irene and I joined George in the bar, fitted out with a giant screen. That night, France was scheduled to play Brazil in the World Cup. George became famous in the hotel for being the only supporter of France, the former colonial rulers of Syria and Lebanon. The next day, we took the desert highway back to Amman and noted poor sad structures standing lonesome by the highway. The wind descends from the sky in columns and small and gentle swirling sandstorms move across the horizon.

CULTURE AND THE ARTS

WE DROVE TO THE NORTH gate of Jerash for a special performance of Mozart's *Requiem* and an unusually beautiful ballet performed by the French Ballet d'Europe. TF1 and France 3 were filming the performance. There was a pit for the Orchestra of the National Music Conservatory of Jordan and the Choir of the Faculty of Music of the Holy Spirit University of Lebanon.

Yolaine, ever vigilant in her friendship, pulled us into the VIP section reserved for the ambassadors. We were sitting on cushions in the smaller of the two amphitheaters, with stones cut high to fit the length of the human form between the hip and the foot. Scenery and costume designer Jean-Michel Bruyère had clothed the dancers in white—the girls in knee-length dresses open at the front or in pants, and the men mostly bare-chested in loose-fitting pants or tunics with loose leg-socks. Stark lighting from the left onto a white sheet made the ancient makeshift stage billow off the amber stone, visual poetry celebrating the greatness of mystery and unpredictability in a setting composed of air, wind and stone. This requiem to the dead celebrates life, and the greatness of the ephemeral. The ballet began with the dancers lying on the stage and then coming to life, mingling, body over body, and one with the other. As the choreographer wrote in the program, "During the whole Requiem, lines are spreading and extending, re-birthing perpetually in a subtle respiration."

Bob asked, "Do you think the Romans would have imagined that we would still be sitting here two thousand years later?"

I said, "Yes, that is probably the way they had planned it—for the Roman Empire to last forever."

After the Italians won the World Cup the day before, this country whose history is so intertwined with the Roman Empire, burst into excited frenzy with fireworks and horns honking well into the night.

WHAT NOT TO WEAR

I WAS REMINDED THERE IS a dress code. Doing an errand at 8 pm at a hotel, I was standing under the awning with some people. There was a large, powerful, gray-haired man in a suit. When he saw me in my white linen sleeveless dress, he turned to me with hate in his eyes and murmured something to his wife who was dressed in an elegant pantsuit. Another outfit crossed off the list. On my return, Bob remarked how emotional Arabs are: "The soldier guarding the house told me that he cried each time I left the house and that he waited for me to return."

PEACE CONFERENCE AND LITTLE PAPER BALLS

I TOOK A TAXI TO THE Royal Cultural Center and the driver gave me a thumbs-up, telling me, "American women, tops." The Royal Cultural Center - built in 1966 and housing a theater/cinema and exhibition halls - stands on the outer limits of Sports City with a soccer stadium seating 25,000, a dozen tennis courts, a tennis stadium for matches, three Olympic-size swimming pools and a huge auditorium.

An Israeli scholar and speaker asked if she could sit with me on the bus. I noticed she was looking at the length of my white blue jean skirt (to the knee) out of the corner of her eye. She asked if I had been pelted with little paper balls from cars driving by in the street. No, I replied, I hadn't experienced harassment, any more so than anywhere else. That took her a few minutes to digest: "Well, perhaps you drive [which is mostly true] and live in a good neighborhood [which is also true]."

She said women wear the headscarf not only to get a husband but because they are harassed. She told me she was one of eight Israeli Jews attending and would speak about the exodus of Jews from Arab countries. I told her how I was told that they hate Israel in this country.

With a wan smile, she said, "Well, yes, of course, the Palestinians do. But can you imagine if seven million people were to actually get their land back. It's impossible."

I asked why everyone couldn't live together the way they do in Jerusalem, noting, by and large, how well Jews and Arabs seemed to get along. She blinked and smiled, "Prime Minister Olmert is very right wing and in any case, is not allowed much leeway either by the parliament or by his own party."

FUNDAMENTALISM HAS KILLED JOY

HAMZAH, ONE OF KING HUSSEIN'S sons by Queen Noor, spoke briefly, in the place of King Abdullah, who had been called away. He descended the stairs in Arab dress, while elderly men murmured homages to the prince, touching their foreheads and bowing slightly. Then Prince Hassan, president of the Club of Rome and of WOCMES, the (2nd) World Congress for Middle Eastern Studies, welcomed the thirteen hundred participants from seventy-eight countries. Intrigued by his remark on friends and enemies, I was reminded that Prince Hassan is the 42nd generation descendant of the prophet Muhammad so that his interpretation of the Islamic ideal, as interpreted in Medina, holds weight.

He began by saying there is a long tradition in the Middle East of the search for enlightenment but that currently there is a "human dignity deficit." He said that *fundamentalism had killed joy* and that aesthetic "uplift" was essential for moving from discursive to intuitive knowledge. He said that the Middle East was in the middle of the smoking zone of the debate about WMDs and that all should be concerned about "MAS", "mutually assured survival". He predicted that the war on terror would peak in the next few months and for it to recede, job opportunities needed to be created: "There needs to be a culture of participation rather than a culture of sheep."

Hassan quoted *La Croix*, a French Catholic newspaper, which, in an editorial, claimed that the emphasis had shifted from oppressed Palestinian people and the unresolved Jewish question to the plight of ten million Christian Arabs. He said the three Abrahamic faiths should rise above politics. He joked that once he spoke to Shimon Peres who told him, "We are surrounded by enemies," and he (the prince) had replied, "You think you've got problems. We are surrounded by friends!...Saddam Hussein has ten billion dollars in bank accounts outside of Iraq. Wouldn't it be wonderful," he said, "if it became an endowment to rebuild the churches, the mosques and to develop a pro-active initiative for social change since religion is about people, not just buildings?"

He invited the Muslims, Christians and Jews at the conference to develop a deeper understanding of each other, to build up the knowledge bases in the Middle East, to develop human dignity. "We, the tolerant ones, are the silent majority, the silenced majority."

CHILDREN OF ADAM NOT ISLAM

"THE FUTURE," HE SAID, "is either one of ethnic and sectarian strife, surrendering to extremists, the 'privatizers' of religion, or the future is with us. Let us remind the world of the Muslim intellectual tradition. Farina Allen from the *Observer* wrote, 'Freedom of speech is not an absolute. It has to be in the service of something.' We must stop thinking of ourselves as children of Islam but rather as children of Adam... Muslims should eradicate hunger. The Gulf States have $500 million a day in income....If we ignore the human context, it will become a time bomb... The bombs facing us are not the obvious ones but those of poverty, environment, and illiteracy... St. Thomas Aquinas was an Algerian. I ask the three faiths: we've come this far in science, how far have we come with humanity?"

Then he quoted Ecclesiastes...there is a time to love and a time to hate... "Stop focusing on the internet—which is obviously important—and start focusing on the inner-net. The virtuous reality is that we are children of the past, masters of the present, custodians of the future. Forgive another speech," he said, "from an arrogant pedant. Edward Gibbon, the great historian, once wrote, 'When the freedom they wanted most was freedom from responsibility, Athens ceased to be free.' Altruism, a sense of mutual interest, the recognition of human dignity, the fact that 35,000 people die of hunger every day, reconciling interest and responsibility—this is our future. Groucho Marx once said, 'Military intelligence is a contradiction in terms.'" He concluded, "Even if the Day of Judgment is near, there is still time to plant a tree."

FILM FESTIVAL

THE WOCMES CINEMA COORDINATOR, Lina Khatib, Professor of World Cinema at the University of London boycotted her own festival; protesting the naming of an Israeli teacher on the staff of a school in the West Bank's occupied territories as a panelist, she had taken the films and gone back to Beirut.

Thanks to Maysoon Pachachi, we had copies of the Iraqi films, *Baghdad Days* by Hiba Bassem (Iraq, 2005) and Maysoon's own film called *Return to the Land of Wonders*. Maysoon is the daughter of Adnan Pachachi, widely known as the James Madison of Iraq, and the sister of my childhood friend, Reema, with whom I was inseparable when our families were living in Washington in the 1950s. Adnan was one of a handful of people who created the Iraqi constitution and who made it his personal crusade to include a bill of rights.

In the question period afterwards, I asked her if she believed, as her film seemed to be saying, that the Americans should leave Iraq. She said her personal opinion was that the Americans should leave. Afterwards, Maysoon knew me immediately—"Emmy!" she cried, to my surprise—and privately told me the troops should stay but they must change—and create a civilian relief force, to stop the destruction of schools and mosques, and start providing adequate electricity and drinking water. Most of all the Americans needed to stop arbitrary arrests, killings and other violations of the Geneva Convention. If the U.S. combined bringing in 20,000 new troops with as much money going into humanitarian relief—medicine, doctors, food and water—then it would all be over very shortly.

In a panel discussion the next day, Lebanese anchorwoman Mrs. Khormy, wife of the slain Lebanese journalist, was saying that in the 1950s and '60s, women were more liberated in Egypt than they are today. Egyptian cinema directors and other artists had liberated the Middle East from the domination of the Ottoman Empire. Egypt became a pole to attract Arab thinkers. She spoke about the Arab renaissance and the subsequent rise of fundamentalism.

"We have to ask ourselves," she said, "how this renaissance failed and jihad became the alternative. We have to examine the corruption in Arab societies. We have to be proponents of the separation between the state and religion. We must not think that the world wants to kill us, but look with openness toward the world. We must believe there are some Americans who take a position against the killings in Palestine. The direction is against Americans and we must encourage dialogue, must make it an option. We must reject the culture of death."

Muslims disagree with what the West conceives of as jihad. The conquests of all of North Africa and Arabia and parts of Europe by Walid and Suleiman were partly religious and partly for political gain, like the Crusades. Louis XIV, Napoleon or Hitler were purely political. Jihad is the struggle of the inner being, out of the darkness and the chaos to ask ourselves why we are alive. It is the search for meaning. Nowhere in the Qur'an, I was told, is there anything supporting violence except in self-defense. It is the prophet's personal reflection on how to empty your ego and achieve compassion—a practical, day-to-day religion. [15] Author Mark Gabriel

---

[15] Reza Aslan explains in *No God but God: The Origins, Evolution and Future of Islam,* "Like puritans of other faiths—militaristic or not—the jihadists' principal goal is the 'purifying' of their own religious communities. In other words, their first target is not the West, or Jews, or Christians, or Zionists, or Crusaders, or any other outsiders (what the jihadists term 'the far enemy'), but those hundreds of millions of Muslims who do not share their puritanical worldview ('the near enemy'). Their agenda can most clearly be observed in the civil war they have launched in Iraq....Of course, that is not to say that the far enemy is not a target of jihadism, as New York, Madrid, and London can testify. But it is mainly as a means to galvanize other Muslims to the jihadist cause that most of these attacks against the West should be understood. The attacks of September 11, 2001, for example, were by bin Laden's own admission specifically designed to goad the United States into an exaggerated retaliation against the Islamic world so as to mobilize Muslims to, in the words of George W. Bush, 'choose sides.'...Thus, the day before the London bombings, one hundred and seven of

explains in *The Meaning of Holy War* that the prophet Muhammad only sanctioned war when there was a just cause, in other words, when Muslims were persecuted or attacked first.

To those against whom war is made, permission is given (to fight), because they are wronged.

—Surah 22:39, Ali translation

In the question and answer session, Prince Hassan was asked whether there was one world-class university in the Muslim world. Bilkent University in Turkey has as good a reputation in the sciences as any Ivy League school, he replied. He said that the brain drain was a brain gain, because the Arabs who study in America share their knowledge on their return (although many stay in the U.S.) He hoped for a return to a culture tolerant of the three Abrahamic faiths and open to ideas and innovation, stretching from the Mediterranean to the Red Sea. He said it was easy to develop a siege mentality and less easy to develop economically. He reminded the audience that the greatest achievements of the Arab world pre-date the discovery of oil.

Hassan's answer to peace in the Middle East was supranational humanitarianism. "Democracy must not be talked about in connection with sovereignty…we must work on putting oneself in the shoes of the other. Water has no nationality and no brand name." He quoted Aldous Huxley, "nationalism is a common misconception of governments… The focus should be on inclusion not exclusion." He proposed creating an intergovernmental organization, a combined EU and UN for the Arab world. "Remember," he said, "Europe created the Coal and Steel Community not so long ago and oil reserves could be the basis for a similar organizational

---

the world's leading clerics and scholars, representing every major sect and school of law in Islam, gathered in Amman, Jordan, where, in an unprecedented display of intersectarian collaboration, they issued a joint fatwa, or legal ruling, denouncing all acts of terrorism committed in the name of Islam. The Amman declaration was not only a tacit (if belated) acknowledgment of the civil war raging within Islam, it was an attempt by the clerical institutions to re-exert some measure of authority over those who have hijacked Islam for their own murderous causes. It didn't work."

unity, bridging the gaps between the haves and the have-nots," and reminding everyone that this year, the 60th anniversary of the creation of the United Nations, that Dumbarton Oaks should not be forsaken.

"There are 1.2 billion Muslim poor and the underlying strife associated with that calls for a new socio-economic vision beyond national interest which will be forgotten when the oil runs out. We must remember the natural rights which come with pluralism and the deep chasm of empathy and goodwill on both sides—West and East. The Muslim world needs a better communications strategy," he said, "than the response to a cartoon by burning down an embassy.

"The budget for Homeland Security is $35 billion. We live in a security-oriented society. We are brave enough to point out when Jerusalem is going the wrong way but we are not brave enough to point out when Medina is going the wrong way.... We must develop an impulse of rejecting the reflex to demonize the other!"

The prince urged going beyond blaming Zionism and neo-Islamism, beyond regional identities, to Ishwa—inspiration. (Loud applause—standing ovation.) Racism, hatred and fear continue to obscure the road to peace. The king hosted a gathering of Nobel Laureates in Petra, attended by Israeli Prime Minister Ehud Olmert and Palestinian President Mahmoud Abbas who vowed to meet to discuss the two-state solution and to revise academic textbooks to rid them of hatred and to set up a Palestinian-Israeli civil society forum to improve discussions. (Meanwhile another Israeli rocket was fired into Gaza.) The conference recommended creating a forum involving Nobel Laureates and civil society leaders from both sides—a "peace partners initiative," to be launched on the **eastern** side of the Dead Sea in November 2006. (Since the war with Lebanon broke out only a few days after the conference, the peace initiative on the Israeli side of the Sea has not taken place.)

GLACIAL RECEPTION

THE NEWS FROM GAZA was bad and the effect sobering: the Israeli offensive had killed more than forty Palestinians because of the kidnapping of one Israeli soldier. At the lunch given by Udo and Yolaine, a chill was in the air: no words needed, just an icy reception from Palestinians and Jordanians.

Dozens of Israeli tanks and bulldozers were shooting at houses and tearing through greenhouses. UN officials cited the same drastic problems as those in Iraq—water, food, electricity, and sanitation. Sixty-five U.S. citizens of Palestinian origin left Gaza on that Saturday in a convoy escorted by U.S. consular officials. Moreover, recent news reports of U.S. soldiers raping and murdering an Iraqi girl combined with the Haditha massacre by Marines had fueled calls for the 127,000 American troops to go home. Animosity toward America filled dinnertime conversations but Bobby noted wryly that after dessert, they asked him if it was possible to get visas to America for their children.

Although the incrimination and isolation was ever-present, Udo and Yolaine, our friends, went out of their way to make us feel at home. We were served a special Brazilian rum drink (Caipirinha) with quartered limes, sugar and ice—a drink that declares the afternoon a holiday. The Brazilian national dish (feijoada) is a delightful combination of beef and beans with white rice, accompanied by a sauce of various colors of hot peppers, some finely ground semolina to cover, and a side dish of shrimp in a coconut sauce.

The French economic attaché was talking about a new scheme for how French exports to Jordan are re-exported to Iraq. When sending new machinery into Iraq, they first remove the parts and send them separately; then they destroy the rest of the machine because otherwise it will be stolen and resold. "No problem," the Iraqi middlemen say, "Everything will be fine. We make many business." Once across the border, it is reconstructed, he told me.

At my end of the table the guests were all male, while Bobby's table companions were women. He dutifully avoided the topic of Israel and delighted in the interest in upper-class English women who take lovers. I mentioned that in researching my first book, *The Lodge Women, Their Men and Their Times*, I discovered my great-great-grandmother, Sally Frelinghuysen, would often visit Winston Churchill's mother, Lady Randolph, Jenny Jerome who, one historian estimated, had had 294 lovers! (Sally had been President Chester Arthur's mistress while her father was Secretary of State.) Jane Digby, the subject of one of Yolaine's talks, was Pamela Harriman's great-great aunt. After divorcing her husband, the Viceroy of India in 1830, one of the first divorce suits, Jane had several affairs with Austrian, Greek, and notables of other nationalities, before marrying a sheik, seventeen years her junior and they lived in Bedouin style in Damascus. Speaking of the courtesans, "les grandes horizontales", Yolaine said, "J'admire beaucoup ces femmes," (I very much admire these women) "because they gave everything up for love. " She then got up and led everyone in a little carnival dance. At another French group meeting, one of the ladies murmured she was going to have a "dirty weekend" at the Dead Sea and I asked her what that was. She looked at me as if I were Bambi. I was told that because women marry so young, often to men they hardly know, having affairs is not so uncommon in a land where men are allowed the flavor of the month.

OUR FRIEND THE KURDISH PRINCE

DONATELLA, THE FRENCH AMBASSADOR'S wife, invited us to the July 14th party and we asked if Saywan could join us. She looked a little shaken when we told her that Saywan Barzani, of the famous Barzani clan, and a polyglot who received his PhD in French from the Sorbonne and wrote his thesis on the history of the Kurds, was the Iraqi ambassador to Italy; he and his family would be staying with us and we were hoping to bring them along. Whenever he and Bob *se promenent à Paris* he gets horrified looks because he is the image of a terrorist with black hair and black bushy eyebrows and a wide face; he took Bob with him for safe-keeping. The feeling was mutual. There was at that time a frenzy of Iraqi reconstruction and Bob was bidding on an electrical project where no one else would go.

As the festivities at the French Embassy had got under way the night before, Zahran Street was swarming with police. The residence, nestled inside a spacious garden with jasmine and other flowering trees, has a small pool just outside, which women in pretty summer dresses and high heels could easily topple into. Donatella greeted her guests in a long pale green strapless dress of Indian silk. Bob introduced me to David Hale, the American ambassador—young, agreeable, and relaxed. He was happy that King Abdullah had just condemned Hezbollah's kidnapping of two Israeli soldiers and the killing of seven. "Mais personne ne parle des morts," Amb. Saywan Barzani, known for his wit, quipped, "donc il faut rester vivant."— *No one talks about the dead so one must remain alive.* Israelis called it a declaration of war, blockaded Lebanese ports and bombarded the Beirut International Airport, forcing flights to divert to Cyprus. Hezbollah fighters fired 100 rockets into northern Israel, hitting Haifa, Israel's third largest city. Two civilians were killed and ninety-two were wounded. Israeli bombing in Lebanon had killed fifty-five and tourists were flooding out of Beirut into neighboring Syria or to Amman.

At the Masnaa border post, 15,000 foreign registered vehicles, mostly from the gulf, had crossed into Syria. The Lebanese were crossing the border any way they could and had packed the hotels here. Everyone was worried that another Lebanese civil war would break out. Damascus sent the guns and Tehran sent the money to finance Hezbollah; the king was not happy with either Syria or Iran. Nor was he happy about Israeli reprisals in Palestine for a Hamas-led attack on Israel and the kidnapping of one of their soldiers. He had also opposed the Quartet's support for withholding funding from Hamas that refused to recognize the state of Israel. The day before the U.S. vetoed a Security Council measure condemning the Gaza offensive; this would not endear us to our new Palestinian friends.

NASRALLAH

ANTON JOINED US AT NOBILE and we asked him what the chances for Middle East peace were. He said that there was a greater chance now than ever because the Arabs felt they won the Israeli-Lebanese war, he proclaimed jubilantly, "Eighty to one hundred Israeli tanks were knocked out! We've never done that in any previous war with Israel." Nasrallah, the Hezbollah chief, was a hero and there was a newfound confidence; they felt (naively) that Israel was now more willing to give ground, even to give back the land they had won in previous wars.

Anton had invited his friend, Ica, a red-headed Rumanian married to a Jordanian, and editor of the opinion pages at the *Jordan Times*, who reminded me that one man's terrorist is another man's freedom fighter. "Your country's rights and freedoms have been curtailed and you are taking it because they have bamboozled you into believing it is in the name of fighting terrorism. What is terrorism? Since Cain and Abel, there has been terror and cruelty and violence. How do you fight terrorism? Why we are upset with you around the world is because you are letting us down. The U.S. was the land of the free without the fear of persecution and now your people could disappear without a trace. Until ten years ago, you were respected but not after Guantanamo etc. How many of those killed in the World Trade Center attacks would be horrified by the freedoms that have been undermined today in the name of freedom?"

Bobby asked her, "What about the way we treated the Japanese during World War II? What about President Lincoln suspending the right of habeas corpus? In war, you do things at variance with human rights. The civil rights of combatants are not important, maybe incorrectly, maybe correctly. We are not perfect."

HOW RICH PALESTINE WOULD BECOME

ONE NIGHT WE WERE DINNER guests of another Palestinian and his wife originally from Jaffa. We tried to avoid the topic of Israel, but to no avail. Our host was saying that the Palestinians in Jordan were constantly going back in history and mulling over the events and mistakes of the past forty year war with Israel, a form of self-flagellation which he found appalling. "Hallas!" (*Enough* in Arabic) "Let's move on—from being the victim of Israeli aggression, the losers, and search for solutions in which we are the winners."

I asked them if they would favor a one-state solution in a parliamentary system where everyone is represented so that everyone could go home if they wanted to; many Palestinians say they would never return. Because the Palestinians would far outnumber the Jews, Bob said this proposal was considered unrealistic and that both the Palestinians and the Israelis would reject a solution that denied them national identity. Our host suggested a demilitarized zone rather than a Wall; in spite of himself, he kept returning to the same controversies of the past. Bob made the point that the hatred between the two sides over a tiny piece of land prevents any solution that does not establish two secure and independent states.

Our host spoke about Oman being considered the most stable country in the Middle East. The Gulf States will ensure that any country controlling the Straits of Hormuz is a stable one. Speaking of religious communities in war and peace, Bob said brightly how much better the situation was now in Northern Ireland. When I added, "And how much richer Ireland has become!" everyone suddenly turned and looked at me. I tried to change the subject to the worst of the world's problems: climate change and the general destruction of the planet but to no avail.

VISIT TO KURDISTAN

SAYWAN BARZANI, THE IRAQI ambassador to Italy, convinced me to accompany Bob to his native Kurdistan. Saddam Hussein, trying to subdue and eventually exterminate the Kurds, razed the trees on the mountains, Saywan explained, and destroyed whole villages—both his father and thirty-nine members of his family were murdered. Saywan's brother-in-law was the current prime minister.

Since the late 19th century, the Turks, the Russians, the Armenians, the British, the Germans, the Syrians, and the Iraqis, among others, have invaded Kurdistan (sixteen times since 1937). When you count the war against the Kurds, the war against the Shia, the war against Kuwait, and the war against Iran, he estimated that Saddam killed 2,000,000 people and caused unimaginable suffering to the families of all the Iraqi people. In the Kurdistan region, one sees very few middle-aged people. Most were killed during Saddam's Anfal campaign in the 1980s.

Now thanks to the Americans, free from Saddam's control, they were eager to broker a peace in Iraq, Saywan said. The Kurds and their world-renowned Peshmerga militia, embraced the American invasion, but had a difficult relationship with the Arab majority in Iraq. They are politically and geographically part of Iraq, but Bob quipped, "not so you'd notice."

Kurdistan's distinctive regional flags were ubiquitous but the Iraqi federal flag was banned from the region. Saywan said that the Americans should learn from the French who have always had the most commercial dealings with the area not only because they have always had the wisdom never to invade them but because they put a high value on their civilization.

In 7000 BC Iraq was called Mesopotamia, situated between the Tigris and the Euphrates rivers, the oldest known civilization; it is rich in natural resources, the legendary place of the Garden of Eden and the Tower of Babel, and strategically located for trade and commerce.

The Sumerians, (c. 4500-c. 2340 BC), a matriarchal society, invented writing in 4,000 BC, along with the mathematical functions of multiplication and division, the lunar calendar and the modern system of time based on the numeral 60. The Sumerians built Ur, (of the Chaldees), mentioned in the Bible as the home of Abraham. In 3700 BC, they invented the wheel. After the Sumerian Akkadian period, the Babylonians divided the days into twenty-four hours, each hour into sixty minutes and each minute into sixty seconds. The Assyrians, under the forty-three year reign of Hammurabi, wrote the first code of justice—282 laws carved on a stone monument, eight feet high and clearly intended to be read, (currently on display at the Louvre Museum), the most famous of which is the presumption of innocence, "an eye for an eye", and "let the buyer beware."

From Amman to Kurdistan, we flew west over the Syrian Desert, with flecks of green on entering Iraqi airspace. After touching down at Erbil, a city of one million, we were met by the Barzani family. Two muscular Peshmerga guards ushered us into a Lexus LX and drove us thirty minutes into the hills to the village of Saladin, named after the famous Muslim warrior, 1138-1193 AD, a Kurd born in Tikrit, who in various campaigns drove the Crusaders out of the Middle East.

Salah-al-Din (in Arabic, meaning the righteousness of the faith), educated in Damascus, founded the Ayyubid dynasty of what is now Egypt, Syria, Yemen, Iraq, Saudi Arabia, the Hejaz and southeast Turkey. The nation-state concept of frontiers and boundaries is not indigenous to the region. Saladin became sultan of Egypt in 1174 and marched on Damascus in 1181. In between those years, he left Jerusalem in the hands of the Crusaders (which the Crusaders had captured in 1099), as a buffer state until he could gain control of Syria. In 1176, an attempt on his life by a Syrian group, the Hashashins, (incidentally the origin of our word, *assassin*) failed.

In his battle to drive the Crusaders from the Orient, Saladin besieged Karak in 1183. The Crusaders lit bonfires there to communicate with Hebron just across the Dead Sea and thence, the message was carried by horse to crusader headquarters at Jerusalem. When Saladin took Karak, it was the end of the crusades because it was so strategic. In 1187, he captured Jerusalem. In the third Crusade led by King Richard of England, Saladin showed a chivalrous side by sending his personal physician to treat Richard's wounds. Richard suggested that his sister could marry Saladin's brother and Jerusalem could be their wedding present. In the Treaty of Ramla, 1192, the city would remain in Muslim hands but be open to Christian pilgrimages. By the time he died in 1193, Saladin had given all his money to charity.

We were staying in a government guesthouse on a perch overlooking

Erbil and behind us to the north was a mountain range of barren hills similar to those we saw driving between the Dead Sea and Petra. These mountains are partly snow-covered even in summer. The guesthouse was a gilded cage under heavy guard. In the computer area, one of the guards was playing a war game. I wondered whether he was fighting Saddam's forces or Turks in his mind. He ceded the computer to me without stopping the game and I found myself under tank attack with troops in American-style uniforms firing at me. I accidentally killed a video soldier trying to exit the game, and suddenly the warlike mentality struck home.

Les Kurdes: Destin héroïque, destin Tragique by Ambassador Bernard Dorin (whom I later met in Paris) explains: "The saber is the symbol of the Arabs whereas the knife is that of the Kurds." In this way, one can cite a Kurdish proverb revealing them as a war-like population: "The gun is your friend, the knife is your brother." Another Kurdish proverb full of wisdom, perfectly illustrates the specificity of the drama of the Kurds in the region: "A drowning man clings to whatever is on the banks of the river, even a serpent!" The Kurds have always been condemned to make alliances with one of four predatory states in order to survive and advance their cause— Syria, Turkey, Iran or Iraq.

In the lobby on the guesthouse television screen, we saw that Hezbollah was continuing to bomb Haifa and Israel was responding in southern Beirut. The French had condemned Israel but the Americans at the G-8 summit argued that Israel was provoked and therefore should not to be condemned. Bob said Syria and Iran were the real source of the problem and it would be more logical to bomb them than poor Lebanon. I said, and then it would be World War III. Bob waited a beat and said: "Two and a half."

We caught the image of President Bush as he was being overheard, saying to Blair on an open mike at the G-8 conference in St. Petersburg, "What they need to do is get Syria to get Hezbollah to stop doing this shit and it's [over]. Can't we get Kofi Annan to call Bashar Assad, [the Syrian leader], to make something happen?"

I was alone in our guestrooms as Bob made his business rounds. Suddenly Ambassador Barzani came up, taking pity on me. As we descended into Erbil he explained that 2300 years ago Alexander the Great waged one of the largest battles in history here to take Erbil away from Darius of Persia (the Macedonian and Seleucid era occupation of 331-129 BC). After defeating him, he went south to Baghdad and then deep into Persia where he destroyed Persepolis. Under the Greeks, the system of bringing water from the mountains to the plains was developed. But the plains of Erbil are among the poorest in the world today and the perfect symbol of that poverty is the Citadel, one of the longest continuously inhabited communities in the world. Squatters and poor families inhabit this city of 780 people. Had the Mongols succeeded in taking Erbil, Saywan explained, they could not make that claim to fame because everyone would have been annihilated. It is only because the Macedonians refrained from slaughtering the population that some remnant of that time remains.

CHAPTER FIVE
August

VISITING FORMER PRESIDENT GEORGE H.W. BUSH

ALL SUMMER WHILE VACATIONING in Massachusetts, we had been hearing about the widening of the 2006 Israel-Hezbollah War—34 days in July—in Lebanon, Northern Israel and the Golan Heights; we were waiting to see if the UN brokered cease-fire of August 14 would hold. We imagined that some of the refugees would still be in Jordanian hotels on our return. Israel's destructiveness with American backing would have made heroes of Hezbollah, no doubt, making our lives more difficult. Beirut was in ruins again.

After sailing in Maine with my father, we drove to Kennebunkport to see our friend Nancy Ellis, President Bush Sr.'s sister, who had worked for my father in his race against Ted Kennedy for the Senate in 1962 and who had helped Bob when he was chairman of Republicans Abroad France during her nephew's second run.

On this bright summer day, we were sitting on bar stools at the kitchen table, chatting when Nancy came in from the porch with Bob and pulled up a (low) chair. We offered to give her one of our stools but she refused. I told her that she was like the Muslim clerics who step down when they preach in the mosques because humility is the most highly prized virtue in the Middle East. She looked surprised. I spoke about how the Arab states suffer from the Israeli occupation—that they felt humiliated and needed to be part of the dialogue for Middle East peace.

I mentioned how much we were enjoying living in a country so full of Biblical tradition—where Moses saw the Promised Land from Mt. Nebo, where Christ was baptized in the Jordan River, and to be near the Sea of Galilee contiguous to the archeological ruin of Um Qays, Israel to the west, and the starkly dark hills of the Golan Heights to the north. I said how Christ is revered as a great prophet in the Qur'an and that it contains two more miracles than in the Bible, one of which is that Christ spoke like an adult when he was a baby. I told them the story of our trip to Bethlehem and our ride with the quiet Hamas driver in a white cap who took us to the shrine where Mary's milk had come in. I told them that I had asked him what it would take to bring peace to the Middle East and that he responded, "When the heart is white."

"What does that mean?" Nancy asked; "*our* hearts are red like valentines. Isn't your heart is white when you are dead?"

"He was speaking metaphorically, that a white heart is a pure heart full of goodwill, honor, integrity and transparency," I explained.

Bob mentioned the unemployment problem—that birth control does not exist—which leads to too many mouths to feed, not enough employment and poverty-related wife- and child-abuse. Families with ten children are not uncommon because that is how women achieve success, a universal condition even though young people tell us that the chances for advancement, for success, were not good. Everyone there dreams of going to America, particularly those who criticize the American government most harshly—many have children and grandchildren in America.

I reiterated what Prince Hassan had said in his opening remarks at the Middle East Peace Initiative Conference that there is nothing wrong with what Karen Hughes said about job creation as long as it includes a dialogue with the people along the pipelines. He also said Arabs didn't need the movie *Syriana* to remind them of that. Nancy's daughter mentioned the movie and its powerful, vivid portrayal of the way in which youngsters whose families are employed (or fired) along the pipelines are conscripted to serve as terrorists. I added that Bob had learned from diatribes sent to him by Al-Qaeda that the radicalization also has to do with the injustice against Palestinians.

After lunch we spent an hour with President Bush Sr. He welcomed us in his small, un-air-conditioned office. He later drove us (rather fast) in his golf cart to the pool. He encouraged us to swim but I said I'd left my suit in the car. He said, "Oh, we have plenty of suits." It was a wonderful slice of Americana with the former president chatting with family and friends on a beautiful day by the sea. Although sunny, there was a kind of haze in the sky that one might see in Maryland not Maine. Nancy looked at the sky and said, "I don't like it," referring to the state of the climate.

The former president told us how much he admired Prince Hassan, and his brother, King Hussein, and how annoyed he was that Queen Noor (formerly Lisa Haleby) begged the U.S. Congress to allow the Middle Eastern countries to repell Saddam Hussein in their own way and asked Congress not to interfere.

"Hassan is a brilliant man," the president said.

We got up to leave and he looked me in the eyes and asked, "Do you think they like us there?"

I allowed for a long pause and then told him, "Prince Hassan spoke eloquently of the importance of a dialogue at the conference a few months ago. I think they would appreciate more of that."

"Well," he said, "They should have it."

Later in the year, his son, President Bush, moved toward a more serious dialogue with Middle Eastern countries.

On my return to Jordan, I met with Hana and asked her why Queen Noor had spoken out so forcefully against the first Gulf War before a U.S. congressional committee. Why was King Hussein opposed to the UN and the U.S. decision to defend Kuwait militarily against Saddam Hussein's aggression? "He wanted the Arab States to resolve it internally," she said with some emotion. It was up to an Arab brother to get Saddam out by diplomatic means. Bob reminded me of President Bush Sr. complaining to French President Mitterand about Queen Noor and how Mitterand simply replied, "C'est une belle Americaine!" as if that justified anything. Bush repeated his complaint, but Mitterand simply sighed and said, "Ah, quelle femme, c'est une belle Americaine!"

CHAPTER SIX
September

THE PROBLEM OF EL

WHEN AL-QAEDA ATTACKED the American Embassy in Damascus recently, the Syrians defended us perhaps in order to show they were anti-Al-Qaeda. On the Air France flight back to Paris, I was seated next to Donatella, the wife of the French Ambassador to Jordan who told me her husband had been reassigned to Tel-Aviv. I showed her an *IHT* article about Prime Minister Ehud Olmert authorizing the construction of another 690 homes for settlers in the occupied West Bank— Ma'ale Adumiin, and Betar Illit. In the face of intense American, European, Palestinian opposition as well as from Israelis who favored the adoption of the roadmap, the plans were on hold. It would connect Ma'ale Adumiin directly to Jerusalem by building an area called El, cutting off East Jerusalem from the rest of the West Bank.

She said, "Even the Americans are against it."

After reading about the murder of a British tourist at the Roman (2nd century AD 6,000 seat) theater in Amman, I asked her if there was reason to be concerned about safety. She shrugged and said she was concerned; there was an American diplomat murdered in front of his house four years earlier, she said, to protest against American-Israeli injustice toward Palestine and the bombing of the hotels the previous November.

"There are highs and lows," she said, "but it is a concern."

Going into Iraq and the failure to stand up to Israel had opened a Pandora's box of woes. The Jordanian people favored Hezbollah. Jordan had contributed no troops to the UN force.

Majid, our friend and driver, had crossed into the security area in order to procure a visa for me and bring me through customs. His face was subdued. For the first time, I noticed in the airport lobby, there were two illuminated yellow signs—"Praying room for Women" and next door, "Praying room for Men." It was a balmy night. In his car, Majid became his old flamboyant self, a crazy fun-loving guy. He broke into song, the first of which was about a poor man who was very lucky, the second was a joyful rendition of *al maya*—when you have water, you have everything. Everything is the will of Allah and he shouted "Allahu Akbar" joyfully. "I am happy because I have my garden, I have my family. Politics and diplomacy, and all the governments of the world are crazy. Just nice people are important."

That's what the people of the world should know about the Arabs— that they want to mind their own business and enjoy life with all its many beauties. Then he sang another song about a flower who cries because she has just been cut and when she asks the man why, he replies that it is to give his beloved. In a soft voice he remarked that Ramadan—the Muslim period of fasting—was coming up in twenty days. "Ees vary nice." To see the banquet with all the food prepared for the evening but not to pick up your fork until 6 pm. "You can't even kiss your wife! I don't eat at 3 am. [when it is also permitted]. You feel very healthy."

I told him I was a bit concerned about returning to Amman after the British tourist had been killed in the forum the day before and learned that it was to settle a score with Israel, presumably because of the Balfour Declaration. He said, "Oh, that was a madman; you have that everywhere. Miss Emily, you know you and Mr. Bob are very much loved here. You are very lucky," (and if you are loved you are protected by your Muslim and Christian friends). The suspect, a 38-year-old Jordanian named Nabil Ahmad Issa Jaaoura, had two brothers who were killed during Israeli attacks on Lebanon in 1982. He told police he had waited until his children were older to commit the crime.

I asked him, "Do you think I should wear a scarf on my head, Majid?"

He said nothing.

I said, "The people in the street support Hezbollah, true?"

Then Majid, all the while proclaiming he didn't want to talk about politics, became agitated: "There are thousands of Lebanese and Palestinians in Israeli jails. Hezbollah takes two soldiers. Why do they not release the prisoners? Why do they not want peace? Under Clinton, the government was much better. This man has a nice face. I like the face of this man, President Clinton. What do you think of his wife, Hillary, for President?"

THE AIR WAS FILLED with red sand, riding on strong desert winds, that sometimes turns to muddy rain. Sometimes the sand reaches as far as France but here it covers your car, and invades your eyes and leaves its residue over the terrace and inside the house. Over the summer, while workmen were putting in the new floor downstairs, they moved our belongings into the living room and left the windows open. Our maid forgot to close the windows, and sand from the desert started swirling over everything—clothes, books, and computers. No one thought to put everything under plastic. Old bread and broken ceramics were lying on the green marble top of the half-moon chest we used in the entryway. Our cat, Puffin, looked stricken and thin. The water from the floor polishing got into the linen; photographs of our children in frames and a valuable painting were stacked on the floor in a room with water from under the doorsill only inches away.

THE BAPTISM SITE AND OTHER WONDERS

MAXWELL, OUR ELDEST son, had arrived the previous night from New York. Bob asked him, "What do you think of Amman?"

"There are no women on the street, or they are covered and in groups," he answered. Max carries his tall, thin frame with his shoulders straight back. He noticed a public demonstration where the men were demonstrating on one side and women on another. Then he added, "It's an urban planning nightmare, a place that was never intended to be this big. But the people are nice and it's a good jumping off place for other places."

Max, who is trilingual, was impressed by the influence of Arabic on our own language, that more than 900 English words are taken from Arabic including admiral, artichoke and algebra (courtesy, as mentioned earlier, of Al-Khawarizmi, the father of algebra, and author of *Kitab al-Jabr*).

To celebrate my birthday, we invited Hana, Faazi and their son Ali, Max's school chum, to dine at Ren Chai. Faazi, who was minister of culture before he was ambassador to the U.S. in the 1990s, invited me to speak since it was my birthday. What interests me most interests everyone else, I said: when will peace come to the Middle East?

"The only way to peace in the Middle East," said Sharif Faazi, "is when the Palestinians acquire their legitimate rights."

Max mentioned how dramatic it was when, after Bush spoke at the General Assembly, President Chavez of Venezuela lit a match, crossed himself as a way of cleansing the podium saying, "The devil has just been here."

The king's speech before the U.N. General Assembly the day before had called for justice; he spoke of "a deep sense of urgency"—that never had it been more important for the Israelis to withdraw from the occupied territories. He said that there could be no just global order when aggression and occupation are permitted to take the place of international law.

In that morning's *Jordan Times*, I was surprised by the vehemence of an editorial by Michael Jansen, who explained how the Muslim world feels aggression from the West and how extremism is a response. Speaking of the Pope (Benedict), Jansen wrote, "What he fails to see is that it is the Muslim world, rather than Christendom, which is today under siege by the Christian U.S. and its Western allies. Furthermore, the siege is total: military, economic, cultural, and social. Muslim activism [is a] reaction to this siege."

The day before, six men including two Iraqis and a Saudi were sentenced to prison terms from fifteen years to life for planning to launch attacks against hotels at the Dead Sea and Aqaba "because they were frequented by Americans and Israelis." Al-Qaeda in Iraq claimed responsibility for the foiled attack. Some of the suspects rented apartments in Zarqa and Jabal Hussein, Amman, in July 2005. Authorities seized 3.6 kilograms of PE-4A heavy explosives which one of the suspects had concealed inside a children's construction game. Naturally Bobby decided this was the time to travel as the rates were lower.

The day before we began a short three-day tour of Christ's baptismal site, a short drive from the Dead Sea, (which the Bible specifies is on the east side of the Jordan River), Petra, one of the seven wonders of the modern world and Aqaba. Max and I approached the site where Saint John baptized Christ. The Israelis, on their side of the sea, also have a site where *they* claim Christ was baptized. The river has been reduced to a stream barely six meters wide and two meters deep, long since withdrawn from the actual site of the baptism a mile away. On the other side of the river is an eyesore—a large cement building with a fence and an Israeli flag.

In 1994 when Israel and Jordan negotiated a peace agreement, and the place, no longer a military zone, became an archeological site proving the veracity of the true baptismal site. Many Israelis come here instead of going to theirs to the west. Local lore has it that this is where Elijah ascended to heaven in a chariot and that that was the reason why St. John (from Bethany) brought Christ from Nazareth to this place to be baptized.

In the soft growth arching over the paths leading down to the site, with filigreed greenery like asparagus ferns swaying in the salty air of unmistakable gentleness, the visitor can almost feel the presence of Christ and St. John, here where they lived. At the riverside, thrushes and birdlife are abundant. The guide spoke of how "Christ's message was to have faith and not to worry and to be peaceful. If you lose touch with yourself, you come here and find it again." Afterwards, Christ spent forty days on what is known as temptation mount at Qumran.

The next day we set off for the castle at Karak on our way to Petra. The topography (between the Dead Sea and Karak) resembles very closely the Scottish highlands with patches of heather and sheep tracks cut into the sides of the mountains. At Petra, after walking the kilometer-long siiq, the sight of the Treasury is most impressive. An English visitor confessed she was "gobsmacked." The archaeological sites being rebuilt by Brown University are meant to show how the Nabateans lived 2,000 years ago. We walked the 2.5-plus kilometers from the treasury and up the mountain to the "Monastery"—a magnificent Greco-Roman temple converted to a Byzantine Greek Orthodox church 2nd century AD, a great tribute to the builders of the day who managed to perform heroic architectural feats. The Bedouin donkey riders vied for our business, reminding me how the Bedouins are a proud race, and one quick to show their emotions.

We left the Nabatean kingdom at sunset, a brilliant sky of every color bathing the valley and setting off the jagged cliffs, and continued to Wadi

Rum, with its dramatic rock formations rising from the red desert sands; thence on to Aqaba, made famous in the film, *Laurence of Arabia*, through its exploration of the Anglo-Arab conquest of the Ottoman Empire. The Germans in alliance with the Ottoman Empire built the Berlin-Baghdad railroad, an offshoot of which ran between Istanbul and Medina, passing through Aqaba, which is where T.E. Lawrence and King Faisal's armies attacked the railway from their base in Wadi Rum.

Aqaba's topography, seen from a distance, resembles the background of the *Mona Lisa*—the jagged rocks and the gray-blue mist dramatically and mysteriously framing the winding road. The whole area here is known as Wadi Musa because the prophet, Moses, is said to have walked from Egypt to Mt. Nebo through these mountains. As we approached the port in the semi-darkness, we could make out two enormous guardian mountains and past these giant cliffs, the bright lights and fortifications of the most official checkpoint among the dozen smaller checkpoints between Amman and the Dead Sea, Petra and Aqaba.

In the morning on opening the curtains in our hotel room, our desert-weary eyes were refreshed by the sight of the brilliant blue ocean and a panoramic view of the harbor filled with all manner of conveyances—a pleasure cruiser, nine freighters, jet skiers, fishermen, scuba diving teams, and tourist boats. The port of Aqaba, inhabited since 4,000 BC, has always been the lucrative gateway to the Middle East strategically placed at the crossroads of four countries (Jordan, Egypt, Israel and Saudi Arabia), a meeting place for the Levant, Africa and Arabia). The museum, located at the fortified castle dating to 111 AD, was originally a Nabataean port, but the Roman X[th] Legion led by Fretensis began the "via nova" there in 116 AD. In the Byzantine period, Yuhanna ibn Ruba, the bishop, made a treaty with the prophet Muhammad in 630 AD, securing the safety of his town during the Muslim conquests. The castle under Uthman ibn Affan, 650 AD, had strong affinities with late Byzantine Palestine and Coptic Egypt. Appropriately, the castle had four gates: the Sea gate, the Egyptian gate, the Syrian Gate and the Hijaz gate. The inscription dating from the 8th century AD over the Egyptian gate, a handsome round arch and the best preserved, is the Qur'anic verse called the Throne verse (Ayat al Kursi) for the protection of the ancient city. Over the northwestern gate of the castle during the 10 century AD, a Byzantine lintel common in churches in Jordan and Syria in the 4th to the 7th c. AD, a Greek inscription translates as "May Jesus Christ Triumph."

When the Muslims settled there, they built a settlement next to the older Byzantine site and named the new oriental town, Aqabat Ayla (later contracted to Aqaba). Under the Mamluks, the castle became a place where the pilgrims on the annual Hajj to Mecca rested. Pilgrims from Egypt, Syria and the Maghreb journeyed through here and it became particularly prosperous under the Abbasids of the 9th and 10th centuries. Al-Muqaddasi, writing a century later, called it "the port of Palestine on the China Sea and the storehouse of the Hijaz." Lovely blue-green Chinese celadon jars from the northern Song period, 1st to the 11th centuries, testify to the long distance reached in commerce connecting the entire Indian Ocean with the Far Eastern trade in silks and spices. Cargoes of grains, oils, fruits and nuts from the Mediterranean region sailed out of Aqaba for Arabian cities and throughout the entire Red Sea as far as Aden and Ethiopia. There was a column, called a "milestone" with Islamic writings on it for measuring distance.

BEIRUT WHERE THE FOUR ELEMENTS MINGLE

BEIRUT HAD BECOME A home away from home, only an hour's plane ride from Amman, and we were happy to bring Max with us. Lebanon is in many ways the sister country to Jordan, with most of the elite here, all my female friends, having gone to the American University of Beirut. I celebrate when they celebrate. I mourn when they mourn. The trilingual greeting in Beirut is typically cosmopolitan : "Hi, keefak, ça va ?" (*How are you?* in English, Arabic and French.) The war formally ended on September 8 when the Israelis lifted the naval blockade of Lebanon and we were the first tourists to arrive in Beirut since the war. The Meridien Commodore in Beirut is where the journalists stayed. Bob joked that he had what he facetiously calls a "Frequent Bomber" rate, a corporate rate for those who survived any hotel bombing. Interestingly, on the door keys and the cocktail napkins was written: "Teachers open the door but you must enter by yourself—Chinese proverb."

There was a part of the city struck by the war in which 10,000 bomblets with their six-claws were yet to be defused and were still hanging from the wreckage. This region was strictly off limits. Lebanon had recently suffered dramatically from the war between Hezbollah and Israel who bombed the airport and key bridges. Universally regarded as rich, educated and influential, the Lebanese diaspora, mostly of Christians, throughout the world is estimated at 14 million people, a veritable exodus, beginning in the post-Ottoman era through 1967, compared with the country's population of 4 million (60% Muslim and 40% Christian), with the largest concentration outside the Middle East in Brazil (eight million as well as six million Syrians—greater Lebanon—all mostly Christian). Beirut, a city of great beauty and one of the oldest continually inhabited places in the world, was a ghost town, full of fruits and flowers, with no one on the street or in the newly rebuilt cafés.

The city forms the western point of a diamond with Tripoli to the north, Tyre to the south, and Damascus to the east. On the trade route from Athens to Aleppo to Alexandria, Beirut has, since the Bronze Age, been the gateway from the West to the "Orient." Ottoman-style architecture, still pock-marked by the wars of 1975-1991, sits on a spit of land jutting into the Mediterranean in a basin framed by white-capped mountains. At dinner the previous night near Pigeon Rock, the traces of the 1975-1991 war between the Palestinian, Christian and Syrian-backed private militias was obvious, with bullet holes etched into the cement walls of the high-rises close to the Mediterranean sea.

Hatred of America's support for Israel made people suspicious towards us, and the hardworking and friendly Lebanese tepid in their greetings. I caught the tail end of a documentary on Beirut TV—the image of a gun pointed directly at the viewer: "The most powerful weapon in the world," the announcer says, "oil." Actually, the world's most powerful weapon is water. The case in point is the Sheba'a farms on a plateau in southern Lebanon, rich in water. Syria took it in 1956, then the Israelis when they took the Golan Heights in 1967. At that time the United Nations was trying to determine who owns it. In the meantime, the Israelis had developed a complex system of water distribution that deprived both Jordan and Lebanon of their water rights.

I came down to the Meridien restaurant to join Bob and Max who were trying to understand what a businessman there was up to. A loud-talking American named Richard was in the breakfast room, trying to "kick butt", as he put it to his boss via cell phone. He complained to his Arab friends, "Please habibi [dear man], our clients are upset because things haven't happened, the cars haven't been delivered. We need the SUVs. Leave Tyre early, 0500. I need you. I don't understand why people aren't returning my calls. It's insane. No one knows what's going on here." We wondered what his project was all about but he was so outrageous it was hard to believe he wasn't putting on an act.

Bob: "I think he sells toilets—probably in Iraq."

Me: "Probably SUVs and toilets."

Max: "A professional 'crappeur'..."

Bob: "Obviously they know it's him and they don't answer their phone."

Max: "Wouldn't it be fun to take a soft pie and calmly put it in his face."

Me: "That's the kind of American who gives us trouble."

Since our tour started in the afternoon, Max, Bob and I had walked the streets of Beirut in the morning. Near the port, a beautiful 19th century pink villa drew our attention—typically Lebanese with Ottoman-style architecture, long oval windows forming the front porch, surrounded by fruit trees of every variety.

Max: "I want to go to the Hezbollah rally."

Bob: "For or against? Or should we split up? It's important we hedge our bets."

Max: "I like to watch the Divine Comedy. God is checking us out."

As we were returning to the hotel to be on time for our tour of Beirut, I noticed a beautiful woman getting out of a Range Rover and going into our hotel—Georgette, tall, with auburn hair resembling Botticelli's Venus, a 28-year-old Maronite Christian archaeologist.

Since 3000 BC, the (biblical) Canaanites, Phoenicians, the Greeks, Romans, Assyrians, Babylonians, Byzantines, and Ottomans all settled this land. The remains of what is believed to be Noah's Ark were discovered in southern Turkey on the mountains of Ararat in 1987, and the Semitic people are descended from Sam, Europeans from Ham, a redhead, and according to Georgette at least, Africans from Yafit, who, cursed by his father, according to legend, was turned black.

Canaan means *low earth*—where the Nile meets the land—and archeological tablets of their civilization have been found in all of Lebanon, and between Iraq and Syria, Palestine and Suez and parts of Jordan to the west of Mt. Nebo. The word Phoenicia means "purple people" from the beautiful dyes that dressed the kings of Europe. The reign of these coastal navigators lasted from 1180 to 333 BC, when Alexander the Great conquered the region and the age of Hellenism began. According to Georgette, the Phoenicians who sailed to Greece and returned, moved inland and became Philistine, the origin of the word Palestine (Goliath was of course a Philistine).

Three thousand years before Christ, Aramaic, the language of Christ, was the lingua franca. When the Empire split between Western Rome and the Eastern Empire, the Middle East was controlled from Constantinople but Aramaic, Syriac and Hebrew still existed thousands of years later. Christ visited Tyre and Sidon and Cana of Galilee and the "Lebanese" were the first martyrs, thrown to the lions by the Romans, she said. Eventually the whole coast was Christianized.

Like Iraq, Lebanon is a melting pot conquered by the Assyrians, the Persians, the Greeks, the Romans, the Muslims and the Turks. In 337 AD, when the Roman Emperor Constantine converted to Christianity, the Christians persecuted pagans. From the 4th to the 6th centuries, the Maronites, (notably, St. Simeon of Stylite) were a peaceful mountain Christian sect whose goal was to convert the pagans (who believed in Baal or the Greek gods) to Christianity. In the 7th century, many Christians became Muslim. The word in Arabic for yoghurt is *leban* and the country got its name from the white mountains close to the Lebanese coast.

From the 16th century to the end of World War I, (1518-1918), Lebanon was part of the Ottoman Empire which also included Turkey and Syria—its beautiful architecture with long oval windows, and fountains in every room and every court, have made their mark on the city called "The Paris of the Middle East." Fakhreddine II, a 17th century Christian Maronite prince living in the Chouf mountains, was honored with the title of King of Kings for driving the Turks out of Lebanon, avenging the death of his father Fakhreddine I. (He is also a hero in Jordan and his name figures in one of the best restaurants in Amman—Fakhreldin).

The Place des Martyrs was originally built to celebrate Lebanon's freedom from the yoke of the Ottoman Empire after World War 1. From the post-World War I period until 1943, Lebanon was a French colony. During the Lebanese civil wars of 1975-1991, Beirut was divided between the Christian east and western Muslim sectors of the city and Bob asked Georgette to point out on the map where the "Green Line" between the two sides was. A book salesman told us that *Mein Kampf* in Arabic was a best-selling book in Beirut. Bob commented, "It's by someone who hated both the Jews and the French so it's a sure winner here."

Bob asked Georgette, "It is said the Islamic Jihad kidnapped the American journalists and Terry Waite [in 1987]. Who do you think kidnapped them?"

She spoke generally, "Always in the question of taking hostages—be they Shiite, Sunni, Palestinian, Syrian, or Israeli—it's a question of an exchange."

The Ottoman prince, Bashir II, whose palace, Beit ed-Dine, was called "la maison de la foi" (*the house of faith*), a place where one could take refuge for three days and no one would ask why. In 1799, when Napoleon took the Suez, he asked for Bashir's help and this was granted on the condition that he would help Lebanon attain its independence from the Turks. The French were not happy and the Turks were not happy that Bashir was acting as a double agent, so he was sent to Istanbul where he was killed and then buried in Armenia. Later, Bashir's remains were transferred to the palace here and laid beside the remains of his first wife (he had two) in the garden of cedar trees. It looked like a set for *Romeo and Juliet* with Ottoman style open balconies overlooking gardens and vines, and flowering plants hanging from doorways.

The doorstep leading into the reception area was in the shape of a greeting—two hands joined together, signifying welcome. In the reception room for the viziers (ambassadors), emirs (princes), imams (clergy), and other notables, one stepped up higher than in the room for the people, onto a carved marble surfaces and the divans were covered in purple velvet embroidered in gold. Georgette explained that the star of David engraved on a silver plaque predates its adoption by the Jews. For all Semitic religions, she said, this oriental symbol of earth and the sky, where four elements co-mingle—fire, metal, water and air—has implied the harmony and mastery of the elements.

The Phoenicians took ancient images such as a house, a square with a triangle on top, and saw in it, the symbol for image "B" (she drew the house and the "B") for the Arab word *beit*, for example—house—and thus began the modern alphabet. The original image for the symbol "A" was a bull, an inverted A.

I asked Georgette, "Is this an Arab country? Are you an Arab?"

"Maybe, as a Maronite, I have traces of Arab ancestors, including the Yemeni people who they say came here; the Palestinians came from Greece to the Mediterranean coast, but unlike the others, we, the Maronite Christians, are indigenous to the area."

"What year did Lebanon begin?" I asked.

"When Fakhreddine II fought the Turks in the 16th century," she replied.

At the end of our trip to the Chouf Mountains yesterday, I asked Georgette, "Will there ever be peace with Israel?"

"Never," was the answer. "Israel will always remain our enemy. Syria would sooner make peace with Israel than we would."

"Why is there so much hate?" I asked.

"I don't know," Georgette replied, "because in some ways it's so illogical as Syria occupies us as well, but that's what we were taught in school. We have been invaded and bombarded so many times but the Lebanese love life. The second day after the end of the war, it was as if nothing happened. We live life each day as if it was our last. We dance and sing and then go back to work."

But the joy emblematic of the Lebanese had suffered. Everyone was depressed.

Our last night in Beirut I had a dream about men in white suits, gloves and masks, spraying a poisonous ooze of thick gel in corridors that was seeping under the doorsteps and sapping the spirit of the city. The name of the gel was *fear* and in my dream, I was frantic, "We have to put towels against the threshold."

When I got up, I understood the nightmare of a democratic society— that any ooze can turn up and seep under your doorstep. Suddenly you wake up and discover what you have lost. The very thing that draws people in the Middle East to Beirut—freedom—can also lead to its demise. It is easy to take freedom's abundant heritage for granted, to forget the meaning of citizenship and leadership. This land, blessed with both mountains and sea, a Garden of Eden under siege, is a microcosm of an entire planet in jeopardy.

EAT WITH THE JEWS, SLEEP WITH THE DRUZE

MAJID PICKED US UP at the Jordan airport and was scratching his head, trying to remember an expression, "Eat with the Druze and sleep with the Jews." Then I thought about it a little and asked, "What about "Eat with the Jews and sleep with the Druze?" Because what the Jews eat is kosher and with the Druze, you are always safe, no matter what you believe.

"Yes, yes, oh, Emily, my Queen."

Bob is frustrated on all sides: "I called my New York bankers and asked them, 'What have you done?' They tell me, 'Nothing.' I called Paris to ask the same thing. They say, 'Nothing.' After six months, the third floor is still in ruins. I call. Again, the answer is, 'Nothing.'"

RAMADAN

RAMADAN BEGINS TODAY and for the next month, Muslims will fast from dawn to dusk. The beginning of Ramadan depends on the sighting of the crescent of the new lunar moon, hence the crescent on many flags of Muslim countries. Last night on our return from Mount Nebo, Max and I went to pick up a few things at the Cosmo supermarket. Tonight, it was chock-a-block with people stocking up on food in preparation for the evening feast—great chunks of lamb in plastic, piles of fish to grill. We were told that in the evening, the streets of Jordan will be empty—everyone will be at home, breaking the fast.

We were also told not to expect as much from the workmen. Everyone was walking around in a kind of blur. No one can drink or eat anything after sunrise and until sunset. Everyday events take on a heroic quality. Sometime in the 600s AD, the prophet received his original inspiration for the Qur'an—and the muezzin's voice has an eerie quality—a high-pitched castrato wail, followed by a quiet, low-voiced prayer.

Muslims believe that the Qur'an is the literal word of God which was received by the Prophet Muhammad directly from God. Ramadan celebrates the revelation and its beginning falls on a different day every year, at the appearance of the first crescent moon, and this year, a month prior to the last week of October. "Maybe the 27th," Emad guesses. Every day in this season, Ramadan is one minute less. On the first day, the breaking of the fast is at

6:35pm; on the last day, it is 6:00pm. Amman is a barren city during the day until 6:30 pm. when Muslims can break their fast… the iftar. About 9:30 pm, one heard the streets come alive again and families congregate and gossip and drink coffee. The guys across the street were playing volleyball. The hotels hosted Ramadan evenings and comedians entertained into the night.

Emad taught me that God instructed Muslims to pray, bending at the waist to the ground four or five times and the prophet added another two times. He told me the names and times of the prayers: 1) Fajr at 5:00 ending at Shorook at 6:29 at sunrise, 2) Dohr at 12:27, when the sun is vertically over your head—4 bends plus two, 3) Asr at 3:51 when your shadow is as long as your body—"you can pray from 4 to 6:25", 4 bends plus 2, 4) Maghrib at 6:24, at sunset, you pray seven to eight minutes, bending 3 times at the waist then another two for Allah. Then there is the breaking of the fast, Iftar, at 6:30, which lasts until the last prayer, 5) Ishaa, from 7:43 to 9:15, when the last hint of red leaves the horizon. At Ishaa, during Ramadan, you bend 7 times plus 14 or a total of 21 times.

Like the Jews in the temple, Muslim men and women pray in different sections of the mosque. Mark Gabriel's *Jesus and Muhammad: Profound Differences and Surprising Similarities*, explains:

"When Muhammad visited paradise and hell (during the Night Journey), he reported: The Prophet said, 'I looked into Paradise and found that the majority of its dwellers were the poor people, and I looked into the (Hell) Fire and found that the majority of its dwellers were women.' In Muhammad's day, women had to be careful not to walk by the men who were praying. That's because Muhammad said that if a woman walked by a man who was praying, his prayer would be cancelled out and he would have to start his time of prayer from the beginning again. Muhammad's second wife, Aisha, reported this teaching, along with a mild protest: 'The things which annul the prayers were mentioned before me. They said, "Prayer is annulled by a dog, a donkey and a woman (if they pass in front of the praying people)."'"

AT MIDDAY WHILE EMAD and I were window-shopping for ceramic tiles, we found ourselves near the royal residence, by the giant mosque that can seat

10,000. Emad asked me if I would mind if he went in to pray, and I told him of course not. I asked if I could wander through the outer courtyard. He said, "Fine." I got out of the car and admired the Ottoman style, the newly planted trees and the wood screens built for shade, and the four wooden decks on top of the spires presumably for the muezzin. When one of the guards saw my Western presence (I was wearing a skirt to the knee, a long-sleeved shirt and sandals) he came over to me, angrily gesticulating with his hands (*What are you doing here?*) with an angry look on his face.

"Marhaba," (*Hello*), I said and, "Saba al xeer," (*Good morning*).

Though his face softened a bit, he didn't respond.

I said, "I am waiting for a friend of mine who is praying."

"Oh," and then he said, as if I were a cow, "You can go and sit there", pointing to a chair a little further away, at the corner of the mosque.

I stood amidst the trees on the outskirts of the mosque near the chair and prayed while the sweet wail of the muezzin inside wafted through the open air. Another guard smiled, and said that I could sit down in the chair, which they moved to an opposite wall. I thanked him and continued to pray standing. After I had finished praying, I finally sat down, on the off chance that I might be arrested if I didn't.

Emad came out and explained, "Women can pray in the back," dismissively. All you have to do to become a Muslim is to say, "I believe in Allah," three times, he added encouragingly.

YESTERDAY THE *JORDAN TIMES* contained an item about the 13th honor killing this year, the second in a two-week span—a brother confessed to murdering his sister: "Because our sister left the house without our permission and her behavior brought us disgrace." A shepherd discovered the body in a canal in Karak, with burn marks on her body and traces of gasoline. The two brothers had driven their sister from Irbid (in the north near Umm Qays) to a deserted area near Queen Alia International Airport, outside of Amman, beat her up, then strangled her. The brother then drove to Karak, south of the Dead Sea, and dumped her body in the canal, after trying to conceal their actions by attempting to set the body ablaze. At the *Jordan Times*, I had met the crusading reporter, Rana Husseini, author of *Murder in the Name of Honor,* who told me the punishment for these murders is anywhere from three months to seven and a half years.

I had a chance to ask Emad about this most recent honor killing and what Islam says about it. The 26-year-old murderer told investigators he tortured his sister after medical examinations proved she was not a virgin, then strangled her. I asked Emad if this was within Islamic law.

"You know many people do bad things in the name of Islam," he answered.

"What would have been the appropriate punishment?" I asked.

Emad responded, "If she was married and committed adultery, then under the law, she would have to be killed but if she is single, well then, just a beating."

The criminal court prosecutor charged the woman's young killer with the premeditated murder of his 22-year-old sister. An editorial commented, "If death eludes them, women in such situations are left to languish under house guard to protect them from their fathers, brothers or husbands who have vowed to shed their blood in a misguided act of purification."

There is a case of one woman held in protective custody for fourteen years, depriving her of her basic rights to live a normal life.

Al Aqsa Mosque

Anglican Church

Amman Citadel

Aqaba

Bedouins, Wadi Rum

Birgesh Cave of the seven apostles,
Ajloun Mountains

Black Iris, national flower

Bethlehem and the Wall

Bob and Majid

Bob at Arafat's grave

Desert castle visit with Jane Taylor

Bobby with Bedouins after suicide attack Nov. 2015

Brazilian party, 3rd inflammatory remark

Choir in Galilee

Damascus gate, Jerusalem

Emad in our dining room

Desert castle

Emad on his phones

Iraq al Amir

Emad putting in ceramics where the wall was falling down

Jerash North Gate

Jerusalem girl scouts

Jerusalem

Pella

Machaerus

Petra necropolis

After Mozart Requiem

Muxeibe near Syrian border

Palmyra

Petra, Qasr al Bint

Qasr Amra fresco

Qasr Amra fresco

Qasr Amra fresco

Spices, Jerusalem souq

Wadi Rum campsite

Wadi Rum

Wadi Rum caravan

West Bank farmer

West Bank Church of the Nativity, Bethlehem

Qasr Amra, 1st known zodiac in round

West Bank Wall

CHAPTER SEVEN
October

MAJID TOLD US THAT THE U.S. government had just given Jordan $50 million in aid and that when coupled with $5 million from the king, the king was able to give every civil servant a one hundred dinar bonus that year. Iftar banquets were being held at all the country's orphanages. He told us that because we found a beautiful house and our family was healthy, we should give thanks to God by sacrificing two sheep for our many blessings. So I told Majid to bring the sheep on Friday, the holy day, in the middle of the holy month of Ramadan, when the poor people may have run out of the food to break the fast.

"Why not," he replied. "You must distribute it with your own hand."

Majid went to the slaughterhouse and when they cut the sheep, he consecrated the offering saying, "This is for Emily, this is for Robert, this is for Maxwell, and this is for George."

He brought the warm lamb cut in cubes in one-kilo plastic packages and we distributed it to Palestinian refugees from the '67 war with Israel villages outside of Amman and also to refugees from the '48 war in a neighborhood closer to the city. It was thrilling for us to meet people from Jenin, Ramallah, Haifa, Bethlehem, Nablus, Hebron, Qelkilliah, Tulkaram, Jericho and Arifa; to say the words, "Hada Ilkom" (*This is for you*) and to hear the words, "salaam ideeki" (*Bless your hands*), and to respond,

"Uideeki"—(*And yours as well*). As we drove through the narrow streets with low brick buildings on all sides, we saw sad, tired faces suddenly come to life with broad, sweet smiles.

Little children followed the car, waving and singing, as it wound its way through the poor villages. I noticed one beautiful fifteen-year-old girl in a headscarf being aggressively teased by a gang of boys. I wondered how long it would be before she would see the veil as her liberation. For a beautiful woman, the taking of the veil is like putting on your armor, it seemed to me, to escape the indignity of harassment. Finally, we went to a Bedouin tent near the Holiday Inn in the northern part of Amman and honked the horn. A large woman in a black chador emerged, her face showing, with several desperate looking children around her. She took the meat indifferently, without a word.

To these people and many others, Israel is perceived as a mere blip on the screen of history. The feeling among Palestinians (the mirror image of Israelis about Palestine) is that "we will outlast them." In speaking of the wars against Gaza, the last year-and-a-half blockade, distinctions aren't made here between America and its client state, Israel. The U.S. is just another in a long line of colonial powers who came to conquer, beginning with the Greek and Roman and ending with the Ottoman, English and French Empires.

Perhaps to understand the missions of foreigners here, I was told that there are hidden microphones under all the tables at every major hotel and all the cafés Westerners prefer (like Book@Cafe). It echoed my feeling that at our apartment our telephone calls were constantly monitored. I even caught one of the spies who had fallen asleep and had the nerve to announce himself—"Just a minute"—before connecting me.

We resumed our Arabic lessons. If driving in Amman makes your head spin, try learning Arabic. Interestingly, there are no separate present and future tenses—they are one and the same. I wondered if T.S. Eliot was influenced by orientalist philosophy in his "Burnt Norton" since his notion of present and future are also merged:

"Time present and time past

Are both perhaps present in time future,

And time future contained in time past."

The timelessness of the place is best understood through the language—and learning Arabic became our daily, determined pursuit. By managing the greetings easily, the softness of the life, the ease and the elegance opened out to us and the scales fell from our eyes. We were then placed in another category, not the dreaded colonial imperialist but human beings struggling to understand another culture. All the horror and fear of "the Arab world" seemed a chimera that didn't fit the reality. Another mysterious world opened up, a journey through multiple layers of ruins, circuitous conversations, with as many sayings and shades of meaning as there are silks and spices.

Sallem, which means *bless*, in the command form means both to "say hello" and to "give up". In a literal sense then, in the tribal Arabic world, when told to "say hello," it means "give up" at least for that moment, and implicitly, the moment of meeting is blessed, in other words, "peace."

Arab proverbs tell you something of the soul of the country. Nyla was telling us, "Once I was with a group of women in mourning and the widow of the man who had died suddenly said, 'The world is like that, sometimes with you, sometimes against you,' (translation: *Idyna haik, yom alak ou yom aleek*) and everyone burst out laughing, because it was said at just the right time."

She told me she was in mourning for her cousin and was still just wearing white and black and had told her brother, "the drunkenness went and the thinking is coming," (translation: *RaaHat issakra u ijat il fakra*)— meaning *you are drunk with grief, you don't think*, and he laughed and laughed. "I had a student once—the wife of the Japanese ambassador who was so apt at proverbs, she made everyone laugh. A group of women were all bragging about their children and she said, 'The monkey in the mother's eyes is a gazelle,' (Il qird bi9een ummo ghazal) the equivalent of, 'Beauty is in the eye of the beholder.'"

THE TERRORISM STARTED IN 1967

WAR AND PEACE MAY have been the topic on everyone's mind but as in France, eating well takes precedence. Ren Chai was the new hip place. Outside on the huge terrace, new age techno on hidden speakers in Japanese gardens mingled with subtly fragrant Chinese cuisine. The main restaurant, made of stone, was surrounded by a huge terrace, enclosed by slats of teak fences, intertwined with wisteria; strong lights shot upwards on tall palms.

We invited Riad and Nora, our neighbors.

The Middle East crisis was not so much America's fault, Riad was saying, "Actually, it is all the fault of the British. Maybe that is why their flights are being targeted and why Tony Blair is working so hard to find a solution. Anyway, going to an embassy now is like going to prison."

On a flight from Amman to Miami via London, their daughter was waitlisted. The British embassy insisted no transit visa would be required but she was sent back to Amman.

"There will never be peace in the Middle East," Riad was saying, "because it is in the interest of both the West and the East to keep the Middle East weak."

The latest buzz, according to Riad, was that this last war in Lebanon was instigated by the U.S. to test the strength of Iran before the Americans decide to go into Damascus and Tehran. The Chinese meanwhile were cooling their heels. "Terrorism really started in 1967 when the Israelis took the Golan Heights from Syria, part of Lebanon, and the Jordanian West Bank.

"We didn't mind being ruled by Jordan," Nora interjected, referring to the pre-1967 years when there was easy passage from Amman through the West Bank to Jerusalem.

"The Israelis still want more land," Riad insisted. (Later in the year, we saw the new settlements being built on Palestinian land to the north, south and east. Israeli bulldozers were working hard building a wall on land that wasn't theirs, goading an extremist defensive reaction.)

Thanks to Abbas, a new coalition government was formed with Hamas officials who thought they could use the ruse of intentionally resigning to be rehired under another name in order for the Quartet to get the aid money flowing.

"Even if the big powers did want a strong Middle East," Riad said, "the Middle East itself would smother any free trade that brought prosperity. A Palestinian couldn't get a visa to Saudi Arabia because they were afraid he would compete with them and take away their jobs. The Arab League is not a league of friends, but Jordanians survive by being amenable to everybody."

REFUGEES

AT THE BRAZILIAN AMBASSADOR'S residence, there was a seafood and vegetable terrine, Brazilian beef tenderloin, and a (dietetic) passion fruit mousse—all served by white-gloved Sri Lankan waiters.

Yolaine, customarily astute, commented, "You know passion fruit has nothing to do with passion; it's called that because the thorns of the fruit resemble the crown that Christ wore during the Passion."

Janvier de Riedmatten, a Swiss director of the UN High Commission for Refugees Iraq Operations, told me: "If you have a valid passport, you are allowed to stay three months and then you have to leave. (Unless you are rich and then you are allowed to renew it for another three months.) If you have $150,000, you can get a residency permit. There are 700,000 Iraqi refugees in Jordan, both Sunni and Shia, evenly balanced. Some in Amman, are people of means, others are poor. For those here longer than three months, Janvier has been trying to convince the authorities not to force them to return, to renew their visa.

Jordanians feel they have done enough to help the Iraqis by letting them in their country—by giving them safe haven—and there is widespread resentment that they have driven up property prices. Although the government downplays the presence of Iraqis for the negative feeling the prices create, it certainly makes the landowners I know very happy.

The poor are of course the ones who suffer because the government is cautious about recognizing refugee status, "They already have the Palestinians and they fear the Iraqis will be here forever," Janvier lamented. "Although our refugee attestation is not recognized by the government, the UN gives them one because it might help them with the police. There is no major forcible return but for every day you have people coming from Iraq, you have people going back to Iraq. If you recognize our paper and give them refugee status, you leave open the possibility that they will be here forever and this they do not want. They live in hiding. There are one hundred or so who line up outside my office every day and they are very scared."

I told him what Naba, my Iraqi professor friend, told me joking darkly, "To get Iraqi refugee status, you have to be dead." But Janvier responded, "That's not true—you can only get refugee status if you are out of Iraq." Bob added that there are camps at the border.

FINDING WAYS AROUND THE CORRUPTION

ZARA, OWNER OF THE Lines gallery—wife of the impressive central bank director here who was voted Central Bank Governor of the Year for the MENA region by the *Financial Times,* in 2009—has become a good friend. Like her sister, famous for her work with Amnesty International and Human Rights Watch, she is piercingly honest. Thanks to her sister's reporting on Saddam Hussein's abuses, the case against him held. Ironically, her current assignment was to make sure that he got a fair trial and it was one she didn't like at all apparently.

Zara, her sister, and her brother, Mansour, are the children of a former prime minister of Jordan; she summed up the central issues. "Imagine the centuries of poetry, history and law in the West from the renaissance on and compare that to life in a Bedouin tent," Zara was saying about the post-golden age days in the Arab world. "Secondly, think of the pain of the 1967 war: the Arab countries have never been able to accept the reality of Israeli's existence. Without diminishing the importance of their cause and their abandonment by the West, Palestinians quibble over minute and irrelevant details of the past forty years. Third, the Arab nations—where dire poverty lives alongside great wealth—often detest one another; the Gulf States are unwilling to help their poorer relatives. Since they are run by dictators, their emergence from ignorance is slow; only democracy lifts societies out of the Middle Ages," she said. "Until the problem of poverty is solved, the Middle East will always be a cauldron. The best role and only effectiveness the West has here is by not interfering and intervening in their cultures but finding ways around the corruption to solve the problem of poverty. Everything else—from environmental degradation to the jihad—will be resolved because the people at the top would cease taking the share owed to building up the country and put it into infrastructure and jobs."

I mentioned how difficult it was for Bobby to work in the Middle East because of corruption. The most effective counterinsurgency in Iraq was to create incentives to oppose the insurgency—safe streets, job creation, clean water, reliable electricity, and ample gasoline. We learned from Vietnam that insurgencies wither on the vine without popular support. You paid the local mafia to protect the electrical lines so there was also an economic reason for the local population to oppose the insurgency. Without safeguards, you got a series of corrupt, unstable leaders who simply pocketed the money, made little effort to get the economy going and spent their time squabbling over power and graft.

MY CHOIR

I WAS LUCKY TO FIND a good choir here. Shireen, a Christian Arab originally from Palestine, the brilliant music director and conductor of the Dozan Wa Awtar Choir, was a thirtyish brunette with sparkling brown eyes. An Oberlin graduate, she was energetic, generous, and gifted. As the November 8th anniversary of the bombing of the three hotels approached, security was tightening. Our choir would be singing the Mozart Requiem that night at the Hyatt in memory of those murdered. The attack on the tourists the week before, (the attacker's anger was over Israeli aggression in the Lebanese war twenty years earlier) and the equal frustration among Palestinians, had made me curious as to just how exposed we were here given our alliance with Israel.

After choir rehearsal the previous night, I asked Shireen, "Do you think Americans are targeted in Jordan?" checking what Majid had told me. "The Arab culture is very hospitable by nature. They might have their political opinions about what's happening, but they are always eager to show off their generosity more than anything else. I don't believe Americans are targeted. People might also think that Israelis might feel uncomfortable, but you would be surprised to know how accepting many are to the Israelis despite the ongoing injustice in the occupied territories."

Known for her honesty, Shireen was kind enough to accord me an interview. Her father, George, born in Egypt to a Palestinian father and an Egyptian mother, owned the Amman GM dealership. Her chic and beautiful mother was born in '47 in Ramleh, a small village near Jaffa, the ancient port and oldest part of Tel Aviv, and grew up in Lebanon. Her parents left their house in Ramleh because of threats to the locals and could not imagine it was actually part of an ethnic cleansing campaign. "Fear was engraved in their hearts as the soldiers drove around announcing through speakers, telling people to leave or their houses will be targeted and blown up. Though this never happened, people left. They packed up and naively thought they were coming back the next day. They never went back; they made a life in Jordan, and died in Jordan. Palestine never died and reclaiming it was a constant dream in the generations to come."

After graduating, she returned to her ancestral homeland in 1998-2000 to teach, part of a UN project bringing Palestinians back into Palestine to work. Although based in the Ramallah conservatory, she also taught at the conservatories in Bethlehem and Jerusalem, and in the refugee camps and trained teachers in Nablus. Shireen believed that the two years spent in the West Bank were the most rewarding for her as a teacher. Students were hungry to learn and making music was extremely rewarding. Having a UN visa gave her permission to travel anywhere in the West Bank (including the Israeli side). It also allowed her to circumvent the extensive security checks at the border permitting her to visit her parents in Jordan in less than two hours.

She came from a liberal family, in which her parents were open-minded about her going to America to study, to choose music as her career, to live alone. But she never felt a sense of belonging until she went to live in Palestine for two years. "I remember standing on a rock by the beach and Jaffa and thinking – *Oh, now it makes sense*. As if my personality fit the feeling of living in a fishermen's town and not the tribal desert of Jordan. My identity somehow matched my behavior. I somehow felt freer. I don't know how to explain that. When you are in your twenties, you do a lot of soul-searching (at least I did) and for me that was a turning point in learning and understanding myself more."

"Regarding the right of return?" (a controversial part of the peace negotiations) I asked.

"I doubt it would be easy to go back," Shireen, whose parents are Palestinian Christian, responded. "My father has been living in Jordan since 1948 [after the Nakbe] so that's over fifty years now. He has established his business here. Will it be easy for someone like him to pick up and go back? I don't know, but having the choice would be incredible; being able to reclaim his home in Jaffa would be a miracle, but let me stop dreaming for now. Israel claims that it needs to defend itself and thus the weaponry, the building of settlements, and the Wall (both of which are illegal by international law).

"The constant separation seems crucial for their existence. Let me ask you something, why would you need to defend yourself if you have not done anything wrong? Don't misunderstand me: they are not only to blame here; as I also believe that the Arab world too has failed its people. The leaders have not done justice to the Palestinian cause and those who are suffering are many, some still living in the refugee camps. I consider myself one of the lucky ones."

The night before, the inaugural concert of the newly established Amman Symphony Orchestra was held at the Al Hussein Cultural Center to coincide with the celebration of King Abdullah's 45th birthday. Traditional Arab and classical European Western music was performed by what the *Jordan Times* called a newborn, professional orchestra (though almost every musician in the National Orchestra auditioned and won a place in the Municipal Orchestra).

"It is very exhausting and lonely to be a conductor in Jordan," and so she now lives in Canada. "I am also an artist and not a fund-raiser. Funding is scarce and the choral culture is very young. One thought proposed was to create the Amman Symphonic Chorus alongside the orchestra. By teaming up with them, both parties would benefit. Unfortunately, this did not materialize. I think this too was a turning point. I was always hoping for the country to recognize and nurture what I have been doing for Jordan [being the only choral conductor with a degree]. Now I know strength comes from within – so working inside out is more empowering than outside in. Does that make sense?

"Don't forget, I am a woman too. This is true anywhere in the world: a woman standing in front of orchestras is not easy. But I will tell you with confidence that the resistance is far greater here. There were a number of issues that arose during our *Requiem* performance. I couldn't have done it if the first violinist did not have my back. He would guide me step by step and also managed the orchestra members well. After the second performance of the *Requiem*, it became easier and I've been told it will become even more so in the future. Another factor to remember is I come from a relatively well-off family. This makes my task even harder. People just assume that I don't need the money and I can do the performances for free. The attitude is different. It just makes it more complicated. Lastly I feel that I want to be inspired again. There is not enough choral music happening, not enough discussions and stimuli. I miss the challenge. Somedays I wonder, how long can I keep going?"

"Is Jordan a center for culture in the Middle East?" I asked.

"Everything seems like it is being done for instant gratification and not long-term envisioning and developing," she answered. "Also, there doesn't seem to be a balance for how the 'culture' is being enhanced. There seems to be more focus on construction and more buildings and not enough on people, the arts, education, culture, music, parks and the urban environment. Culture builds civilization not the other way around. Also, culture is intertwined with education. You cannot have one without the other.

"A simple thing like reading a program in our concerts seems like a challenge. We have had audience members come up to us after a concert and ask us things like, 'Who wrote this piece?' or, 'Who sponsored you?' How are we expected to develop, if we are still faced with questions like, 'Why do you need $5000 for a sixty member orchestra?' 'How do you expect me to pay $20 for a concert? It's too expensive.' These are just a few of our many issues.

"Here is a story for you: a few years ago we were invited to perform at a conference which his Majesty was attending. It was related to Microsoft and Bill Gates was attending too. The organizers asked us to prepare a twenty-minute performance that was going to take place just before Iftar. Our contract states that no service of food will take place during that time- allowing 800 people to listen to the music. His Majesty was supposed to stay for the Iftar and thus this was truly the opportunity for our music to be heard. Unfortunately, his Majesty walked in, shook hands with a few people and had to leave. Though this was a disappointment, we still had 800 people who would hear our music. Unfortunately what happened after he left the room was out of a movie. 790 people left immediately after his Majesty walked out. The only remaining table was a group of ten doctors. We performed for them, but my heart ached that night.

"We did 'A Night at the Opera' at the Citadel in September, 2005, before the November bombing. I had an ambitious vision to bring in an orchestra, soloists, and a large choir. The budget to build a stage with the lights was around 30,000 JD. Nobody would pay it. A generous donor stepped in at the last minute. In order to cut costs, we needed to sell 500 tickets; we thought the most we could charge was 35 JDs ($50). Nobody would pay that. It was too expensive. Three days before the concert we managed to sell one hundred tickets. Then, as an experiment, we announced that the attire for the concert was formal. We set it up in a way to prepare for a 'gala' night. We had red carpets, lit the Citadel with candles and even had small bottles of wine to sell at the door. This was new for us.

"The formal attire strategy worked. Between Monday and Thursday we had sold over a thousand tickets with people begging at the door. Just before we went on stage, there were another hundred people with no tickets who wanted to come in. We had one thousand, five hundred people show up! There weren't enough chairs. We had people perched on the ruins in formal dress, some in their tiaras. After the concert, people were telling us that 35 JD was too cheap for what we had done. Afterwards, they realized how much work went into it. But what do you make of this?"

"The conservatory is moving downtown from West to East Amman. Will that make a difference?" I asked.

"I am in favor of the move. The hope is to bridge the gap by opening channels to the poorer neighborhoods. It would be great to create a core constituency, to have a place—like the Royal Cultural Center or the Amman Municipal Center—so that musicians, instrumentalists, singers, audiences and sponsors, could contribute to such an organization and to the cause of building culture through music. We need that kind of consistency. But I would lie to you if I didn't say that I am skeptical if any of that will happen anytime soon.

"America is fascinating. Oprah says, 'Support this,' people go out and support it. I felt there was a sense of community in the states. I don't feel it as much here. As a society, we are extremely family-oriented, very caring and with a sense of duty toward reciprocating socially, very courteous. However, outside the family, the sense of community seems to be lost. But I do feel it in the choir. We have managed to build an incredible community."

"If you were to stay in [return to] Amman, what would you do?" I asked. "If the symphonic choir materializes, then I would do a lot—major works like requiems on a regular basis, masses (B Minor Mass is one of my favorites) and all the classics, concerts (Christmas, Easter, maybe operas). I came back to Jordan with a vision to create and recreate music; to build communities of singers and though the path is difficult at times, I still hope for it; sometimes even pray for it. There is something beautiful about our culture and people. The hospitality, generosity and overall kindness is very present. There is a lot of heart and that's what keeps me going."

MARWAN

THROUGH ANTON, I OBTAINED an interview with Marwan al-Qasim, Foreign Minister from 1980-1984, Chief of the Royal Court 1984-1988 and 1995-1996, Minister of State in 1976, Minister of Provisions in late 1976 to 1979, and Deputy Prime Minister and former Senator. I noticed a large signed photo of Saddam Hussein with Marwan in the library. My initial question had to do with the way the Jordanian government functioned.

Their Chamber of Deputies is just like our Congress. The Senate or House of Notables is chosen by the king but under the constitution, it cannot be a random choice; they must have a long and distinguished service in government or in the army. Traditionally former prime ministers are members of the senate. The king's council which now numbers about forty must be completely credible and considered a valued asset to king and country.

Is the justice system just?

"The judiciary has been deteriorating over the years. It was always looked upon as the just arbiter and people felt secure in that they could get a fair trial. Everyone knows it's the final term of reference. We will suffer from this deterioration that has been heavily influenced by the executive government. The Ministry of Justice should be immune from political pressure. The judiciary should not submit to a change."

Because Jordan is not an oil-producing country, the government depends on foreign assistance, customs, and transit trade. Jordan, a poor country, relied on British subsidy till 1956 then on Arab and Western assistance during the Cold War era. The country is geographically well-situated. That's why they were originally called Transjordan—anything from the Red Sea to Syria and Iraq used to go through Jordan, from the desert to the Mediterranean. Income taxes here range from 35-70 per cent plus the taxes charged by the universities and by the municipalities. Those whose taxes are deducted from their salaries bear the greatest burden—civil servants, bureaucrats, the middle class and the military. Many rich people find ways of not paying taxes and there is almost no inheritance tax.

In 1976 when he was Minister of Provisions, prices were shooting up and they had to curb unbridled inflation for the sake of the poor. If it had been left to the merchants, prices would have gone through the roof. So they monitored and priced seven major commodities—wheat flour, frozen protein like fish, chicken, meat, and milk were placed at cost plus 5 per cent administrative charge. During the embargo against Iraq, their annual national revenue increased by $2 billion in light industries by selling clothing, canned food, water and medicine to sustain Iraq's consumption. They had leverage because of their location. Iraqis knew how important Jordan was. During the embargo, Jordan kept Iraq alive with commodities, services, and exports. That was no longer the case. "Iraq is in total disarray," he said, with Iran and Syria now supplying Iraq.

"What is your reaction to the war in Lebanon this past summer?" I asked.

He responded, "Hezbollah has been the only force which has successfully checked Israeli aggression. Their discipline on the battlefield exposed the weakness of Israel with all its military hardware and technology. This was the first time since 1948 that an Arab country was able to repulse and defeat the so-called invincible power of Israel. In Palestine, the first intifada in 1987 was little more than a spontaneous uprising of people throwing stones as a sign of resistance to the inhumane occupation of Palestine by Israel. In the second intifada, the Palestinians learned a lot about how to respond to Israeli aggression and occupation from the Hezbollah's successful eviction of Israel from southern Lebanon in May 2000. "

"In what way has the West failed Jordan?" I asked.

He got up and brought Bob Woodward's *State of Denial: Part III Bush at War.* "I quote, [George] Tenet [director of the Central Intelligence Agency under Presidents Clinton and Bush] said, 'We have created Jordanian intelligence. Therefore we own it. We have bought the Jordanian intelligence.'"

At that point, I said, "Jordanian intelligence is very impressive. Jordan is the only stable country in the Middle East. By the way, how do you do it, is it by word of mouth?"

He smiled and then assumed a serious tone. "America can help install peace, but not maintain it. They cannot act on an ad hoc basis."

I said, "Agreed, but in the first Gulf War, didn't Bush Sr. go in with a coalition of twenty-three countries?"

"You whip nations to stand by you and as a result of such an imposition, you intensify disaster in the region. When you talk about occupying a country to install democracy, you are not going to make it any easier. Egypt, Saudi Arabia and other Gulf and North African states are America's moderate allies in the invasion of Iraq. The question I pose to you is, are any of them genuine democracies, or do they share the same so-called democratic values of the U.S.? Let the governments run their countries without outside influence. The closer a country gets to the U.S., the more vulnerable it becomes, as it loses credibility with its own people," Qasim remarked, sounding a lot like Obama.

"But," I asked, "the Weapons of Mass Destruction. What was all that about?"

"David Kay," Marwan began, "who was hired by the CIA as one of the inspectors in the 1990s, was asked to check over 900 sites and he led the team again in 2003 and there were none."

"Why wasn't Saddam open about it?" I asked.

Marwan answered, "He wanted to give the impression to keep the Shia and the Kurds scared. It was for internal reasons."

THE COMMANDER

THE COMMANDER CAME to dinner with his wife (and mother of their three small children.) She was dressed traditionally in a headscarf and a long dress embroidered in the Palestinian style. Bob said that of all the women he had met, those in their traditional headscarves were the sweetest in Amman. The couple were from Zarqa, the birthplace of the deceased Al-Qaeda leader. The commander spoke with feeling about how Zarqawi was a traitor to the religion of Islam. They invited us to dinner at their house and we of course accepted with pleasure. We told him that the yells and grunts from the soldiers in training were disturbing, not to speak of the real-life video games. He was asked by the builder not to make noise until the apartments in our building were sold, was told that it upset people to see soldiers rappelling off the roof and simulations of house-to-house searches, shooting and blowing up (fake) bombs. Though sympathetic to his mission, I told him, it continued to be difficult living with war.

At dinner, the commander proudly told us his unit would be training some female recruits soon. Hanne Ulrichsen, Norway's deputy ambassador, told us young blonde Swedish women were training thousands of Iraqi police here, rotating in six-week shifts with no harassment. The next day, for the first time, I heard some female grunts in the morning exercises, from women performing martial arts in the yard—another great video game from our picture window. Fifteen women in navy blue pantsuits with white, pink, brown and green headscarves and navy caps were watching how to be fitted out with the rappelling belt. Some women and children sat and clapped as they descended. At the end during a running drill, the women chanted, "My mother is safe because I am a soldier."

The soldiers loved loudspeakers. 7 am and they were testing the mikes over at the diplomatic corps next door to the army unit. An awards ceremony was taking place that morning. The awards presenter gave a little speech, followed by the grunting cheers of the corps—three times, then a scream like "Allahu Akbar" and clapping.

A PRIVATE MILITIA

GUNFIRE PRACTICE AND LOUD cries of the drill sergeant could be heard early in the morning and late into the night. The neighbors were hopeful that the rumor of the police facility moving farther to the outskirts of the city was true. That morning, Bob went over to see the commander and they let him speak to his assistant, Muhammad, by phone, who said, "What's the problem?"

"Noise" Bob replied, "It is not normal when we hear gunfire and the cries of the volleyball players at eleven at night."

"That is our job," said the vice-commander.

As a joke, to get his attention, Bob replied, "Then we will form a private militia."

The commander got on his motorcycle and drove out to meet with Bob who had been detained by the guards. "Private militias are not allowed," Muhammad said.

Bob replied, "It was just a joke."

The vice commander said, "Everyone around here knows we are here," as if to say, choosing to remain living here is *your* business.

"It upsets my wife," Bob said.

The commander responded, "Please tell her to accept our apologies," and then set off a huge explosion as he left.

Early the next morning, a huge (fake) bomb was exploded in the guardhouse just under our terrace. A soldier, hardly recognizable, in desert fatigues was poised on the roof of the guardhouse just below us; in the yard, soldiers in a training exercise surrounded a car and held two men at gunpoint. Another van drove up and soldiers jumped out and threw another bomb in the guardhouse. Everyone clapped. The soldiers rappelled off the roof yelling, "Allahu Akbar."

THE WALL

YOLAINE, THE WIFE OF the Brazilian ambassador here told me of conversations she had had with the wife of the Palestinian representative in Madrid who was convinced that a Middle East peace was hopeless. Now with the Wall that separates Israel from the West Bank, whole families were cut off from one another.

"They cannot even visit their dead," she said, with tears in her eyes, "and they cannot go to work to support their families. Children cannot go to their schools. They have no water and no glasses to pour water into. The shape of the wall suddenly deepens into Palestinian land. One little thing will set off conflict and the cease-fire will be broken. Neither side is ready for peace. The Israelis give back some Palestinian land and then they come in the night and uproot olive trees, the Palestinians' only source of livelihood—trees that take fifteen years to grow. It's evil. All that exacerbates the problem."

Katerina's three-story house in Haifa (Israel's third largest city, a port near Mt. Carmel) was lost during the 1948 war.

"She can never go back," lamented Yolaine.

Naturally, many of the residents, who were not radicals, who depended on salaries from Israel, were increasingly likely to sympathize with Hamas's refusal to recognize the state of Israel. If only, my friends here told me, the United States would cut off their military armaments to Israel, especially the bombs, to express outrage. True that after Israel and Egypt, Palestine received the largest amount of foreign aid but how could Palestinians believe

Americans were their friends when they saw that the missiles heading in their direction were American made. During the Lebanese war, the European Union appealed to Turkey to hold up the transfer of American missiles destined for Israel. Yolaine surmised that there were easily 100,000 Lebanese in Amman hotels over the summer. I asked her about the September murder of the British tourists at the Roman theater and whether Westerners should adopt a different sort of dress, particularly in that part of the city. Dressed in a white piqué dress with red cherries, she said, "We can't let them frighten us. We wear what we want."

A ROYAL WEDDING

THE NIGHT BEFORE, HRH Princess Basma, (sister of King Hussein and Prince Hassan), celebrated the wedding of her son Ghazi Timoor Al Daghestani to Samanta Mahdi Saifi. In the Queen Zein garden just below us, King Abdullah and Queen Rania mingled with the other guests at this elegant black tie event. Stars were projected on the surface of the octagonal tent and strobe lights set up near the band flickered as the performers sang. The music was mixed—both Western and Eastern pop. Nancy Ajram, the famous Lebanese singer, who had flown in from Beirut, dressed in a long silver lamé gown, wowed the crowd. Bob and I watched in fascination alongside the sniper who had come to survey the scene quietly. We danced on our terrace under a full moon.

Echoing the opinion of some foreign policy specialists that moderate Arab states deserved recognition, King Abdullah said in an interview with *Time* magazine that day that, "A lot of moderate countries are feeling isolated. I don't think people are taking us seriously. [Predicting what has actually happened.] The world will be doomed to years of violence in the Middle East if there is no major effort by 2007 to resolve the Israeli-Palestinian conflict." Describing himself as an optimist, he said that without urgent efforts, he didn't think there would ever be a Palestinian state. The king also expressed concern that the region's troubles could multiply with the crisis over Iran and Iraq. "I don't think the Middle East could afford another war. A war with Iran would sort of open a Pandora's box and one from which I don't think the Middle East would recover."

VISITS FROM CONDI RICE

HISTORIANS GENERALLY AGREE that the expansion of Islam was both political and religious but what is less known is the many years of peace between Muslims and Christians. When President Bush misspoke and used the word "crusade," it was because in America, the word has become part of Western vocabulary and has ceased to be associated with the religious wars. But people here are well aware that the neo-cons—Wolfowitz and Cheney, the architects of the Iraq war—had the backing of the Christian evangelists. They questioned the motives of this administration. Bush never meant "Islamo-fascist" to have anything to do with Islam but with Al-Qaeda and other terrorists who use Islam for political purposes. Nevertheless, to run *Islam* and *fascist* together in one word was ill-advised. These oversights, compounded by innumerable other insensitivities, not only make Americans seem ridiculous and ignorant but offensive and dangerous. The result endangered the lives of Christians and pushed moderates here into the arms of the extremists.

The U.S. Secretary of State finally turned her attention to the Arab world, flying to Jordan, Lebanon, Syria, Saudi Arabia, Egypt (and it turned out Iraq), before heading toward the Palestinian territories and finally, Israel. The U.S. aimed to strengthen ties with moderate Arab states –Saudi Arabia, Egypt and Jordan—since Iran concerned the Gulf States, influencing both the situation in Iraq and in Lebanon. Condi Rice and King Abdullah met in Saudi Arabia for talks about how to rekindle the Middle East peace process. Even though Secretary of State and a former National Security Advisor, she was widely perceived as "dreamy" here.

At a business dinner, my partner repeated what Salwa had told me: that a show of force was needed—to keep the Iraqi temperament in check; it also seemed to explain why the clerics in their fiery Friday holy day speeches micromanaged instruction on Islamic law. He believed that history would bear out Colin Powell's strategy of "overwhelming force"—requiring more than the 155,000 troops in the country—over Secretary Rumsfeld's light, technologically advanced, agile units.

Israeli Moshe Arens, twice defense minister, contradicted what Georgette had told us in Beirut, that no one had won the war. "It is a defeat for Israel [because] that is the way it is perceived in the Arab world, and perception is reality…. It has changed the feeling for years that no coalition of Arab forces would be able to defeat Israel," the *Jordan Times* reported.

MAURICE AND ANDRÉE'S FARM

IN THE CAR ON THE way to the Maurice and Andrée's farm northwest of Amman, Nyla told us there had been nothing here for miles around when her family first came to Amman from Haifa in the 1950s. Nyla remembered how in those days Christians were put into prison for breaking the fast before iftar—drinking coffee or tea in public places during the day. (Lent, the Christian season of fasting, here means giving up all animal products, including eggs and cheese.) I remembered seeing photos of public hangings for greater crimes near the downtown mosque. I am careful with my Muslim friends not to drink (even) water in their presence and I warn Bob about any affectionate advances during the day.

The grove of fig and grape trees and wisteria vines provided shelter for the ample terrace; a light breeze played with the leaves, mingling with the sound of laughter and music. Two Iraqi musicians played the oud, the more ancient version of a lute, and an Arab version of a bongo drum. Of the forty guests, one of the ladies joined in with the professional Iraqi singer, making the evening exceptionally festive and warm. The small house with the antique ceramic tile floor and the colorful sofas lining the walls in Ottoman style were originally appointed.

Andrée's hostessing gifts were on display: spicy tomatoes and yoghurt spread on fresh bread followed by goat cheese dumplings, fried outside in a round copper dish. The older ladies, dressed in their long silk robes, played with the flame. When I admired them, they offered their dresses to me. Naturally I refused (the required) three times. The eternally youthful Andrée, our hostess, was wearing a bright pink and turquoise tunic and pants with large oval rhinestone earrings from Beirut, setting off her huge brown eyes.

Large washing basins had been transformed into serving dishes and the magnificent spread included chicken with large lentils and baby onions; wrapped grape leaves with rice; a huge salad with egg-shaped cheese encircled by tomatoes; steaks sizzled on the grill in front of us while Anton was cooking frogs' legs.

We knew quite a few people there and realized we were the only Americans to have been included in this cherished circle of friends. I wore an embroidered Ventilo top and a long beige skirt cut on a diagonal. Through Anton, I met Palestinians from Jaffa and others from Haifa, who had lost their land after the war. George, the handsome mild-mannered father of my conductor Shireen, who owned the GM dealership, described how he pushed her musically. He introduced me to an architect, and his wife, Maurice's sister, also active in electricity in Iraq. "But now," the architect said, his eyes hot and his nostrils flaring, "It is run by gangs." His passion was Bronze Age pottery and he offered to show us his collection.

During dinner, Maurice came and sat with us and told us he was from Salt, which preceded Amman as the first capital of (Trans) Jordan in the 1920s. I said, "Oh, then you must know where Job's tomb is."

"Who? Oh, you mean *Ahyub*"—the Arabic name for Job—"the one famous for his patience."

I said, "The guidebooks say he's from Salt," and a loud conversation ensued in Arabic between our friends about Job and his burial place. "We have a lot of prophets buried here, you know," Maurice said jovially. "Elisha [Elijah], I think, but I am a businessman, I don't know much about our prophets."

Bob punned, "You're a businessman so you should maximize your prophets."

Maurice, who is Jordanian, studied in a Jesuit school in Jerusalem in 1965 and received his post-graduate civil engineering degree in Baghdad from Boston College, a Jesuit school with a branch in Iraq.

PARTITION PLAN

ONE NIGHT ON BBC WORLD, Adnan Pachachi, the grand old man of Iraqi politics, was asked about the idea of partitioning Iraq into Sunni, Shia and Kurdish areas, an idea under consideration and rejected as an option by the Baker-Hamilton Study Group

"You can't do it. They [the sects] are all mixed up," said Pachachi.

Then he was asked what was his solution to the sectarian strife plaguing the country. Echoing Hana and Queen Noor's reasoning on the first Gulf War, he responded that a peace settlement could only come about if the

Middle East region supported it. When pressed, he said, "I'm sorry but this is the *only* way."

Bob added, "Eight times a day I hear, 'No matter what we say, don't leave us. The Shia militia, backed by Iran, will invade us.'"

At the gym, I met Irwin, who worked in Baghdad ten days out of every month helping the U.S. government with security and telecommunications. He said that when you give the local sheik a percentage, it is not a bribe; it is including him in the process and that otherwise you run the risk of incurring his wrath. If Americans did not do this, he said, they were only profiting from the situation. There was a huge incentive for creating community goodwill by realizing that sharing the wealth creates firm foundations between two cultures.

LITERATURE

WHEN PEOPLE HERE SPOKE of the late Columbia Professor Edward Said, the revered historian and author of *Orientalism* (translated into thirty-six languages), born in Jerusalem, Palestine in 1935 and died in New York, 2003, they bowed their heads as if honoring royalty (or a prophet). Mahmoud Darwich and Mourid Al Barghouti were also widely read. And yet, author Diala Khasawneh wrote in the *Jordan Times*, "Censorship has become internalized: whether the socially shameful, the religiously 'haram' [taboo] or the politically dangerous. Little space is left for creativity and self-expression."

She cited great Arab novels like *Seasons of Migration to the North, Sultana, Women of the Sand, Cities of Salt, Stone of Laughter,* and *The Yacoubian Building* by Egyptian Ala'Al Aswani [2002]—officially, the bestselling Arab novel and at that time a recently released three-hour feature film—and Amin Maalouf, Naguib Mahfouz, Emile Habibi, and Ibrahim Fawal's historical fiction about the Israeli-Palestinian crisis, *On the Hills of God.* Other friends had recommended *Guests of the Sheik* and *Islamic Feminism* by Elizabeth Fernea. Although Jordan's literacy rate was 86 percent, few books were sold—it wasn't that people couldn't read, it was that most people didn't read. My French group were voracious readers but they were apparently in the minority and most people relaxed by playing cards. A Russian civil engineer married to a Jordanian was regularly teased for reading books. Some attributed this to the difficulty of the Arabic language but this was also becoming increasingly true in America as well.

In an interview in *Paris Match*, Queen Rania spoke about Jordan: "Every country in the Middle East is unique. Perceiving the reality hidden behind general impressions and stereotypes is important. Take the question of the veil in Kuwait, for example; one must see that for certain women, it is not at all a symbol of oppression, but a symbol of modesty and devotion to God. One must approach the question of women in the Arab world within their context and surmount superficial perceptions."

The queen went on to remind the readers that Bin Laden's message was laden with talk about justice. "Very well, then," she said, "Use it to smash him. We must absolutely believe there is a solution, even if the means already used have failed. It is not because the method has not succeeded that we should abandon the objective, peace."

"The principal enemy, you are saying, is fear of the other?" the *Match* interviewer asked.

"Yes, fear reinforces mistrust. The nourishment for fear is ignorance. And the cause of fear is the lack of a dialogue." Marguerite wrote in her novel, *Emily L.* "Causing fear is what constitutes evil." It is often said that the war on terror enhances terrorism.

During Ramadan, the early morning threading of calls from a quartet of muezzins has mystical resonance, resembling a hive of bees, high-pitched and intense like the hurried flap of a multitude of angels' wings. We were close to Eid Al Fitr, the festival that marks the end of Ramadan when the prophet is thought to have received the word of God to write the Qur'an. Emad expressed his disappointment that I would miss Eid because I was due to leave Jordan for Paris and New York the following day.

Chapter Eight
November

O N THE PLANE RETURNING to Jordan, I met James, a sandy-haired young man in his early 40s, whose keen understanding for the failure of Iraq's economy struck home. James, whose family owned a farm in western Massachusetts (my home state) for three centuries, was the top agricultural counselor at the embassy in Baghdad. We invited him to join us later at the Four Seasons Square Bar, appointed in gold leaf wallpaper, where he, like Naba, recognized many distinguished Iraqis.

After four years of government service, he was leaving soon to start his own business in Iraq (Director of J&S Foodstuff Trading DMCC).

"The Iraqis are a lovely, dignified, gentle, and sophisticated people," he began. "Iraq is a rich country with $223 billion in assets. 99.9995% of all Arab peoples are peace-loving. But those in positions of power don't want to use their power correctly—they don't want to take a chance to come up with an aggressive plan to turn the country around, a plan that would require change. They don't want to draw attention to themselves; they want to keep their heads down.

"They hate the middlemen whom they recognize as the mafia. But right now, it's every man for himself rather than working to form a consensus that would allow the effective functioning of a business model. There has to be a certain trust that the business model will survive—the concept that even if you don't get your way one day, you will the next time. Many Iraqis are making money in business because they know they can fleece the Americans. They are not building toward a national consciousness. They have no collective sense of wellbeing. There is no self-confidence."

James gave the example of the Port Authority at Umm Qasr (mother of all castles) at Basra, an estuary which empties into the Persian Gulf, that, among other things, discharges wheat. The previous year, the U.S. had 72 percent market share. The American Embassy wanted to bring a fourth berth on line with a private British company because there was a backlog of ten ships waiting in the Persian Gulf outside the port, costing the Iraqi Treasury $25,000 a day. The Port Authority resisted because they wanted to use their equipment and make the additional $100,000, regardless of the cost of "demurrage"—the costs to the government for delays in discharging. Much like the tribal mentality, the port didn't realize that, if it brought in a private company from Dubai or Kuwait or Jordan, which could think beyond a few days or months, it would have a better reputation for efficiency and bring more business to the port.

Muqtada al-Sadr, according to James, controlled the Ministry of Transportation governing ports and four or five other ministries— agriculture, health and culture. [It is widely known that Muqtada al-Sadr is mentally retarded, heavily medicated and relies on the reputation of his father to gather support for his cause. His bodyguards were nevertheless quite helpful to Bob.] "The Shiite mafia doesn't like working with the U.S. even if the aim is to improve Iraq's finances, not to promote U.S. business. There are Iranian agents throughout the Iraqi government."

James was saying the real problem in Iraq was that there was no access to international suppliers so entrepreneurs had to go through traders in Turkey, Jordan, Syria, Kuwait and other countries. These traders were making huge profits because the international suppliers did not sell to Iraqi buyers. The Iraqi buyers hated the middlemen because they knew they were getting overcharged but they didn't know whom to talk to or how to get the credibility to open a business, or how to open a letter of credit to do business.

Putting them in touch with the original source appealed to their dignity for three reasons: first, because they would be held hostage by the usual suppliers; second, because it would improve their marketing; and third, because they would have technical assistance on the food safety system of certificates.

COMMEMORATING THE DEAD

ON NOVEMBER 10 AT THE La Salle Church, the Dozan Wa Awtar Choir and the Jordan Conservatory Orchestra were due to sing the complete version of Mozart's *Requiem*. But the Hyatt Hotel, the principal sponsor, asked for one of the movements to be sung on November 8 to commemorate those killed in the suicide bombing of November 9, 2005 (while Bobby was staying there). Recalling Bob's phone call—"It's alright. I'm alive,"—that night sent a shiver through me.

Shireen, our conductor, a powerfully creative spirit, remarked, "We artists have many dreams, but many times, we need somebody to make them happen." She was offered the Zara Expo (a circular mall within the Hyatt complex) but preferred to do it on the circular stairs in the center of the Hyatt Hotel lobby on all three floors. Her friend, Barbara, said, "That's a brilliant idea. Let's make it happen." But had it been someone else, they could have had an attitude, "What do you mean on the stairs?"

Candles on the three levels lit Hyatt's circular stairway and Shireen conducted from the central landing as groups of families of the survivors gathered on the three floors shattered in the violent attack. The sea of quiet and melancholy faces responded to the pathos of this masterpiece and gave power to the performance. People were crying. It was a happening, a personal connection with the families of those who died there. "One must have faith—that's what really puts it together at the end of the day," she added.

Music erases all nationalities, class and gender or religion, there is a feeling of goodwill in the common pursuit of excellence. And this music has particular resonance in the bloody, war-torn region where requiems for the dead are an everyday occurrence. The suffering was invading my dreams. The gruesome images of leg piled unnaturally over leg, bodies scarred or bloated, blood everywhere, children crying, shaking in fear, speechless, continued day after day; it was forming a dull knot of pain in my stomach.

Through a fellow chorister on the night of the Mozart *Requiem*, I met Kenneth, Prince Hassan's speechwriter and press secretary—a thirty-seven-year-old Irish lawyer, journalist, writer, and graduate of Trinity College, Dublin and the School of Oriental and African Studies, University of London. We discussed how U.S. citizens give up their old countries and swear allegiance to the flag; here, other things are more important. People belong to their tribe, family, religion and village. What matters here is not the individual but the collective—the family, one's ancestors, the tribe or tribes to which one belongs.

"The ancient caravan routes from Beirut to Baghdad have always been welcoming toward foreigners. There is no dislike of Americans. There is hatred of what they are doing to the region. The Americans don't give the Middle East the credit they are due. But as Churchill once said, 'You can always rely on the Americans to do the right thing once they've exhausted every other option.' So now they are talking to Damascus and Tehran," Kenneth remarked in his light-hearted Irish manner.

Once upon a time, Westerners spoke of this place at the very edge of the Western world, as being where the macadam ends, and the ancient Silk Roads—bandits, Bedouins, desert—begin. Today, we are in the middle of what could be Armageddon and the future depends on understanding Arab culture, appreciating the people and carrying on a dialogue with them.

THE BULBOUL

IT WAS MID-NOVEMBER and I raised the blinds at sunrise when my night owl came to bed. I was up at 5:08 in darkness at the second call to prayer. The sky turned from black to red to rose to gold. Just before six, it began to take on a teal green hue with the slightest hint of blue that bathed the contours of the jebel on the other side of the wadi. The falcon-like crows were flying through their fir trees; small birds chirped morning greetings. From the terrace I warmed up my voice, and had an attentive listener—a small white face, black and white head, a black breast, a long delicate beak and a long black tail, the markings of the famous Iraqi nightingale, the Bulboul. Thinking perhaps he was hungry, I put some bread on the terrace balustrade. He ignored the bread and paced at the window, chirping, and flapping his wings on the glass door, trying so desperately to get in he left his feathers on the windowpane. I considered this an immense compliment, that a bird who sang with such beauty would find a kindred spirit in me.

The previous day I had gone before the Royal Academy of Music jury—a young blonde Russian with cat-like eyes and a sweet smile sat next to the rudely yawning Mr. Othman, who was grading my mid-term. I sang

"Lascia Ch'io Pianga" from *Rinaldo* and Robert Franz's "Err Ist Gekommen" (*He Is Coming*). I managed better than average marks, in spite of nerves. I am relying on the Arab proverb, "What comes from the sky/heaven, the ground receives." ("Illi biji min asama, tittla??a Il?ard") meaning, in a word, *whatever.*

KINDLY TYRANTS

I WAS IN THE HANDS OF kindly tyrants. The climate—dryness and sand—is really hard on the eyes and must be looked after. The same is true for the throat. At the end of the Arabic lesson that day, Nyla, famous for her remedies, gave me sesame seed oil—tahini—which, when mixed with honey, is an effective remedy for sore vocal chords. Svetlana had ordered me not to sing for three days after the jury.

From this perch I considered the intense pride of the Arab peoples—their sense of decency in the midst of cruelty, their unpredictability—the mix of docility and aggression—and finally, their different view of the very notion of time.

"As regards their concept of time," said Bob, who loves the Arabs, "They make the French look like German Protestants."

Bob was meeting with the Jordanian prime minister and finance minister and, for the first time since our arrival here, he was dressed in French tailored finery. Even without water and oil, the stability in Jordan makes it the new center of the Middle East. Amman is a sophisticated version of a desert island where you rely on the diesel truck to keep the heat on and sometimes if, in the construction phase, you go over your city ration, you rely on the water truck.

Barrenness brings out Arab ingenuity—if you can't find something, you make it—from furniture to faucets to fix-its. For certain things, like fabrics and lighting, you find a wide variety of specialty goods—like elegant Italian and German lighting fixtures (because people here have passion for beautiful lighting.) What we thought was the outer edge of civilization is the place where West meets East, where you can find the best of both worlds.

I spent hours on that day with Emad, the creator of our closets in the penthouse, measuring and debating the size and look of the kitchen, closets, and bookcases. Instinctively his ideas were correct—Arab ingenuity rules again. After three hours of this, my eyes were tearing—from the dust, the sun, the smoke of their cigarettes, and from impatience. Emad thought I was crying and promised, "We will do it all together and have it for you before Christmas."

The living room, with its walls of desert beige in swirls and the faux marble corniche to match the design of the fireplace, was a success but empty paint cans, dirty plastic sheets, cigarette butts and boxes, sheet rock, plaster, sponges in pails, and dust littered the apartment. Bob said, "It's like the Kurds and the Arabs—I tell the Kurds, 'You have to check with Baghdad,' and they say, 'No, we will handle it;' and I tell Baghdad to check with the Kurds and they say, 'No, no, we will handle it.' So there's no communication, weeks go by and no work gets done."

But finally, the trompe l'oeil on the cornice which I made the painter re-do three times looked fabulous. MamdooH arrived early in full Egyptian regalia—boots, with a hose over his shoulder and kefi, to clean the mess left by the workmen. Nader, our electrician, an Egyptian Christian, showed me the green cross on the underside of his wrist that had been pierced by needles when he was six or seven. It was the orthodox cross (of equal length) and embellished with what resembled a little flower at the tip. When it faded, he had it redone. He was from Asut, 360 miles south of Cairo, near Luxor and Aswan, where Mary, with the baby Jesus, escaped during the time of Herod. (There are annual pilgrimages to Mary's house now a church on a hilltop.)

BEIT HANOUN

FAMILY IS SO IMPORTANT here and the smallest suffering reverberates in every household. So when there is a very large suffering, the air is thick with recrimination. The *Jordan Times* cover photo showed tiny bodies swathed in white, being lowered into graves in Gaza and, alongside, a picture of a large group of weeping women. Nineteen people—all members of the same family—mostly women and children—were killed. Jordanians were appalled that the U.S. provided the weapons technology the Israelis used in the raid which missed its target and fell on Beit Hanoun. The U.S. vetoed yet another UN Security Council resolution condemning Israel's attacks. I was ashamed of my country. One Palestinian woman screamed, "I lost my whole family; is there anyone who is still alive? My husband, my mother, my children, my sister. But I swear in the name of God, we will not surrender; this is our land and here we shall live and die."

Bob's response was, "The Israelis say the same thing when their citizens are attacked by suicide bombers and terrorist infiltrators."

"But it is nowhere near the same magnitude," I argued. "This is overkill!"

The lead editorial in that day's *Jordan Times*, echoed in every world newspaper, concerned the recommendations of former U.S. Secretary of State James Baker's commission on Iraq. Already he was known to favor opening channels to Syria and Iran—what my Baghdad friend confirmed was already taking place and putting the U.S. at odds with Israel—"giving the green light to Israel to strike Iran's nuclear facilities would be the last thing it [the Baker report] would contemplate." A decade later President Obama, following Baker's advice, seemed to have closed that chapter.

On that day when Jordan honored the late King Hussein's birthday, the *Jordan Times* quoted a young student who recalled how, "Hussein was a leader that never ruled by blood. He killed no one, and sometimes pardoned those who attempted to kill him."

At the HSBC bank, Michel, a kindly-looking man with salt and pepper hair, greeted me. "I am Christian," he began by saying, in accordance with a long tradition of establishing personal relationships with clients. "Arab Christians were the first in Jordan, before the Muslims," he told me as if that would surprise me.

"Yes," I said. "It was only around 600 AD that Christians began converting to Islam."

"The problem," he said, "is Bush and the Pope; they are making life for us [Christians] very difficult. We have no problem with the American people. We have no problem with Clinton. Have you ever heard of Arabs having problems with Americans?" he asked.

"Not Arabs maybe but Iranians do," I answered.

"Well, yes, [Iranians do] with blondes," he said.

"Blondes?" I asked.

[Years later Saywan Barzani, then Iraqi ambassador to the Hague showed me a photo of an ISIS leader with long hair and wild eyes and next to it, his enemy—a beautiful blonde.]

One of his assistants came in to ask a question. When she left, he went on: "I am from Jerusalem," he explained. "My mother's house is ten minutes from the [Church of the] Holy Sepulchre. Have you been there?"

I told him that I had. I asked, "Shouldn't the Arab League be stronger?"

"No," he remarked (in an appraisal that is hardly politically correct), "One Arab in a room is a genius. Ten Arabs in a room are idiots. They fight; they go on strike. It's the opposite with the Japanese: one Japanese is an idiot. In a group, they are geniuses."

When I mentioned to Emad that our mutual friend, our banker, Michel, had told us that the original Jordanians were Christian, he smiled nervously and explained that Jordan was the stopping-off place for people making the Hajj (the annual trip to Mecca in Saudi Arabia, to commemorate the birth of the prophet.) Jordanian ancestry is also Syrian, Turkish, Lebanese, and a tiny minority from Russia and the area surrounding the Caspian Sea—the Caucasus, Turkmenistan and other parts of Central Asia. Because the Hashemites came from Mecca, some Jordanians are also of Saudi origin, others Bedouin, and at least fifty percent Palestinians from the coastal plane.

The richness of the Middle East tapestry is revealed in the weekend edition of the *International Herald Tribune,* a historical detail the Israeli hard-liners against Iran may have missed. Souren Melikian noted the similarities between the early Hebrew and Qur'anic texts in the earliest dated medieval Hebrew manuscript, 903-904 AD from the Seleucid era, "The manuscript format is identical to that of small Iranian Qur'ans of the 10th century, pointing to shared aesthetics in scriptural tradition. The earliest near complete, dated manuscript of the Bible, copied in 929 AD, is believed to have also come from the Genizah....The Latin version of the Bible prevailed and the Palestinian prophet, Yeshu, under his Latinized name, Jesus, was depicted wearing a Roman toga..." from an article entitled "Many Bibles: a Puzzle of Fragments" at an exhibition at the Arthur M. Sackler Gallery in Washington, entitled, "In the Beginning."

BITHIB MOOZ? AND KOLI HAWA

NYLA, FRESHLY COIFFED WITH blonde streaks in her auburn hair and dressed in a thick yellow and navy three-quarter wool jacket, took us to her "farm" only thirty minutes outside of the city. Typically generous and fun-loving, she decided to take advantage of the drive to have an extended, interactive Arabic lesson. She proceeded to explain in Arabic the words for everything we saw—street, palm tree, buildings, land, etc. "Sayid Bob, do you like bananas?" she asked, in Arabic, "Bithib mooz?"as she passed a fruit stand. At her country estate, there are two security entrance gates. Olive trees line the driveway; after the harvest she sells me the oil at a good price. As we were leaving, Nyla performed a tricky maneuver onto the highway that she hoped the police would not see. I drew in my breath. The maid warned her in Arabic.

Nyla answered, "**Koli hawa**"—literally "*eat air*"—which is the Arabic way, of saying "shut up." I thought she was chastising me for scaring her. She said, "Oh no, I was talking to the maid. She is very outspoken. I would never speak to you that way."

THE SECOND INFLAMMATORY EVENT

KATYA AND I WERE HAVING tea with Lebanese and Iraqi friends at the Four Seasons. The Cuban consul said his Lebanese wife's family had taken refuge in Jordan over the summer like many other thousands. "We are used to living with the absence of stability. Why can't we live with the first rising of the sun?" he asked, endearingly poetic, his large eyes wide open.

Another friend there, Luke, an Iraqi intelligence analyst whose sharp good looks had just won him a job as a male model in a cell phone commercial, remarked, "At any given moment in Baghdad, it's worse than it's ever been. Iraq has everything—it's the cradle of civilization, it has the sea, the mountains, it's rich in agriculture and oil, with strong tourism potential."

Katya commented, "Well you know the saying 'Patience is a virtue: seldom in a woman, never in a man,'" and then smiled and giggled so naturally I could see why so many men had fallen for her.

Katya gave a small dinner in our honor—Anton and Salwa, Roland and Katerina, and a few others. At her villa in the lush Abdoun neighborhood, the house was old enough for ivy to have grown on the outer court; and had turned red and yellow as it does in the fall in America.

"Up until 1988," she said, "the monarchy was fully in control. Now the monarchy shares power with the parliament."

"How do they control the country?" I asked.

"Through conversations with people. By word of mouth," she explained.

Others have said there is wiretapping, and monitoring of conversations.

"Of course this occurs," said Salwa, "but this is a fair regime...not bloodthirsty, like so many others."

Katya had prepared a generous table—avocados with shrimp, lamb, chicken, and lasagna. The seating was open and on my right was the spouse of a diplomat who told me that it was true that Jordan's hierarchical monarchical system afforded it stability in the region. "The parliament is nothing. This sort of control means that all the creative people, the innovators, leave and go where the money is—to Dubai or to one of the other Arab Emirates. Kuwait makes $80 billion a day in revenues, can you imagine? What do they do with all that money? And only a third of it goes back into the community."

When I asked the group if they thought *we* should leave, I meant Iraq. But I was surprised to realize that they all thought I meant we— Israel/America—should leave Palestine, such is the mindset equating America with Israel. Roland asked Bob, "Tell me one other country that colonized another and got away with it."

"Our own," Bobby responded, "we took the land away from the Indians and twenty-six million square miles."

"That's old history," Roland responded, but you could tell the wound was deep.

"The U.S. had had an embargo on selling arms to Israel until 1967," Bob told Roland, "because they didn't want them to fight the Arabs. France provided all their weapons until the '67 war."

Roland, a Frenchman, fumed. Every time Salwa opened her mouth, pursed in anger, Anton told her, "We often disagree with our American friends but we don't say anything against them at the dinner table."

Later, Bob asked me privately if I had noticed how many times people say they are going to kill someone. This penchant for creating controversy just for conversation seems very French, a quality descending from his Swiss French ancestors, no doubt; seeing how wounded our friends are by the colonization of Palestine, I asked him, "Is this really necessary?" Apparently this discussion became highly controversial. At future parties we went to, we were welcomed with Indian whoops and war-cries.

JORDAN'S SISTER

IT CAME AS A SHOCK THAT young, handsome Industry Minister Pierre Gemayel, a critic of Syria and a rising star in the right-wing Christian phalangist party in Lebanon, was assassinated this afternoon. Amal (the Shia party formed by Imam Musa) and Hezbollah may soon be forming a joint government. Amin Gemayel, the father of the latest martyr of the cause of a free Lebanon, then spoke, "I can't put into words this tragedy. The martyr was victimized for a cause. My son was murdered. I call for self-control, self-restraint to protect the cause. I call on all those who loved Pierre who worked for the cause for which he worked. I have only one hope—tonight is a night of prayer, of the meaning of a martyr, and to consider how he wanted to protect our country—other than violent reaction. [There will be] no exchange of accusations. We shall adopt a responsible position, we should preserve the integrity of Lebanon."

He did not call for revenge. Walid (Wally) Jumblatt, the Druze leader, arrived to offer condolences.

They were blaming Hezbollah and Syria and Iran. The pro-Syrian Lebanese President declared that Gemayel's assassins were conspiring against Lebanon. There were calls by the Phalangist party to go to war against Syria, although their client Hezbollah had condemned the killing whilst maintaining that the government was illegal. The Security Council was calling for the establishment of an International Tribunal to investigate the murder of Rafik Hariri, a former Prime Minister of Lebanon, in February 2005. Many accused Syria of having orchestrated the killing and a UN inquiry had produced evidence to support this.

Suddenly, Majid dropped in and said, "Wally Jumblatt has a 'thin face,'" an Arabic expression meaning he sides first with one, then another (their version of our expression *two-faced*). We watched Saad Al Hariri, son of the assassinated Hariri, give a short, sharp condemnation: "They are carrying out what they want to do—the sequence of assassinations they promised. The International Tribunal will judge. God is great."

I felt the isolation growing even in our small circle. When I appeared at a gathering of friends, their rage assaulted me—America's one-sided foreign policy blatantly favoring Israel over Palestine and our intervention in Iraq strikes a chord that vibrates alarmingly in this region—a region that has suffered from numerous occupations—Persian, Assyrian, Turk, Greek, Roman, and British. Bob's debate with Roland at Katya's—comparing the Israelis taking land from the Palestinians to America taking land from the Indians—had been making the rounds. In the ancient Bedouin tradition of courtesy toward visitors and support among friends, Anton walked to our house the next day to give Bob support, something Bob, a seasoned political debater, didn't feel he needed. But I did and thanked Anton. But I could feel the sense of helplessness and frustration. They could not go to war for their land and their good manners and traditions prevented them from even being rude to a foreigner whom they are supposed to welcome. So they were sullen. I admired their fortitude and their wisdom and was deeply ashamed of my country's duplicity regarding the Palestinians—all talk and no action. It reminded me of the way King George treated his rebellious American colonists and why we fought in 1776.

I went to see Kenneth to prepare my interview with Prince Hassan. Until 2002-2003, Prince Hassan was seen as someone who could draw together Shia and Sunni and there was talk of him becoming King of Iraq (as his Hashemite cousins had been until the late 1950s), according to Bob. When Abdullah became King, Prince Hassan left the government and had since been working at his foundation, the Royal Institute of Inter-Faith Studies (RIIFS), among many other organizations.

Kenneth told me that when he came into a room with Prince Hassan, people assumed he was American and were greatly relieved to hear he came from a country that had experienced the same sectarian strife. That the British Empire was the original cause of the Middle East unhappiness had apparently been forgotten. "There is nothing dangerous about Islam," Kenneth told me. "What *is* dangerous is these extremists who can hijack an entire religion and there's no central voice to say it is wrong. In the Catholic faith, we have the Pope to do so; in the Anglican faith, we have the Archbishop of Canterbury. In Sunnism, there is no central voice. It was easier when, under the Ottoman Empire, the caliph could issue the party line through the religious leaders throughout fifty states that were predominantly Muslim. There is no moral center for the Islamic Sunnis. They are searching in the dark particularly because politically they are so weak."

For centuries under the Ottoman Empire, the three Abrahamic faiths got along. Since they were not expected to fight Islamic wars, in lieu of military service, Jews and Christians were required to pay a tax and the empire grew rich through this tax. In Hejaz, Saudi Arabia, where the Hashemite tribe originated, the kings of Hejaz were called Sharif and held the keys to the Kaaba, a stone structure made of a black meteorite, the center of the Islamic world, which was also worshipped by Abraham who first recognized it as a holy site and revered it. Like the Christian prophets before him, the prophet Muhammad objected to the golden idols that crowded the Kaaba and removed them. When the Hashemites guarded the holy sites of Mecca and Medina, there were four independent buildings for the schools of Sunni and Shia surrounding the Kaaba and the area was a center for discussion and debate. For centuries, the empire extending to Red Sea coast was a center of learning.

The prince wanted to see the Middle East region return to its roots, extending from the Mediterranean to the Red Sea, when borders and nationalities meant very little, to the time when the exchange of ideas was common to all Arab cultures and fundamentally part of Islam. Ethnicity was not a big issue: the Ottomans married Circassians, Kurds and Slavs. The three Abrahamic faiths lived together side by side. The nation-state was something imposed on them by Europe—a concept forged over centuries in a foreign land. There is little difference between Syria, Jordan and Iraq, which is why it makes it so easy for extremists to cross the borders.

"When the Wahhabis, a strict fundamentalist Islamic sect, took over, they hijacked the center of Islamic civilization by destroying the four structures housing the Sunni and Shia sects; they have used the prophet's anti-idolatrous message for commercial gain. It would be as if a strict fundamentalist sect from Arkansas suddenly ruled America," Kenneth said. "The Hajj suddenly changed under the Saudis. Ironically, according to an architect—Sami Angawi—the destruction of Mecca and Medina is taking place using the prophet's anti-idolatrous message. It is not just depictions of people and ancient monuments, it is the prophet's own house as well as that of his wife and his mother. In Medina, you could see everything—where the prophet's prayer room was, where he slept. They were given a week to excavate it and then it was bulldozed and made into an apartment building because it was prime real estate.

"The Wahhabi sect of Islam has also distorted the prophet's message about women. The Qur'an is progressive in giving property rights to women [women were only allowed to own property in England in the 19th century]. The Qur'an says that women should dress modestly but, except for his brides, nothing about being veiled. Likewise, nuns, the brides of Christ, are veiled. But under Byzantine and Persian rule, it was a sign of exclusivity and status to be veiled and live in seclusion. [No doubt they were influenced by the climate also.] When the Arabs conquered all of Byzantium and Persia, their culture filtered down to everyone. Not that it helps women now; the chador in Saudi Arabia and Iran has become an essential part of their life. What is important is to understand there is nothing so strict in the Qur'an.

"There was a Saudi hadith that a woman couldn't ride a camel; that became a law that a woman couldn't drive a car. But this again is a corruption: in the prophet's time, women rode camels and horses and fought alongside him in battle. The Qur'an is against intoxication but there is nothing that says you cannot drink alcohol," Kenneth continued. "The prophet speaks of wine at celebrations though later hadiths forbid it.[16]

"The Bishop of Bethlehem is an Arab Christian and has been so forever. The U.S. misses this—that the Christians and the Arabs are together here. Traditionally, in Arab culture, every Christian family has had a Muslim family as protector. When the Crusaders took Karak, for example, the Christian Arabs fought alongside their Arab brothers against the European Christian invaders. Saladin's wife was Christian. Islam recognizes Abraham and Christ as great prophets and all three faiths believe in one God, the same God. The only difference is that in Islam the prophet Muhammad received his revelation from God and was the last of the great prophets. The Holy Bible comes to us 'after the fact' through the Greek tradition of reason, whereas the Qur'an is the revelation of the word of God.

"The point is that we are all worshipping the same God," Kenneth explained. "St. John Damasy, an 8th century Umayyid Greek Orthodox Christian church, founded by Christians in Damascus, wrote about Islam as a Christian sect, not a different religion. The Greek Orthodox ceremony is

---

[16] Reza Aslan, in *No God but God*, states, "The Qur'an initially took a somewhat neutral stance on the drinking of wine, (2:219); a few years later, another verse was revealed that urged believers "not to come to prayer while intoxicated" (4:43).

in Arabic. The nuns chant 'allah, allah' and prostrate themselves. I felt more alien there than a Muslim," Kenneth said.

"The Arabs are concerned that what is driving U.S. politics is the Christian right—they are the ones who vote—and that is why Israel's interests are given a heavier weighting. Forty percent of the land where the settlements are built in the West Bank is Palestinian," Kenneth said. "The Jewish tradition and goal is to rebuild the Temple of the Mount (where the Wailing Wall is) and with it, the destruction of the Dome of the Rock and Al-Aqsa where Muhammad ascended into heaven, before the Messiah arrives so that the Messiah will recognize his holy place. This is ridiculous. The Messiah needs no such place. It is a very bad sign when a group of Orthodox Jews march out of the Damascus Gate in Jerusalem, the Arab sector. They never dared to do that before."

THE ROADMAP IS BACK

AT FIVE THIRTY AM, just before dawn broke, the sky turned red and then settled down to golden hues at the horizon. Small birds were eating the bread on the balcony but were distracted by the noise of a military helicopter that had been circling the city at a low altitude. One bird stayed and looked from our perch, uncertain and uninterested in the bread. President Bush was coming to Jordan to meet with Nuri al-Maliki, the prime minister of Iraq. The King told George Stephanopoulos of ABC's *This Week* that three civil wars were looming in the Middle East.

"I keep saying that Palestine is the core," the monarch told him. "It is linked to what is going on in Iraq. It is linked to what is going on in Lebanon. It is linked to the issues that we find ourselves in with the Syrians."

When Emad, the eternal optimist, came this morning and saw my long face regarding the news, he laughed. I love this about the Palestinians, they assume they are going to win, that one day, there will be a fair two-state solution.

Over drinks, Anton said excitedly, "The road map is back," referring to Hamas' rumored capitulation and the recognition of the state of Israel. "It's all been decided and everything will now happen very quickly. The Americans have put pressure on Israel, the Palestinians will be paid off, they have given Jordan the money for an airport in Irbid. Jordan will become a very important center in the Middle East. They are meeting with Syria and Tehran over Lebanon and Iraq. Hopefully, there will finally be peace in the Middle East."

THE DESERT TURNS TO ICE

AS I WENT TO MY daily workout at the Four Seasons the previous day, the spectacle of a U.S. presidential visit greeted me. There had been a freeze on personal relationships within our circle during Bush's visit as if an ice flow suddenly rendered the desert immobile followed by a thaw after he left. Jordan relies on foreign subsidies because it is expensive to produce anything here and to farm, because water is scarce. Jordan has benefited from its alliance with the West, particularly the U.S., from direct things like subsidies to create businesses and maintain infrastructure but now the debate was how much damage that does, particularly with Bush visiting. Jordan was looking for other sources of income. They would have liked to benefit from investment or financial activities from the Gulf and were weighing the pros and cons.

A pretty young woman with straight blond hair in a burgundy business suit (to the knee) and a badge, in stockings and heels, was pacing and talking on her cellphone outside. Concrete slabs instead of the usual plastic barriers had been placed at the driveway entrance to the hotel. There were no cars anywhere and three big trucks in the parking lot. I learned that day—watching from the spa and exchanging pleasantries while waiting for the elevator—that the young men and women loading computers and wires into huge plastic bins were technical support for the White House. An ambulance stood guard outside the entrance (ready to pull into Security Unit 14).

The security checkpoint had been placed inside with a new X-ray conveyor belt to check bags. A soldier in green with a gun in a white holster stood by the entrance. Two security people surveyed me. An Arab in a long brown robe with a red headdress and his lovely young wife in a headscarf, carrying Vuitton luggage, looked annoyed by the change in mood at the usually obsequiously friendly Four Seasons style, and at having to walk a few meters away in order to retrieve their car instead of standing under the heated Roman awning. There were sharpshooters on all the roofs, and big black vans filled with the king's guards in front of the hotel.

As I was waiting, young men with wires in the backs of their ears watched me. As I re-entered the hotel, a portlier version of the girl outside and her male colleague looked at me as I looked at him. You can recognize the guards by their red woolen caps as opposed to the blue ones in the diplomatic corps across the street. I said, "Alla YaAtik il Affye," (*may God give you health and strength*) and he smiled, obviously delighted that at least one American had taken the time to learn some phrases in his language. As mentioned earlier (it can't be stressed enough), if the American military had known five greetings they might have pulled it off in Iraq—the others would be marhaba (hello), keif haalak (how are you?), il Hamdilla (I'm fine, thanks be to God), saba al xeer (good morning). Once on a plane out of Amman, I happened to meet a mercenary who worked for Blackwater and I tried out a little Arabic on him but he was clearly distressed by it and told me, "I'm trying to forget all that," chillingly reducing all Arabs to bad guy status.

President Bush had been scheduled to participate in a three-way summit meeting with Prime Minister Nuri al-Maliki and King Abdullah II. The last minute cancellation of the Wednesday night dinner meeting was not announced until Bush was inside Raghadan Palace, posing for photographs alone with the king. Prime Minister al-Maliki's no-show of the opening session was a major snub in the context of an event involving the U.S. president, the king and the prime minister. Confusion and conflicting explanations ensued. It was impossible not to read some palace intrigue into the scrubbing of such a meeting.

Al-Maliki had arrived earlier and had had a productive private talk with the king, according to the theory. The Jordanian and the Iraqi decided that a three-way session with Bush was not "the best use of time" and that Bush would breakfast with al-Maliki the next morning at his hotel. Therefore, al-Maliki was already gone by the time Bush arrived on Wednesday night from a NATO summit in Latvia. The president had an abbreviated dinner with the king before heading early to his hotel. Another explanation was that al-Maliki wanted to distance himself from Bush to appease some of his hard line supporters in Baghdad.

An Iraqi acquaintance explained—the king did not want to be caught in a dispute between Bush and al-Maliki and wanted to impress on Bush the importance of a comprehensive solution in the Middle East—bringing the Palestinian question into the equation. A senior aide to Abdul Aziz al-Hakim who was also in Amman, said the Iraqis balked at the three-way meeting after learning the king wanted to broaden the talks to include the Israeli-Palestinian conflict. Two senior officials traveling with al-Maliki said the prime minister had been reluctant to travel to Jordan in the first place and decided, once in Amman, that he did not want "a third party" involved in the talks about subjects specific to the US-Iraqi relationship.

The American spin on "the scrub" was that al-Maliki cancelled the meeting after a classified White House memo expressing doubts about al-Maliki was disclosed and after Muqtadr al-Sadr loyalists suspended participation in the al-Maliki government because he had ignored their request to cancel the Bush meeting entirely. The classified memo by National Security Advisor Stephen Hadley had said that while al-Maliki seemed to have good intentions when talking to the Americans, "the reality on the streets suggested al-Maliki is either ignorant of what's going on, misrepresenting his intentions or that his capabilities are not yet sufficient."

Al-Maliki's deputy prime minister, Salam Zikam Ali al-Zubaie, said he was baffled by the boycott because the prime minister had met Bush in both Baghdad and Washington. "So why can't he see him in Amman?" asked Zubaie, a Sunni Arab. Bush was expected to ask the embattled Iraqi prime minister how Iraqi forces could be trained to halt sectarian violence and mend the Shiite-Sunni divide so that 140,000 U.S. troops could come home.

An Iraqi politician told me, "Bush created all these problems and now he wants the Arabs to fix them." Bush was trying to reach out to moderate Arab nations to alter the dynamic in the Middle East, because it was unclear what other solution was available to him. At the dinner with the king the previous night, the Israeli-Palestinian relationship was discussed as was Syria's involvement in Lebanon. Iraq was not the primary focus of the meal, according to press reports. As anti-Bush sentiment was high, I didn't dare call to ask what had happened. Conversing too much about palace intrigue could have diminished my standing. But the leaking of the NSA memo critical of al-Maliki with the withdrawal of the Shiites from the Iraqi parliament might have been figured into the outcome.

A LONDON VISIT WITH ADNAN PACHACHI

BOB AND I WENT TO London to celebrate to see Reema Pachachi—we were inseparable friends at Beauvoir (elementary) School in Washington when her father, the distinguished statesman Adnan Pachachi was Iraqi consul, later Iraqi ambassador to the U.S. and to the UN in the 1950s.

"What do I call you—His Excellency, Minister, Mr. Ambassador?" I asked.

"Call me Adnan," he replied with soothing charm. The coalition had asked him to be president of Iraq just after Saddam was toppled but he preferred election to appointment and refused the position. "The timing wasn't right. I don't know, maybe I was wrong," he said softly.

Considering all that had transpired without him, I quietly remarked, "I wish you'd taken it."

"I am much happier being an elected member of Parliament [in December 2005]. I walked the streets. People said how happy they were I had come back."

He is currently the head of the Iraqi Independent Democrats— ideologically centrist—the party that believes in a secular democracy, equality for women, separation of religion from the state—"not separation of church and state, separation of mosque and state," he quipped. In 2003-2004, as a member of the governing council, he was the chairman of the committee drafting the new constitution. "Bremer called me the James Madison of Iraq," he laughed.

I told him that I was struck by how highly intuitive the Arabs are, "As if they had a little wire at the back of their heads picking up on what the rest of us don't." I emphasized how uncommonly generous and hospitable they are, much more so than the French.

"We have more in common with the Americans, I think," Adnan said. "We never knew whether our neighbor was Sunni or Shia just the way you probably don't know or care if your neighbor is Protestant or Catholic [though we did for a long time until 1960 when JFK was elected.] Everyone is intermarried in Iraq."

As for what happened in Iraq after Saddam: "You can't expect to be welcomed the way the Americans were after World War II when Europe had been completely destroyed. In the early days in Iraq, the American soldiers were rough. They were looking for weapons and they were trained to kill. They didn't know how to deal with civil disturbance. They offended people and created discontent. People didn't see a vast improvement after Saddam. Their electricity was cut, they had no water, the sewage broke down, and they were queuing for gasoline. The resentment grew.

"The first few months after the war, there was a void. There were no militias. Iran created the militias; then Al-Qaeda and the former Ba'athists. Saddam had let all the criminals out of the jails. All the disgruntled people re-grouped and took up arms. It was so easy to get weapons. There was a breakdown in law and order and the police were corrupt. Now they are so heavily infiltrated by militias, only a very powerful force could deter them.

"The main problem now is the militias," Adnan continued. "They are bolder, stronger, ruthless, and behave with impunity. The Shia government is incapable of handling the situation. Not only are the training of the Iraqi forces and the weapons below par but also the main reason is that they are heavily infiltrated by the militias; many of the most violent are supported by Iran. Until we can reorganize the security forces so they assure the undivided loyalty to the Iraqi state and affirm their allegiance to our country, we need multinational help. It could have been better. We were so full of hope."

As regards the Iraq Study Group recommendations—the James Baker report: "I agree that the United States should get involved more forcefully. It is true that the Israeli-Palestinian question is the key to the whole thing. It would defuse the Iraqi militias. National reconciliation cannot happen without an improvement in services," Pachachi told me, "but this cannot happen until people no longer live in fear, and until we solve the problem of militias. President Bush feels a responsibility to the Iraqi government and is prepared to help us with better training. He thinks that embedding experts in our armed forces will allow them to reduce U.S. forces. But simply embedding American advisors within the Iraqi brigades is not enough—I repeat—not enough to give Iraqi forces the power to defend our country. The total reorganization of the Iraqi forces can only happen with a multinational presence. If the United States and the U.K. are unwilling or unable to master the situation, then a multinational force must be sent in."

I asked, "What about the Arab League?"

"The Arab League," Pachachi said, "is an intergovernmental organization like the Secretariat of the UN. It is as good or bad as its members. It doesn't have the power or a personality of its own and tries to coordinate the actions of Arab countries. There is no military."

I told them that we had been in Beirut in September.

"More than a thousand Lebanese were killed," Adnan told me. "It is very sad. If you don't solve the Arab-Israeli problem, you are just giving a painkiller to a disease. All these conferences are nonsense." Pachachi continued, "Some experts say that, of all the issues of the Middle East, Palestine is one that can be resolved because there are no winners and no losers. Lebanon and Iraq can't be solved, they say, because both sides want to win. Israel realizes it can't win by force. They want to live in peace. Two states will be created."

CHAPTER NINE
December

CHRISTMAS IN AMMAN

WE DIDN'T EXPECT CHRISTMAS to be celebrated at all here in a country that is ninety-eight percent Muslim. If Muslims celebrate in moderation (Jesus is one of their chief prophets), Christians do so with gusto. Never one to pass up an opportunity for perfection in decoration, the Four Seasons lobby is decked out in Christmas finery—evergreen boughs around the room and Christmas trees—nine of them with white lights and balls. We found a tiny tree at the florist near our house and Emad taught me the Arab technique for keeping (Christmas) trees alive—a ceramic pot filled with sand and water. It is a perfect "stand."

Princes from the Gulf are here, their impressive fine gold threaded robes trailing the ground. Hassim, Hussein's son by Queen Noor, is marrying a Saudi princess. The Jordanian prince became very religious all of a sudden after meeting his Saudi wife and decided within ten days to marry her. The neighbors think this may explain the new additional prayers on the loudspeakers. There were some lovely Saudi women in the hotel lobby today. One was not covered head to toe in black; her lovely fine-featured face, with heavy eye make-up, was animated by her happy situation. A fine white fabric scarf covered her head and the robe covering her body did nothing to diminish her thin silhouette.

Nasser, owner of the Alexander the Great antiquities shop at the Four

Seasons, identified the agate of earrings Bob bought me from another dealer as being Sumerian, older than Roman (which is considered almost commonplace here.) It is thrilling to know that part of the earring affixed to my earlobe is 1,700 years old, from the time of the first Christian emperor, and that the stone hanging from it was probably first worn by a Sumerian woman in 4000BC, from the first urban region in Mesopotamia, in modern day southern Iraq, during the Bronze Age. Nasser convinced me to take a necklace of Sumerian beads from the same period—agate, mother of pearl, jasper, and bloodstone. When I wear this necklace, the stones emit heat and their energy has a curative effect on my neck. Once when I wore it at a party of archaeologists, and when they told me, "That should be in a museum," I decided to have it appraised.

At the Anglican Church (the Episcopal Church of the Redeemer whose diocese is in Jerusalem), my choir, led by Shireen, performed a tapestry of Christmas music—beautifully weaving together Arab Christian and Western Christian music. Though I didn't understand the words to the opening song in Arabic, the plea for peace came through intuitively. "Deep River," "I want to cross over Jordan…I want to cross over into campground," had a solitary, chilling ring for all the Palestinians here.

The darkened church with only the glimmer of the lights on the Christmas tree near the altar set the mood. The singers entered by candlelight singing a capella, stopping at every fifth pew, turning to face the congregation and then turning back on their way to the altar. They wore black with a large red chiffon rose in the lapel. At the end, I embraced Shireen and told her, "Congratulations, it was beautiful," and she whispered in my ear, "We missed you," (my workload was such that I was unable to sing two concerts that season). The soprano and tenor soloists caught up with me—one hugged me with tears in her eyes and the other looked stricken. The loss of one member of the group is emotional—each voice counts and when one is not there, it is as if a small part of your body is missing.

In the program notes, Shireen wrote,

"…the kingdom of heaven is attainable here on earth…all we need is for us to open our hearts. 'My kingdom does not belong to this world. I was born and came into the world for one purpose, to speak the truth. Whoever belongs to the truth listens to me.' John 18:37. May our music open your hearts to His truth."

Imagine the U.S. being the cause of the break in the link of the chain of thousands of years of your people living in one region. Iraqi Chaldean Christians whose ancestors have been in the area for thousands of years are forced to flee Iraq. Half the Christian population, many of whom speak Aramaic, have left.

On Christmas Eve, Christians walk from Jerusalem to Bethlehem and try to get past the famous Wall. Madaba—where Moses died soon after he saw the Promised Land from Mt. Nebo—is another big Christian town. Christmas is widely celebrated in Lebanon where Christians comprise up to 40 percent of the population. The Arabic word for Christians is "Il massayiin"—or "the Messiahs," though in the Gulf, they don't think there are any Christians left in the Middle East.

The night before, three Iraqis had come to dinner—Naba, who is Sunni and Haytham, her architect husband, Shia, and May, an Iraqi Christian woman living in Amman who had managed to find a job working with *Doctors Without Borders*. May's son was kidnapped by militias and she paid a handsome sum to get him back. The war had taken a terrible toll on everyone's psyche. She told us of the chaos that now reigned, that the Shia had told the Christians to evacuate their houses and the Sunnis who had been told to evacuate theirs. The Shia moved into the neighborhoods that once were Sunni and vice versa, she said. Yet, before the war, a Sunni-Shia marriage was not uncommon. (In Iraq, having four wives is not widely practiced, "among the ordinary people," as Ambassador Pachachi put it; "in the general population, there are not multiple wives. Because of the Iraq-Iran war of 1980 to 1988, the population of Iraq became 60 percent female, 40 percent male so these women who had lost their husbands didn't mind being the second or third wife. It was legal but kept a secret since, under Sharia law, marriages must be publicly announced.")

The day before, the soldiers had done a little rain dance with drums and bagpipes. Jordan was then in the grip of a drought with 95 percent of the country receiving lower than normal rainfall levels for that time of year. That day saw the first sprinkling of rain since the previous spring and the soldiers across the street ran out into the yard, jumping and dancing for joy. At eight am on Christmas morning the soldiers were already drilling in the yard. Then the bagpipes and drums on the loudspeakers began. We were speculating on whether this was a Christmas celebration or whether in preparation for Eid Al-Adha.

The next day, Max, who was here for the holidays, and I went to the Mecca Mall, "the Mecca of deregulated corporate greed where," he said, "the environment is forsaken for the higher value of consumerism." Max refused to have coffee at Starbucks so we went to the "Blue Fig" where Ralph Waldo Emerson's words are inscribed—"Do not go where the path may lead, Go instead where there is no path and leave a trail." This was my philosophy, why I was here, why I kept the diary though I was not sure that this would ever lead to peace.

In keeping with the tradition of Boxing Day, we visited our neighbors, Nora and Riad, who had also invited some Syrian-Palestinian couples for cake and juice. During this dinner, it became clear how much curious and opinionated women like me are disliked. I told them I was trying to understand the relationship between the moon, the Eid, the Hajj, and the sacrifice.

(Silence.)

I said I guessed that the second Eid, ten weeks after the first, must be a half moon if the first Eid begins with the crescent. Max looked at me. The Arab men sat stone-faced, refusing to look at me.

Then I said how wonderful I thought Jordan was and how well the monarchy worked. Again, Max was keeping his eye on me, sensing that the atmosphere in the room was taking an interesting turn. One of the men said that he did not like King Hussein.

"Why not?" I asked, expressing amazement, as I had never heard that before.

(Silence)

Later Bobby told me that some people hate King Hussein because they thought he betrayed the Palestinians by recognizing the state of Israel.

As a final conversational resort, I tried the sympathetic anti-imperialist argument about how unfortunate it was that the French sold out King Faisal and the Arab world when they claimed Syria after World War I. This time their faces contorted.

(Silence).

I later discovered it is taboo to discuss politics, especially for women. I felt the centuries divide us. The wives, all dressed up, were silent; the atmosphere, dark.

My eyes started to tear, maybe because of the smoke from the fire, maybe because of the fire in their eyes or the hatred in the air. One of the women asked sympathetically about the sensitivity of my eyes to smoke. She said her son was living in Los Angeles (as is so often the case with people whose parents hate America). That appeared to be enough of an ice-breaker for them to suddenly get up. One of the men glanced at me but didn't look as if he wanted to shake hands and the other simply left.

Riad looked a little sick. I steered the conversation back to the main topic which was why Syria and Jordan don't get along. Riad said, "It has to do with the Ba'athist party. Also after the '67 war, the Jordanians integrated the Palestinian refugees into their society whereas the Syrians kept them in camps." Then he quickly turned the topic back to the anti-imperialist argument, "No one wants the Middle East to be strong."

"How do you know that?" Bob asked.

Riad said that there was Russian influence in Syria, Egypt and Algeria, and U.S. influence in Tunisia, Lebanon and Jordan. Bobby said the Israelis refused Russian influence and also defied the U.S. Riad said when he was in Libya, people thought that Qaddafi was a U.S. invention to cause trouble for the Arab states, to weaken them.

Bobby again asked, "How do you know that?"

Then we talked about the poverty in Jordan in a region of so much wealth. Riad told us that the Saudis throw money after "girls"—that one of the Saudi princes had filled a swimming pool with champagne at a resort in Switzerland for his girlfriends to drink. I wondered what sort of religion they belonged to.

RAINING INSIDE

ALL MY DECORATING SKILLS of the previous months had been for nought: it was raining inside our house! Heavy rains, ice and snow were causing flooding. Again water was leaking through the open light fixture downstairs, and down the chimney upstairs and there was flooding in the stairwell. The water had spread into the penthouse living room. Our insistence last June on the importance of insulating the entire terrace with rubber before tiling was proved right. The builder's men, Emad, and various other experts came to check the damage. Miraculously, finally, the builder agreed to do whatever was necessary to fix the roof. (He later retracted the promise.) Coincidentally, the boiler broke down so there was no hot water and no heat. We relied on an electric fan that doubled as the air conditioner in summer and we showered at the spa. Yesterday we had planned to go to Petra but the site was closed due to snow and ice, for fear of a repeat of another year when tourists were killed from flooding in the siqq, the narrow passage leading into the site.

THE WEATHER IS COLD SO CAKES ARE NICE

FOR OUR ARABIC LESSON, Nyla had made some delicious cakes—blueberry cheesecake and small crepes—because "ittaqs barid, fi hilu" ("*the weather is cold so cakes are nice*.") We are planning a trip to Jerusalem due to bad weather in Petra, and Nyla told us it would be easy for Americans to go by car. We will return by air since we read in the *Jordan Times* that the King Hussein bridge would be closed during Eid (this later turned out to be false) and would reopen on January 5th so as to allow the passage of pilgrims returning from the Hajj in Saudi Arabia.

When I announced to our Palestinian and Jordanian friends that we were going to Jerusalem, their voices became quiet and I heard in their tone, a trace of love lost, a half note in their voices, like a sigh or a whisper. They had to wait hours or days or never go home at all and we, as Americans, could supposedly cross over into Israel easily. For Arab Christians as well, there was a tangible nostalgia for a time when they were young when there were no walls, checkpoints, barbed wire or guns; when people wandered freely into each other's backyards without thinking whether they were Arab or Christian or Jew.

Bobby's method of choosing a vacation was to locate the latest disaster because the hotel rates would always be cheaper. When he heard they discovered a case of bird flu in Egypt the other day, his response was, "Maybe they could find us a place on a Nile cruiser after all. Disasters are illusions made worse by the media," Bob said. "Even in Baghdad, there are Westerners who walk down the street in a yellow Brooks Brothers shirt and corduroys."

In the end, we stuck with our plans to go to Israel.

CROSSING OVER JORDAN

NYLA'S CLAIM TO AN EASY crossing into Israel turned out to be optimistic; it was long and arduous—a short sixty kilometers became a five-hour marathon. Every Jew should be forced to cross over into Israel as an Arab; it would remind them of their own historical experiences. We chose land transportation from Amman to Jerusalem, because we were told it was easy for Americans—four hours for an Arab—and less time-consuming than flying. A man in a black wool coat who looked like a bodyguard took us to the Jordanian border checkpoint at the King Hussein Bridge. Of Palestinian origin, born in Jordan, he said he loved his country and happily complied with Bobby's attempt at speaking Arabic until we reached the crossing at the Dead Sea.

The subsequent six checkpoints were exasperating. No signs indicated the procedures; we stood in one line for passport control for an hour, then another to pay a departure tax (5JD). We gathered up our luggage and stood outside on a cold sidewalk for another hour for a bus to take us across the stream called the Jordan River. Once the bus came, it was stopped mid-way and checked for bombs even though as the only authorized transportation, they are already—and regularly—checked for bombs. Once across the stream, the same bridge goes by another name—the Allenby Bridge, after the British general who took control of Palestine from the Turks after World War II.

At the first checkpoint just before the border, we were made to exit the bus and showed our passports to a young Israeli woman and as we were getting back on an attendant again checked under the bus for bombs. We waited for another fifteen minutes while a few V.I.P. vans sped across the border. Finally, the authorities lifted the gate letting our bus pass. I was amazed when our luggage was thrown out onto the sidewalk and one of the officers wearing a reflective orange vest took our passports. We lined up outside at five entry points wide enough for cattle to get through, trying to get the attention of a customs official, and noting that those who showed a little cash got better service. It all had the look and feel of the movies of the Jews in German concentration camps. After about twenty minutes waiting there, a young woman finally cried out our names and we stood in another line, to pass through the metal detectors and another machine that blew wind through your clothes (skirt flying up), checking for drugs and miscellaneous traces of chemicals. At this point, you ended up inside a large customs hall for interrogation.

After thirty minutes of waiting, Bobby had the task of persuading the young female customs official, (wearing Dior sunglasses, her auburn hair pulled back in a clip), not to stamp his passport because he worked in Iraq and other Arab countries, where a passport stamped by Israel precludes entry into the country. She questioned him and checked to see if this was permissible. We waited in another line to be processed into the baggage area—one person took the customs paper and another checked the passport. Finally, we found our bags and headed toward the exit. We had been told that outside, someone from Petra Travel would be holding a sign with our name on it. No one was waiting for us and, exhausted and frustrated, we took a taxi to the checkpoint outside the airport where we found that the van had been forbidden entry and had been waiting for two hours.

From the Allenby Bridge through the West Bank, with Jericho on one side and Bedouin camps on the other, the Jordan Valley—under whatever authority, Israeli or Jordanian—looked exactly the same, dry land on gently sloping mountains. Large herds of goats grazed on what looked like dry earth.

"What kind of grass can they possibly find there?" Bob asked the driver, (not realizing that goats eat the bark of trees or any dead wood.)

(No response.)

Nearing East Jerusalem, Bob tried out his Arabic, in an effort to extract a little conversation from the close-lipped, unemotional Palestinian driver from Bethlehem.

Bob said, "Those high-rises are ancient."

"Are any of those settlements authorized?" I asked.

"That's a naïve question," the driver answered, meaning it was an oxymoron.

Then Bob asked, "Are you for Fatah or Hamas?"

"Neither of them do much for the people," the driver answered.

"What's the difference between them then?" I asked.

"Hamas is a religious organization," he responded.

"If they don't help their people, how can they be religious?" I asked.

"Why don't they recognize the state of Israel and allow the food in?"

"Because Israel does not recognize Palestine," he said without emotion.

Under the Oslo accords of 1993, during a secret negotiation that took place while Bill Clinton was president, Prime Minister Yitzhak Rabin of Israel in direct negotiations with Yasser Arafat, chairman of the Palestinian Liberation Organization, recognized the legitimate rights of the Palestinian people and began the process that would lead to a state. Palestine, with Arafat as its president, recognized the right of Israel to exist. Gaza and Jericho, Ramallah and Bethlehem were turned over to Palestinian rule.

With the intifada, the issue of the settling of the borders fell apart.

If the King David is a Jewish hotel, Palestinians run the American Colony Hotel. We vastly preferred the welcome here to our first at the King David in 2005. The exterior and interior gardens are visions of loveliness with stone fountains and golden walls inlaid with blue peacocks painted on tiles. Although the fixtures are new, the rooms are furnished with antiques and old books and the hotel has the feel of the old world luxury of the Levant. The Palestinian staff are characteristically gentle and cordial. When the standard Arab greeting is intoned genuinely, "You are welcome", the visitor is bathed in *aHlan wasaalan*. French, Italian, German, American, English, Chinese, and African tourists were staying here for the New Year.

In the late 19th century, an American family—the Spaffords, messianic Christians from Chicago—bought the palace, first built for an Ottoman pasha—Rabbah Daoud Amin Effendi El Husseini and his harem of four wives. In 1895, after losing their children at sea, the Spaffords and their Swedish relatives took up residence in the hotel compound and created a commune—making their own bread, providing health care to the local community and soup kitchens in time of war (thus the name, American Colony). The hotel has remained determinedly neutral ever since.

When the British took control of Jerusalem after World War I, the Turkish governor brought flowers to Mrs. Spafford at the hotel to announce his departure; he did not have a white flag with which to indicate the surrender of the Ottoman Empire to the British Empire so Mrs. Spafford gave him a white sheet. The hotel then became a home away from home for General Allenby. It was the secret meeting place between Prime Minister Yitzhak Rabin and PLO President Arafat preceding the Oslo Accords in the early '90s. Lawrence of Arabia told his war stories to Lowell Thomas here; it has also been the home to Graham Greene, John Steinbeck, Saul Bellow,

Marc Chagall and numerous journalists. From '48 to '67 the American Colony in East Jerusalem was Jordanian. In that long lost time, taxi drivers used to take tourists from Jerusalem to Petra to Jerash and back in a day.

We hired a taxi to see the city by night from the Mount of Olives. Going into the Jewish quarter during the Shabbat from sunset on Friday to sunset on Saturday is "very dangerous" according to the driver. No one is allowed to touch anything mechanical and no cars—neither taxis nor police—are allowed inside or they are stoned. (This explains why on the holy day, the elevators automatically stop at each floor at the *King David* Hotel where we stayed in 2005.) As Bob is a night owl, he was pulled outdoors by the full moon and ended up walking the circumference of Jerusalem, entering Muslim and then Christian cemeteries on the hills overlooking the Kidron Valley. Lying on top of the marble slabs of the graves, he felt the spiritual rapture that is commonly known as the Jerusalem syndrome.

Tomorrow is Eid Al-Adha when according to the Bible, the Lord tests Abraham by asking him to sacrifice his son, Isaac whereas, according to the Muslim tradition, Al-Adha marks the moment Abraham's hand was stayed by an angel when he was about to sacrifice his (older) son, Ishmael.

The story of Abraham with his sons, Ishmael and Isaac, is celebrated in a monotheistic context by the Muslims, Jews and Christians, but it actually proceeds from an ancient sacred tradition. In the 8th century BC in Babylonia (modern day Iraq), the link to the divine world was celebrated on the New Year with the sacrifice of a "scapegoat," Karen Armstrong writes in *The History of God,* "to cancel the old, dying year… These symbolic actions thus had a sacramental value; they enabled the people of Babylon to immerse themselves in the sacred power or mana on which their own civilization depended." It reminded me of when Majid went to the slaughterhouse in thanks for the blessings God bestowed on us.

We began our tour of Jerusalem with a perky Christian Palestinian guide at the church where they celebrated the Last Supper (Maundy Thursday). Our Amman friends, the (Muslim) Dajani family, own the property of the famous Church of the Last Supper but Israel claimed it as state property and even had the nerve to offer it to the Spanish government in exchange for a Jewish temple in Madrid. The Dajanis, who had a block of apartment houses in 1948 when the Israelis took over, have been in court over that theft as well as other attempts to take possession of their current

East Jerusalem property. In one exchange with the court, Mr. Dajani told the judge that he also had property in London but that the British government didn't assume ownership and steal his property rights just because he was out of the country.

Then we visited the garden of Gethsemane on the Mount of Olives where Jesus and his disciples often met. A 20th century church is built on the rock where Christ came to terms with the horror of the ordeal awaiting him, and where Matthew, Mark, Luke and John stood guard. The freshly tilled reddish soil of the garden with its thick ancient twisted olive trees, exposed in their rude setting, seem a raw reminder of the evil that took place there. Some people were crying as they prayed. It is possible to pray at night in the garden by calling the priest at the sanctuary and ringing the bell at the gate between 8 and 9 pm.

The Last Judgment is supposed to have taken place just in front of the church in the Kidron Valley. Absalom's tomb is there in a Jewish cemetery on land rented from the Muslims for 99 years. We passed through the ancient wall into the old city at St. Stephen's Gate where Saint Peter's pupil was stoned to death for carrying on the torch of Christianity, long after the death of Christ. On Palm Sunday, Christ started his triumphant procession as king of the Jews at Bethphage on a donkey, entering through the Golden Gate with people singing "Hosanna," our guide told us. (That gate has been closed since the 1500s.)

In the Qur'an, Jesus is revered as an important prophet. Saladin spared St. Anne's (Christ's grandmother's) temple in his 12th century march to take the city back from the Crusaders.[17] The Romanesque church, lovingly

---

[17] Karen Armstrong wrote in *The Guardian*, December 23, 2006, "The Qur'an does not believe that Jesus is divine but it devotes more space to the story of his virginal conception and birth than does the New Testament, presenting it as richly symbolic of the birth of the Spirit in all human beings (Qur'an 19:17-29; 21:91). Like the great prophets, Mary receives this Spirit and bears Jesus, who will, in his turn, become an ayah, a revelation of peace, gentleness and compassion to the world. The Qur'an is horrified by Christian claims that Jesus was the "son of God," and depicts Jesus ardently denying his divinity in an attempt to "cleanse" himself of these blasphemous projections. Time and again the Qur'an insists that, like Muhammad himself, Jesus was

restored by the French with elegant simplicity, is a reminder that the virgin birth is glorified in the Qur'an which includes a miracle not included in the Bible that the infant Christ could speak in full sentences. Mary's birthplace is revered by Muslims and Christians; with its lovely gardens, it was once used for Qur'anic study. To one side is the pool of Bethesda where Christ healed a paralytic on a Saturday, the day of rest, and was chastised for it by a Pharisee, (John 5). Our guide commented practically, "When the Lord decided to do something, time would not hold him back."

The streets of the city were empty for the holiday—the eve both of the Muslim Eid and the Jewish holy day; vendors would not violate the religious intensity of visiting the Stations of the Cross as was the case on our last visit here. Across from the palace where Pontius Pilate judged Christ, station number one, is a small open courtyard with arches, full of sweet-smelling orange trees. A church frontispiece marks the place where a barbed cat-o-nine-tails (a whip with spiked balls at the end) tore into the Savior's flesh thirty-nine times (forty is taboo since the Jews spent forty days in the wilderness). We saw the place where he was tied and whipped (the Church of the Holy Sepulchre houses the column). Across the front of the church are circular motifs portraying the weapons as well as with I N R I, Iesus Nazarenus Rex Iudaeorum, and hands above a bowl, signifying Pontius Pilate washing his hands of the crowd's choice to crucify Christ over the criminal Barabbas.

Inside the chapel are red stones marking the spot where he took up his cross, station number two; station three 100 meters away, he fell for the first time; station no. 4, he met his mother while carrying the cross; station number 5, Simeon the Cyrean offers to help him; at this point we leave the walls of Jerusalem in Roman times. The Wailing Wall is not far. It is the last remnant of the 955 BC Temple of Solomon. The Babylonians destroyed it in 587 BC; the wall was rebuilt by the Romans in the 1st century BC by Herod "to please the Jews," our guide said. All that is left is the wall built around the palace. It encloses the Dome of the Rock built by Walid I in the 8th century AD because here, Abraham first attempted to fulfill the sacrifice

---

a perfectly ordinary human being and that the Christians have entirely misunderstood their own scriptures."

of Ishmael and Isaac, the genesis of the Muslim celebration of Eid as well as the holiest site for Jews.

A sign commemorating the Wailing Wall reads:

"Here Adam came into being. Abraham, Isaac and Jacob served God. The first and second temples were built upon the foundation stone. Jews were chosen by God [and this] as the dwelling place of the Shechinah. David longed to build the temple and Solomon built the first temple here 3000 years ago. It was destroyed by Nebuchadnezzar of Babylon. A second temple was rebuilt 70 years later. It was razed by the Romans 1900 years ago. This is a remnant of the Western Temple Mount. Jews have prayed in its shadows for hundreds of years, an expression of their faith in rebuilding the temple. The Divine Presence never moves from the wall."

We returned to station number six where Veronica (vero=true, ica=icon), wiped the Lord's face; at station seven, Christ fell for the second time; at the eighth station, when a woman approached Christ, crying, He responded, "don't cry for me, cry for yourself and your children;" at the ninth station, near the (modern-day) Coptic Church (Egyptian), Christ fell for the third time while carrying the cross. At the tenth station, near steps on the outside of the Church of the Holy Sepulchre leading up to a glassed porch, He was stripped and his clothes were divided into lots by the Roman guards. Ten feet away, at the eleventh station, He was nailed to the cross, a space currently "owned by the Roman Catholics". Ten feet from there, where Jesus was crucified, the Greek Orthodox Church has dominion. The altar, covered in hammered gold with elaborate paintings and lamps hanging, is crowded with visitors and priests swinging incense. The faithful can reach their hands into a hole and touch the place where the cross stood. Next to it is a window showing how the rock was split by the earthquake, as is described in the Bible. Down a few steps, one can touch the place where he is supposed to have been washed before being laid in his tomb inside a rock that is housed by a Rotunda.

Although Hadrian built a temple to Venus in the 2nd century AD, Constantine ordered the temple consecrated as a church in 325, the Church of the Holy Sepulchre. Constantine's mother Helene claimed to have discovered Christ's tomb and arranged for the rock face to be cut away from the tomb so as not to disturb it and the Rotunda was built around it in 380.

Our guide led us out to the west wall of the old city where the three kings came to Herod, asking where was the new King of the Jews, followed quickly by Mary's flight into Egypt and the slaughter of the Innocents. Speaking of Herod, our guide murmured, "He came in as a fox and left as a dog."

In preparation for the beginning of Eid (the Arabic word for feast), people were either praying or visiting their families, bringing sweets, as is the tradition. I read that even the poorest Muslims struggle to find the money to sacrifice a goat to the glory of God. The Muslim world woke up on the first day of Eid Al-Adha, a few hours before the Eid prayer—to find that Saddam Hussein had been hanged, despite Iraqi law forbidding executions on holy days. Even the moderate governments of Egypt, Jordan, and Saudi Arabia complained that President al-Maliki had breached the holiness of the Eid Al-Adha. In the evening, as the details about Saddam's hanging came filtering on the television news at the Pasha restaurant where we dined on Arab food, I asked Bob, "Who chose this day for his hanging?" "The Americans told the Iraqis to execute him before or after but they did not listen," Bob answered. The Muslim patrons seemed in shock; they all stared at us as we watched in silence.

Our guide told us false information—that we could visit the Al Aqsa mosque if we got there early before the prayers. Our taxi driver, Nabil, who from that time on became our guide, told us that it was out of the question. (An Israeli policewoman confirmed it with her horrified look.) We set off for Bethlehem in the West Bank. Nabil's family were laborers who built the tombs in the Jewish cemeteries and took tourists throughout Jordan, a country that before 1967 extended from Jerusalem to Amman. As we were leaving by the Jaffa gate to the south, Nabil told us the Greek Patriarchs walk to Bethlehem every Christmas Eve Day and arrive by nightfall. "Christians and Muslims are brothers," Nabil told us.

Bet= house + helem=bread in Hebrew, and meat in Arabic. Nabil, of an indeterminate elderly age, his luminous face lined with decades of patience, told us that he had eight uncles who all lived to be between 125 and 134 years old. "We are from the Mount of Olives and in the morning, we eat fish and half a kilo of olives—Bejallah olives being the best—and at night, we smoke Nargileh, the fruity tobacco. My father died at 82 but that was because he smoked four packs of cigarettes a day."

We went a way to avoid the checkpoints since we didn't happen to have our passports with us—he does this for journalists too, he told us. He pointed out Christian houses with Saint George and the Orthodox cross over their thresholds. He said another way that the Qur'an differs from the Bible is that Muslims so revere Jesus that they do not believe that he, Isa, died on the cross. "Nobody could touch him. They believe it was someone who looked like him and that he is still alive."

We arrived for the final twenty minutes of a Roman Catholic service in Arabic and exchanged the peace with the Arab Christians. The church was built on top of the cave where St. Jerome translated the Bible into Latin vulgate: the Old Testament from Hebrew and the New Testament from Aramaic and Greek. Next door is the church built on top of the cave where Christ was born. Manger Square just in front leads to "Shepherd's field," where the shepherds saw the star, only a steep slope of a mile away from the cave used as stables for animals.

An arch built by Justinian 1400 years ago was paved over after horses were driven across the threshold and a smaller door was created, so that you have to bend over to get into the church. In April 2002, when Israel reoccupied Palestine, there was a siege inside this church, and Israeli gunfire killed six and wounded eighteen, damaging the 4th century AD Byzantine mosaics—giant angels that Emperor Constantine's mother, Helena, had had created. There used to be 5,000 visitors a year, our guide told us, and lines crowding to get in to see the site. Now there are a few pilgrims and the city of Bethlehem suffers from 40 percent unemployment. 30,000 of the 52,000 people living in Bethlehem are Christian, we were told. The basilica over the manger is the oldest standing in the Middle East and three denominations claim the site—Greek Orthodox, Roman Catholic and Armenian.

As we made our way to the holiest site for Christians, we helped some French nuns descend the steep marble steps into the cave where Christ was born. Bobby, moved by their readings and singing of gospel stories in French, sat down with them, listening on the steps in front of manger where the Christ child had been laid. Visitors came and kissed the Christ child's bed.

As we left the church, there was a heavy rain and some sleet and we took shelter in Manger Square. We were warned by our guide not to give money to the beggar children as it had become a big problem. When the five- and six-year-olds approached us with their candies for sale, their round eyes so open and hopeful, I hated both our guide and myself for being obedient—our refusal was too cruel, for we saw them passing in the square later with tears in their eyes, hungry and cold from their ordeal.

Snaking our way back to Jerusalem, we suddenly came up against the 700-kilometer wall the Israelis had built within walking distance of a rose stone Ottoman palace—a five-star Intercontinental Hotel, the Jasser Palace—whose owners used to cook for poor people. The graffiti on the Wall read: "Walls can't hide the truth, Mr. President, tear down this wall." On the other side of the Wall is the tomb of Rachel, the second wife of Jacob, among the grave sites of many Palestinians who can no longer visit their dead.

Not far away is the Mount of Temptation in Jericho, where Christ was tempted in the wilderness. Today, a priest lives in the cave that Jesus inhabited for forty days and forty nights. Our driver seemed sure that the baptism of Christ was on the west side of the Dead Sea, near Jericho, contrary to the Bible that claims the event took place east of the Jordan River. A church nearby was opened only once a year, at Easter, to commemorate the occasion.

In the disfigured West Bank, we used the Jews-only bypass route back to Jerusalem. There was no one on this highway and stopping at the checkpoint leading back into Jerusalem was frightening. Nabil reminded us that there were 400 checkpoints in the West Bank. People from Gaza regularly passed the checkpoint to go to work in Israel. The next stop was the Holocaust museum in the valley of West Jerusalem named Ein Karem, or garden of eyes, and the springs where John the Baptist was born. The museum's modern architecture seems designed to lead you slowly through the pit of hate into the valley of despair and monstrous evil so that you hasten to get out. One of the first exhibits that struck me was St. Augustine's 5th century dictum: "Slay them not (the Jews). Scatter them abroad." From the beginning, the exhibit's panel remarks were highly charged:

"From its inception, Christianity was ambivalent toward Judaism. It recognized the Jews' uniqueness as divinely chosen bearers of God's Word. However, Christianity developed a hatred of the Jews for rejecting Jesus as the Messiah who preached a new redemptive gospel, and it blamed them collectively and forever for his death. 5th century Christian theology determined that Jews should not be killed, rather, they should be kept in their humiliated status until they accept Christianity. In the Middle Ages, the negative image of the Jew became entrenched with the charge of deicide. This image led to popular outbursts and blood libels against the Jews especially in times of crisis. In its theological struggles against Judaism and the Jews, Christianity perpetuated and spread this negative image over the centuries and wherever European Christian culture reached."

Looking at the photograph of the tear-stained cheeks of the Jewish children in the Warsaw ghetto and reading a poem by a child murdered at Treblinka, I blinked and saw the cheeks of the six-year-old boys and girls who ran up to us asking for money in Manger Square; it made me feel complicit in this tragedy in the same way we were toward the Jews only a few decades ago.

"The Little Smuggler"
Over the wall, through holes, past the guard,
Through the wires, ruins and fences
Plucky, hungry, determined
I sneak through, dart like a cat

And if the hand of destiny
Should seize me in the game
That's a common trick of life
You, neither, do not wait up for me.

And only one request
Will stiffen on my lips:
Who, mother mine, who
Will bring your bread tomorrow?"

RAMALLAH

AFTER NEW YEAR'S, WE LEFT the American Colony Hotel and headed for Ramallah in the West Bank on the way to Tel-Aviv where we were due to catch our flight back to Amman. Nabil was able to drive wherever he wanted. Ramallah, the capital of the Palestinian state, was clearly poorer than its neighbor but, thankfully, it was peaceful. We ate at a local shop selling "shawarma"—beef with peppers, cucumbers, tomatoes, red cabbage and a tahina and lemon sauce on fresh bread. I visited the local jewelry shop next door and the elderly owner, in his traditional red and white scarf, took off his diamond and platinum Rolex to show me. Business on the street seemed slow. Graffiti in praise of Fatah was everywhere. We paid our respects at Arafat's grave within the walls of Abu Mazen's offices. Bob telephoned the son of Abbas (Abu Mazen, whom he had met on a plane to Frankfurt to wish him Happy New Year).

"Ramallah is a good town," Bob said, "…well-organized."

We noticed there were plenty of (illegal) Jewish settlements outside Tel-Aviv. The huge Wall was going up in the middle of nowhere, deep into the Palestinians' West Bank territory, where there were no security risks. The land is high, rich with olive trees, and green. A shepherd guided his donkey to pull a plow through the land.

"There is no irrigation here," Nabil told us. "The cauliflowers are dark yellow and the fruits are sweeter and more delicious here where there is no irrigation."

In Abud, there is a Baptist church and each village has a little (Palestinian) government school.

We passed a town called Petah Tiqah, where American USAID people visited. "If I told them you were from Jerusalem, they would empty the car and search it." So, instead, Nabil said, in Hebrew, that we were from Petah Tiqah. "Shalom, moushloum ha" or "Peace, How are you? It's okay."

The checkpoint leaving the West Bank for the Tel-Aviv airport looked like a concentration camp—there are no other words for it—with high concrete walls and barbed wire on top, police in uniform and police dogs. The graffiti written on the Wall read, "God will tear down this Wall". As we took our leave, I told Nabil he is a treasure of Jerusalem. "If everyone were like you, there would be no walls, no wars."

His old face smiled back at me through the rearview mirror.

When we entered Ben Gurion airport in Tel-Aviv, we went through the three-hour security.

"Who are you [three]?"

"We are a family. This is my husband and my son."

(Pause, considering looks, discussions among one another.)

"What were you doing in Israel?"

"Tourism."

(Another pause)

"Where do you live?"

"Amman."

(Another pause)

"What do you do there?"

"Work for the reconstruction of Iraq."

"Why did you come to Israel?"

"Tourism."

(Another pause)

"Tourism?"

"Yes, tourism."

Everything was searched, rather perfectly. A man took a plastic stick with a cotton pad and passed it around the inside of the suitcase looking for traces of explosives, no doubt.

I said, "Thank you for cleaning my suitcase."

He looked at me with a faint air of sarcasm. The whole process took thirty minutes. Then we were at the Royal Jordanian counter.

The flight is only 45 minutes. It was a new small plane with leather seats, built by Brazil, the stewardess told me. At the airport, Majid whisked us through customs and on the road told us that there was a lot of anger in Jordan about the execution of Saddam Hussein—to each Palestinian family killed in the intifada he gave $30,000. As Michel, our HSBC banker in Amman told us, Saddam was not liked in Jordan, *he was loved*. Majid told us it was the Iranians who gassed the Kurds, not Saddam.

"They should never have executed him on a holy day," Majid exclaimed in a state of frenzy.

Leafing through the *Jordan Times*, Bob noticed a pro-Saddam rally with 2500 protesters holding up Iraqi flags and pictures of Saddam, condemning his execution, and perhaps also there to honor all the money Saddam used to give Palestinians. The photograph showed men, women and boys looking, variously, confused, frustrated, and angry.

THINK THREE TIMES

AN EDITORIAL ENTITLED "Do Away with Honor Killings," commented, "Fathers should think twice before killing their daughters."

Bobby added that if he had a daughter, he would think three times.

My friend, Jordan's cherished conductor, Shireen, told me, "There is a sad story of a girl from a well-known tribe, a hugely wealthy Jordanian family in Amman, who wanted to marry a really very nice boy, actually. The boy kept insisting. He did not tell her father that he had slept with her, but 'you will have to give me your daughter's hand at some point,' insinuating that he will not have a choice because he might have slept with her. One day, the father invited the boy and his daughter to his house, asked them to come to the office and shot both of them. The father is in prison. If it's proven that the girl actually slept with him, i.e. lost her virginity, it will be considered an honor killing and he will go free."

Another day there was a particularly shocking honor killing in the news. A 44-year-old father and a 15-year-old son from Amman's Wadi Abdoun neighborhood were charged with manslaughter for their role in tying up and electrocuting their daughter and sister, thus becoming the 16th so-called "honor crime" that year. The victim was repeatedly beaten on her head with a wooden stick. Initial testimony given by the suspects indicated that the victim had been married one month before her murder to a man "who asked her to engage in abnormal sexual activities with him and offered her to one of his friends," officials said. The victim fled from her husband's home and the police found her three days before the murder at her husband's friend's house. It was not clear if the woman was forced to stay at the man's house, the source added. The girl was handed to her father who interrogated her for three days. The victim told her father about her abusive husband but her father decided to punish her and beat her. He then asked his son to tie the victim with an electric cord and connect it to an electric socket; they electrocuted her until they made sure she was dead, officials said.

CHAPTER TEN
January

I HAVE ALWAYS WANTED TO live in a glass house. But however wonderful the feeling that the sky is the limit, in summer it is too hot and in winter, too cold …and wet. *Ittaqx zift* (*the weather is horrible*). The previous day, fog, rain and sleet had closed down Queen Alia International airport for four hours. Water was streaming into the stairwell and inside the fireplace, meaning there was a space under the roof (and no cap on the chimney) and under Bauhaus-style glass wall of the penthouse, beneath the cabinet containing beloved photo albums. Two cold fronts had affected this country in the past two weeks. Heavy rain, snow, sleet, hail, strong southerly winds and thunderstorms brought layers of thick fog causing more flooding in the country over the weekend—and an additional 12 million cubic meters for the reservoirs. The cold had caused a shortage of gas cylinders which most people use to cook. Emad dropped by to get a fire going, and said, "I like the voice of the fire." The word for voice and sound is the same in Arabic.

Rain was filling 27 sand dams in desert regions, it was also filling our house—seventeen workmen were here the day before; besides Emad and Majid—Mr. Keilani, a well-known Jordanian architect, our insurance adjustor, and the builder's men—a tall Iraqi engineer, the plump building expert, the lazy-eyed building electrician, the Egyptian night watchman, along with his friends and various laborers—all to correct the mistakes made on the roof. It was the third inundation, and since we had managed to obtain an insurance policy, we were in a strong position to threaten the builder with a lawsuit if action wasn't taken quickly. The edge of the roof needed rebuilding with flashing. Majid also dropped by because he remembered we had had a lot of problems when it rained; he entered just as a workman was putting a cap on the fireplace. Majid asked him in Arabic why Muthana, the builder, had not fixed this—that it had been going on from the beginning—"Really," Majid told us, "this is a mafia man. You should be angry," he said to Bob, his usual taciturn and amused self. "Who do you think you are, the bank?" Majid asked.

Bobby, who sees the comedy in everything, realized this situation was ripe for it. I saw him begin to make faces at me, repressing a smile, and I quickly pulled him aside. "Bob, remember what Majid said. Do not smile. You are not the bank and if you smile, they will laugh all the way to the bank." He went back in and acted the right part. Emad told us the reason why the kitchen carpenters were not there yesterday was because of "the mist in the wadi after the storm." Bob winked at me and told him he hoped the mist had cleared.

When I came down to check the damage the next morning, a workman in the dining room had drilled three holes into the ceiling to let the water through and a man with a blowtorch was burning the concrete living room ceiling—common practice, I am told, for drying ceilings. All our decorative efforts, re-done after the last catastrophe a few months ago, were ruined and even the workmen looked appalled.

Nasser, who was reputed to be the best contractor in Jordan, whistled when he saw how they had blowtorched the ceiling in the living room. The water expert's face turned gray when he saw the dining room where they had drilled holes in the ceiling to let the water through. We were taking the builder and the insurance company to court. The insurance adjustor failed to show; indeed, we discovered insurance companies do not pay out in Jordan. The following day the insurance adjustor came and said that the builder should be put in jail. I handed both him and the lawyer a CD full of photographs of the damage as well as the furniture pushed to the side of the room without water, and the boxes still unpacked after living here almost a year.

ENVIRONMENT AND ENERGY

WAR IN LEBANON, war in Iraq, war in Palestine, war on terrorism; meanwhile in Greenland, global warming had accelerated at such a pace that the permafrost was releasing large amounts of methane gas, it was reported on BBC World News that night. A quizzical newscaster pulled a large dinosaur bone out of the mud on camera. My skin was parched but I lived in the best conditions. What about the average person here, in one of the driest parts of the world?

The children in the schools here were expressing the deteriorating water situation through their art—the Jordan River was depicted as a stream due to drought. With the demographic explosion of Amman, many worried whether the water table would support its growth. Through friends close to the royal family, I was able to see Dr. Walid Al-Turk, Secretary General of the Higher Council for Science and Technology of the Royal Scientific Society, situated in northern Amman, near the University of Jordan.

"Israel is confiscating all the water from under the West Bank, leaving whatever remains to the Palestinians, the drylands", al-Turk remarked, explaining the Swiss cheese pattern of occupation. "They are extending the Wall into wells in the West Bank, confiscating territories that contain water and piping it into their territory. Prince Hassan is looking to pre-empt a conflict that might occur. Any war in the future will be over water resources."

Before the 1960s, a 300-400-meter-wide bridge spanned the Jordan River into the West Bank; now it is a stream. As part of the 1994 peace treaty with Israel, Jordan got a few million gallons back, their share from the Tabereah region (the lake of Tiberias). The Al Karameh dam, fed by a tributary of the Yarmuk River, used to be a major source for Jordan, and Al Wahdah, nicknamed "the unity", had been built a year and a half earlier by Syria to give Jordan the share that had been going to Israel, Al-Turk explained. Jebel Sheikh, in Syria, covered with snow, feeds the Yarmuk. Many rivers in Syria used to end in the Jordan River but the Israelis dammed the Yarmuk River at the top, preventing its flow into Jordan.

The wars of 1948, 1967, 1973, in Kuwait, and now Iraq, brought an influx of people that have had a strong environmental and socio-economic impact on the country. It was not planned and every scientist and sociologist said Jordan would not have enough water to absorb such numbers. Refugees have also had a major impact on land use. Normally, Amman would have a growth of 2.5%, an increase of 20,000 people per year. They ended up with an influx of a million and a half, one million of them wanting to live in the capital city. The Amman downtown stream—Ras Al Ein, the headwater— went under the municipality building all the way to Mahata and Marka to the Zarqa stream; fresh vegetables used to be sold in downtown Amman along the banks of the streams in early '60s that, of course, now was all cement.

So many industries were built in Zarqa that instead of having a water treatment facility and a proper sewage disposal system, they dumped it in the stream and it became toxic and environmentally hazardous, according to Al-Turk.

Twenty kilometers north of Amman, between Jerash and Irbid, is the Baqa'a Palestinian refugee camp, one of six camps built to house refugees from the '68 war, now numbering 100,000, the largest camp followed by Zaatari. There are six dams in the north and middle Jordan Valley— including the King Talal dam. King Abdullah's Canal pumped into Zai, the main treatment plant for Amman, to the north near Salt, and then sent up to the city. Because there was not enough rainwater, the government was attempting two major projects. The DISA project concerned land between South Jordan and the Northeast Saudi Arabian desert, where there are seas of water underground. "We had been trying to bring water to Zai for five-six years but the price did not benefit Jordan," Al-Turk said sadly.

The Dead-Red project was a major source of hope but politics and delays got in the way of progress. Jordan, Israel and Palestine would benefit from reviving the Dead Sea. Initially the project to save it, and provide a water supply for drinking and agriculture was to pump water from the Red Sea over the Moab Mountains between Aqaba and Petra and then down into the Dead Sea, the lowest point on earth. The pressure going up and down would be used to generate energy. The money collected—$1 billion plus— was just for the feasibility study and the Gulf states, the World Bank and the U.S. were supporting that study.

The Sea, over-used for its minerals, is rich in potassium chloride (potash not sodium chloride, the salt we eat, which is of course very cheap to produce.) Potash is a main ingredient used in many industries hence its overproduction. Dead Sea salt and mud are prized throughout the world for their skincare properties and Israel and Jordan are in a race to sell more of it. The problem is that they also take the water with the salt when extracting it, shrinking the Sea by millions of gallons—40 or 50 cubic meters a year, a major ecological disaster. They simply take the water (draining the Sea), putting it in a drying area, and letting the water evaporate. Then they collect the salts and then separate the potassium and calcium.

Besides water and related environmental problems, Jordan had energy problems. Jordan lost what they used to get free—half their oil—and for the other half, they had a special price during the UN boycott of the Saddam Hussein regime. After the new government took over, Jordan signed an agreement to receive Iraqi oil at preferable prices but the country faced a security problem because the oil had to be transferred in tanks. We couldn't find any company who would take the risk of going from here to Baghdad at a suitable price.

The International Nuclear Agency was due to visit Jordan to discuss the production of nuclear energy. At the Arab Summit, countries agreed to work on a regional basis to share knowledge about this possibility. But even Jordan's experts and top officials found this solution laughable since there was not enough water. Dr. Sultan Barakat, Professor, University of York, a member of the governing council of WOCMES and a friend of Prince Hassan, also with the Royal Scientific Society, wandered into the room, "I work on water in Egypt, and the demand for water is going up without a vision of what is to come in ten-fifteen years. The whole economy is unsustainable in the region."

"Is there hope for a regional approach as advocated by Prince Hassan?" I asked.

"We don't feel threatened enough to act as a region, to get together to talk about something. The closest has been the Iraq war. As long as Israel looks westward and is subsidized by the U.S., as long as Israel doesn't need to live in the neighborhood, then we will never be a region. If the U.S. were really Israeli's best friend, it would help it to become an adult and act responsibly by engaging its neighbors instead of treating it as its spoiled child. Maybe when the U.S. decides that Israel should be responsible for its own future, Israel will feel the need to engage with neighboring countries, stop importing people into Israel, new settlers—people from India just recently—and find solutions. We've been hoping that for fifty years."

AN ECONOMY TO MATCH

THE COVER PHOTO OF that morning's the *Jordan Times* showed Palestinians standing next to fruit and vegetable stalls damaged by Israeli troops during a military operation in Ramallah. I noticed it was the same peaceful center street where we were eating hot shawarma sandwiches only five days earlier. Israeli undercover troops burst into the market street, seized four men and exchanged heavy gunfire with Palestinian fighters in the first major raid since the Israelis and Palestinians agreed to ease tensions. Three Palestinians, all civilians, were killed and twenty wounded in the fighting. It could just as easily have been us. I wondered how much longer it would take American tourists to want to go to Ramallah to buy jewelry, how much longer it would take for the Palestinian economy to match that of Israel, in what is, of course, the same country. Palestinian President Mahmoud Abbas, whose offices we admired, said in a harshly worded statement that Israel's peace promises rang hollow in light of the raid and demanded $5 million in compensation for the damage to cars and shops in Ramallah.

I called Kenneth, Prince Hassan's press secretary, and asked: "Why couldn't Jordan take back the '67 land and be the broker with Palestine?"

"That's been suggested," he answered. The Wall extended further into Palestine from the '67 borders. The rumor was that the Israelis were building the Wall as the future border between them and an enlarged Jordan. This country had had a slightly uncomfortable history with its population; they didn't even release official figures here where the Palestinians probably make up 60 percent of the population. If Jordan ever officially ruled over the West Bank, it was a protectorate, i.e. never part of the territory of the state. If they were to absorb the West Bank, there would be many problems not worth the risk. Firstly, millions of Palestinians changing the demographics of the country would entail a certain risk. Secondly, it would probably involve some sort of financial reward from outside parties towards a solution to the conflict that would be seen by many as taking blood money, profiting from an enlarged kingdom while gaining a financial award. It might mean the end of the monarchy. There could be a coup from the army who are pure Jordanian, as they call themselves, or some sort of eventual revolt by the Palestinians.

From Jerusalem to Ramallah to Tel-Aviv, there seemed to be no threat to the Israelis at all—just miles and miles of beautiful land with olive trees and this enormous wall going up and illegal Israeli settlements dotting the hillside.

"You go to Israel, you are back in Germany and the Palestinian people are the Jews. This is the sadly ironic thing. When you see the setup of the Wall with the watch towers and the barbed wire and the armed guards, you just think concentration camps," Kenneth was saying. "Did you see Shimon Peres on the Doha debates? He's such a good PR man. Among the Arab audience, young people around the world were asking questions. Basically Shimon Peres says black is white. 'The Wall marks the border, the Wall is for security.' The Wall is not for security. It hasn't affected the number of attacks. It hasn't been placed in the most dangerous points. There's obviously another reason for it. You reach a point where you don't even bother arguing because unfortunately, there aren't enough people in the world who care enough. Jimmy Carter writes a book and goes out on a limb to say what's happening is wrong. The Palestinians certainly aren't perfect and their leadership is in a shambles but there's a reason for that—it's the way the people are treated.

"Nobody is really welcome. There isn't a strong lobby to defend the Palestinians and unfortunately, you do get the crazies who grab the headlines. Yasser Arafat did them no favors because he was a crook but you have a situation where people are so poorly treated that Gaza has become a desperate society. You have 1.4 million people squeezed onto this strip of land, not enough water and not enough electricity and you get gangsters, as you would anywhere. The Israelis assume that 1.5 million people would go home which is why it's no longer even on the table."

"Isn't there a longing to get back what is rightfully theirs?" I asked.

Kenneth answered, "Most of the Palestinian refugees don't want to go home." (As Mahmoud Abbas has said.)

Given that Israeli settlements, comprising 90% of the West Bank, are unlikely to be withdrawn, the topic everywhere was the workability of a one-state solution or a two-state solution. Kenneth replied, "In Northern Ireland there's no way it could have worked if you had one state and people going home. The problem with the comparison is the longer timeframe in Northern Ireland. The Palestinians are now maybe third generation, grandchildren from the '48ers but they can still remember what they had. But in Northern Ireland it was very different because you had so-called colonizers who had been there for 300 years. If there hadn't been a border drawn in Ireland in 1921, you would have had a civil war. If we had been given full independence as one state, we would have had a much bigger civil war between the unionists in the north and us in the south. Here land was confiscated within living memory and there hasn't been any compensation. Initially, the Palestinians didn't want compensation. [Now the figure mentioned is $40 billion.] They all had their keys and they were planning to go back. The '48ers took their deeds with them. You still have three and four generations living in refugee camps—around Amman, Rafa, and in Syria and Egypt, still living like that."

ARAB PHILOSOPHERS ALL PREACH TOLERANCE

AT THE FRENCH GROUP breakfast tea, Rhada, a beautiful brunette in her 30s, recalcitrant, politically fiery, and intellectually astute, spoke about the 8th century the Abbasid Caliph Al-Mansur who encouraged writers like the Iraqi author, Al-Jahiz, born about the year 776, fourteen years after the foundation of Baghdad. Al-Jahiz grew up in Basra, Iraq, founded early in Islamic times as a garrison city but, by the time of his birth, a major intellectual center, along with its rival, Kufa. From China, paper had been introduced into the Islamic world only shortly before Al-Jahiz's birth. It had, by the time he was in his 30s, virtually replaced parchment, and launched an intellectual revolution. The availability of a cheap writing material was accompanied by another social phenomenon—the rise of a reading public. For the first time since the fall of the Roman Empire, the cities of the Middle East contained a large number of literate people, many of humble origins.

In 8th century Baghdad, Rhada was saying, teachers were chosen at the mosques for their skill in telling anecdotes—lessons revealing their level of knowledge. Through commerce with India, all levels of society—the aristocracy, middle and lower classes, and slaves—participated. Jahiz, from the lower class, stayed up all night copying whatever books existed at the time and translated them into Arabic. "The 9th century," Rhada's father explained, "was the golden age of Islamic literature and the key principle in

Islamic thought at the time was the importance of diversity—that people should retain their identity. At that time, there was an important caliph named Ma'mun, the son of Harun al-Rashid, whose mother was Persian and whose father was Arab. (Ma'mun al-Rashid began his career by tyrannically reigning over his people. Ma'mun's army attacked Baghdad and defeated his brother Muhammad Amin. After this bloody war, Ma'mun became the caliph of the whole territory and ushered in a period of tolerance.)

"Ma'mun's vision was to encourage the translation of books from all over the world and Greek, Indian and Persian literature became known. He built a library of one million books in Baghdad and called it the House of Wisdom (Bayt al-Hikma). He supported free thought in contrast to Sharia law. He defended the cause of reason as opposed to the Islamic Courts. They studied Greek philosophy and science and encouraged freedom of thought, and the discovery of God through reason not through prophets. Philosophy was ruined by the application of the Sharia law, the Muslim caliph said, and those who practiced Sharia law were persecuted at the time. Al Mouatkel (sic) opposed Ma'mun, supporting Sharia law and there was a constant conflict between them.

"Today," Rhada's father continued, "the problem is to know and accept others—tolerance is a problem. If you treat people with justice, you don't have a problem. The philosophers, Abu Zein, Abu Zali, and Abu Haldoun, all preached tolerance, free speech. Al-Jahiz used sarcasm—caricatures—to tell his stories about cosmopolitan Baghdad—a paradise for the rich and isolation for the poor."

Al-Jahiz's book, *Le Livre des Animaux*, taught through anecdotes; those about snakes are most numerous. The first one Rhada told, *L'Orfevre* (The Goldsmith), caused a stir in the group. "A goldsmith asked a woman to come to his shop. The woman had never been to his shop but out of curiosity, she went. On entering, she asked him 'Why did you ask me to come?' The goldsmith responded, 'Because I didn't have an engraving of the devil and I needed to see your face.'" A murmur went around the room of women. One woman commented that this image of a tolerant Islam is not widely known—older than anything known in Europe at that time. What a pity, said another, that the oil-rich countries do not use their money to inform the world about the beauty and wisdom of the history of their literature.

At another meeting of the French club at the home of Ghada, a Syrian woman, whose villa is surrounded by a beautiful garden of olive trees, bougainvillea, lavender and roses, we were treated to a film about how physically damaging negative thinking is—that thoughts and emotions are literally carried inside your cells and through your central nervous system. The film, *What the #?// [Bleep] is this?*, suggested that stepping back, allowing some distance, and accepting the mystery of our existence will make us healthier.

U.S. policy toward Iran was brought up in the most innocuous way: their journey to Iran. One of the Palestinian ladies gently laid a book in my lap illustrating its architectural wonders. One asked when the country had ceased to be called Persia (after the First World War)—a pity, it was decided. Inside the mosque, the cleric sits lower than the "congregation" because humility is the supreme value in Islamic faith. One lady wryly pointed out that the Germans didn't invent the Aryan race (Iranians are Aryans, not Arabs). Persian poetry from the 9th century—like Al Hallaj's verse "I am the Truth"—is universally admired. Another lady lamented how just the previous week, satellite dishes from private homes in Teheran were being loaded into the back of government trucks, censoring broadcasting from the West.

"There is a social principle in Iran called taarof," Michael Slackman wrote in *The New York Times, "The Fine Art of Hiding what you Meant to Say,*" (Aug. 6, '06) "a concept that describes the principle of insincerity—of inviting people to dinner when you don't really want their company, for example." Iranians understand such practices as manners and are not offended by them.... "In Iran, 'yes' can mean 'yes' but it often means 'maybe' or 'no.' In Iran, listeners are expected to understand that words don't necessarily mean the same. This creates a rich, poetic, linguistic culture, ...a multidimensional [one] where people are adept at picking up on nuances. On the other hand, it makes for bad political discourse. In political discourse people don't know what to trust... Taarof is a cultural reality that Iranians say stems from centuries under foreign occupation whether it was the Arabs, the Mongols, the French, or the British, teaching Iranians the value of not showing your true face."

SHE LEFT HER BABY

ONE MORNING I SHUDDERED at the cover photo in the *Jordan Times* of the Israeli police hustling a Palestinian farmer off his land in Bethlehem so that the ten-meter high cement Wall could be constructed right through his olive groves. We were on that land just the previous week among the beloved, familiar trees where one farmer was using a plow and a donkey to hoe the land as they had done for centuries. In Bethlehem, we stood at that wall in the rain and yearned to see Rachel's tomb on the other side of it.

The new French ambassador and his wife hosted a musical evening at their residence. I was drawn by the magnetism of one of Jordan's icons, the legendary Rabiha Dajani, who started the first girls' schools in Kuwait. She was dressed in a brilliant red embroidered caftan. Mirroring my own literary path, Madame Dajani said her first book was a family memoir and her second concerned her life and especially the subject of women. She told us that one of the characters in her book suggests a toast: "Let us drink to the woman who steals, lies and swears—steals my heart, lies in my arms and swears, 'I love you.'" Then she turned to Bob and said, "Women's faults are many, men have but two—everything they say and everything they do." Mrs. Dajani's family, originally from Jerusalem, owned eight of the oldest and most spacious properties on one street in the central city. "One day, the Israelis came in and told them all to leave. We left in such a hurry that one woman left her baby. The Israelis wouldn't let her back in to get the boy. Years later, she went back and found the child, grown into a man. 'Under that floorboard,' she told him, 'you will find some jewellery.' She gave her son the jewellery and left."

THE ARAB WHO LOVES NORTH CAROLINA

THE NIGHT BEFORE THERE had been a little party music emanating from the guardhouse. I learned from Emad that that day was the Muslim New Year. Most of the shops were open so we took a little ride out to Sweileh to check on the availability of the marble for the kitchen—apricot-rose with streaks of green and yellow. On the way, I asked Emad which he was, a Sunni or a Shia. He immediately said, "I am Sunni but you know we don't care about these things and we never ask, not here. We are all Muslims. That is not a concern in Jordan." I asked what the difference was, and he replied, "We believe in God and the prophet and we pray accordingly. The Shia believe in God, the prophet and ten or twelve Imams who interpret the teachings. Anyway, a good Muslim does not care what religion you are. The prophet taught us to care only if the person is good or bad." I told him that as late as 1960, being a Catholic in American politics was difficult and that as a presidential candidate, John F. Kennedy had a hard time because of it.

Behind the desk of the marble shop was Samir Naoum, the owner of "Rosa." After graduating from Virginia Tech in civil engineering, Samir earned his MBA at Mississippi State; he also has a factory in Raleigh, North Carolina. "You know," Samir said, "I love the East Coast and especially, right in the middle, not north, not south. It is so beautiful and the people are so nice. There are real seasons: the winters aren't too cold and there is a fall." He showed us the large fireplace filled with burning logs and told us it supplied more than 50 percent of the heat in the office because of an ingenious fan capturing the heat and sending it back into the room rather than up the chimney. "I don't like to waste all that energy," he said.

Then we walked around the back where all the marble was neatly vertically stacked. A large crane overhead moved on a track and a hook, attached to the crane with a large chain, brought the marble inside to be cut. He showed us all the choices for rose marble; we found the one we liked. There was a brief business discussion in Arabic about how it would be cut and when it would be available—tomorrow (I thought, *boukra, in sha Allah,* but they didn't say it). As we left the shop, I noticed a huge carpet on the balcony across the street and pointed it out to Emad. "Those are used by people who don't have marble floors. Your floors are too beautiful to be covered with carpets—you need small ones," he said.

On Al Jazeera that night, David Frost, speaking of Bush's "surge" of 20,000 troops into Iraq, was the only journalist who dared remind his fellow commentators that the Baker Study Group recommended this surge, followed by a withdrawal.

MASSIVE HUMANITARIAN EFFORT

NABA WROTE ME, "One hundred of my students were killed yesterday. A massive global humanitarian effort is needed to accompany these troops, *the* chief error of the war in Iraq. We cannot give the terrorists opportunities to find shelter. It is not just babies that need help (the Rotary supports operations for Jordanian and Iraqi babies with heart disease), but everyone, particularly young people. I am stuck here. I cannot get a visa, with my S series passport, neither to America nor to Canada."

She told me what Pachachi had also told me a few months ago—that the American military should have been trained in civil unrest—and that a massive infusion of food, bottled water and medicine must be accompanied by troops protecting schools, traffic, and government buildings. Given what I had been told of how heavily infiltrated the Iraqi government and military is by militias, the 20,000 new troops were desperately needed to stabilize the situation—but that these troops should leave within six months and must perform civilian relief."

I THINK I'M A SUSHI

AYHAM SAMARAIE, A LEADING figure from the Samara tribe and the Iraqi minister of electricity 2004-05, escaped from a jail in the Green Zone with the help of his bodyguards. The dual Iraqi-America citizen, who was being held on corruption charges, walked out of a police station on Sunday with the help of private guards who arrived at the station in sport utility vehicles, the *Jordan Times* reported. He told Bob that he told his bodyguards, "Whenever anyone offers you any money to kill me, tell me the amount first, and I'll double it." He asked him if he was a Sunni or a Shiite. "My father was a Sunni, my mother was a Shiite. I think I'm a Sushi." He said Baghdad had been a prison under Saddam but that Iraq would cease to exist if the Americans left.

My Iraqi friend, Naba, came for dinner. She asked me, "Do you know how to tell a Shia from a Sunni? By the black turban." Naba is a Shia on her father's side with a direct line to Ali, the prophet's son-in-law and cousin.

"Where's your turban, Naba?" I asked her.

"I left it at home," she replied, smiling. On her return to the University in Baghdad in August for several days, a young man wearing a white headscarf insulted her because she was wearing pants and a long shirt. "Why is your head not covered?" he asked. That very day, she decided enough was enough and obtained a visa to visit her daughter in Toronto for three months. Men want to hide their wives and daughters from the eyes of jealous men, Naba said, but in the Gulf states, because of the wind storms, covering the head was a physical necessity for both sexes. In any case, fundamentalists were now using this to frighten women but, she said, "We will go on just as we always have."

Georgetown University professors recently invited Naba to speak but U.S. government officials refused her a visa. The mistreatment of Muslims applying for U.S. visas was the subject of much discussion, especially since President Bush's rhetoric about "Islamo-fascists." Even though fundamentalism is opposed by the vast majority of Muslims, all foreigners trying to enter the U.S. (Europeans included) were subjected to endless delays, refusals and bad manners (now much worse under President Trump).

Both the Syrians and the French eat lentils for good luck in the New Year, and at this week's French Club, over a delicious dish prepared by Raymonde, Suzanne told me her family had been in the carpet business for 150 years, bringing carpets from Iran to Damascus since the mid-19th century. Raymonde, a classical pianist, was the widow of Hanna Nassr, a Lebanese whose father (her father-in-law) had started a newspaper in Haifa, Palestine, in the 1920s and who was then asked by King Abdullah I to go to Jordan to start the first newspaper. Her mother-in-law put the children in schools in Ramallah and went with him.

I asked her about the press law forbidding negative press against those in power. "People are very kind here and don't like to make trouble unless there is really something terribly wrong." I told her I was surprised that the Arab press was so fatalistic, so opposed to the American troop escalation. Conspiracy theories abound here—whether that the Jews control the world media or the Americans are only interested in Iran. "The troops are not for the Baghdad militias," she said, "They are for the borders." Katerina said it would not do any good anyway—that Iran would continue to send more and more soldiers and that Iraq was lost to the hands of Iran. "Those poor American boys," referring to their youthful innocence and bravery. "I saw one who was engaged to be married and who had his face blown off and now he has the face of a monster. The poor girl went ahead with the marriage."

In the absence of Bob who was on a business trip, I learned the Arabic expression, "Live long and learn a lot." Today, I learned something, speaking up (in French) at the French group's Thursday breakfast tea for the first time. Nuhad, the group's organizer, had prepared the talk discussing Amin Maaluf's *Identités Meurtrières* (publisher, Grasset, 1998)—the idea that Arabs think that modernism is synonymous with Americanism and the loss of their roots. That the internet is perceived both for its good—in disseminating knowledge—and for its evil—the transmission of terrorist messages. Nuhad was also impressed by Maaluf's idea that we are all a composite of the people around us—father, mother, spouse, environment.

Another woman interjected that her friend's six-year-old grandchild had been shocked by what a Jordanian elementary school teacher had told her, and asked her parents "Is it true we must kill all the Jews?" Hamas encourages the defeat of Zionist politics in Palestine and claims to welcome the Jewish religion but some Hamas textbooks and children's TV shows recommend killing Zionists. (A year earlier, on January 18, 2006, AP reported Ismail Hanieh, Hamas's leader, saying, "Hamas is not hostile to Jews because they are Jews. We are hostile to them because they occupied our land and expelled our people.... We did not say we want to throw the Jews in the sea or feed them to sharks. We just said that there is a land called occupied Palestine. It was burglarized and it needs to be returned to the Palestinian people.")

DESPAIR CREATES RELIGIOSITY

NUHAD CONTINUED, "MAALUUF'S point was that whether one is Christian or Muslim should not be the basis for relationships... Crimes are committed in the name of religion... There is a longer history of tolerance in Islam than there is in the Christian religion... What is bothering the Islamic world is that Christian Europe went so far beyond them, after the golden age of Islam in the 8th century, when they were the intellectual rulers of the world. The Arabs who gave Europe literature and science now show intolerance toward the West. Only through openness can tolerance be accomplished. When the Arab countries felt they had control of the world, they were more tolerant. Despair creates religiosity. Arab countries feel victimized, stamped on, and overlooked by the West. When they were part of the Roman Empire, the Arab people felt happy. Under the Byzantines, people were under a system of beliefs. Now people feel lost. They don't want to be part of the commercial culture of America—the standardization, the globalization. The West is everywhere. With modernization, one loses oneself. The Arab revolt of today is basically anarchism—standing out against standardization, against CNN and Mickey Mouse and McDonalds."

Prince Hassan, in Doha over the weekend at the 25th annual meeting of the Arab Thought Forum, suggested the key to empowering Arabs was to provide basic resources; the lack of vision to deal with the existential needs of a rapidly growing population was driving the region to social breakdown. He reminded his audience that democratization was a process that could only grow from grassroots. The ballot box, the prince said, is a very small part of a process that begins when civil society and a ruling elite, who embrace an ethic of good governance, act in tandem for the community good. In his keynote address, he discussed how state and region are necessarily interlinked. He championed the cause of dialogue in cases of a common human agenda.

Janvier de Reidmatten, head of Iraqi Operations for the UN High Commission on Refugees, told me, "When I was in Basra the last time, the Sunnis and the Shia stopped killing each other and started shooting at the coalition forces in Basra instead. (These were British, Bobby told me later. After the U.N. Iraqi representative was assassinated in 2003, Kofi Annan asked the coalition forces to cover the U.N. personnel there.) Whenever Janvier goes to the war zone, he is in armored coalition vehicles—U.K. or U.S.: "We are always a target. You can see that from the vehicle which has traces of the last bomb that hit it and the last person killed."

"Well," I said, "wouldn't that argue for pulling out of the country?"

He looked straight into my eyes and quietly said, "There would be a bloodbath."

In Davos, King Abdullah called on the delegates of the World Economic Forum to articulate a new vision for the Middle East—"A vision of ordinary life where people can go to shop or work without fear…where ambulances don't face checkpoints to get the sick to hospitals, where young people are able to build families and plan long careers, where the first-grade students of 2017, Israeli and Palestinian, can look back as adults, and have no memory of the conflict years."

NOT A HOLOCAUST BUT A SLOW DEATH

LATER IN THE DAY, YOLAINE asked me to lunch with Hala, the wife of the Palestinian Representative in Madrid who said a one-state solution allowing all the Palestinians to return home and to vote in a parliamentary style election would be impossible—having 1.2 million people eligible to return. "Hamas would be very generous with Israel under those terms. We tried that in 1968 and it was rejected." (Bobby later said the Jews tried it in the 1948 war and it was rejected and now it's not on the table.)

"Yet," another interjected, "they invite 1.2 million Jews to live on our land. That's racism. And look at the way the Israelis track the number of births to Arab homes, comparing them to low Israeli birth rates. That really galls me."

Another spoke of the humiliation of the border crossings—80-year-old women forced to strip naked. Hala told of a reporter who documented the number of women who had given birth at the checkpoints and the number of hours they held the women being rushed to the hospital—and the number of deaths that this caused. Aida said she would rather never return to Jerusalem, where she was born, than undergo one humiliation after another. "The only difference between the Holocaust and what the Jews are doing to the Palestinians is a matter of time. The Palestinians are living a slow death. I frankly would rather die faster."

Maha asked rhetorically, "What is the difference between what Saddam did to his people and what the Israelis are doing to the Palestinians?" All of the women thought there was no difference between the U.S. and Israeli governments. Today the Israelis announced they are expanding their territory and the Wall another five kilometers eastward, ensnaring another 20,000 Palestinians.

The U.S. State Department would present findings to Congress that day on whether Israel violated an arms agreement with the United States when it showered South Lebanon with over four million cluster bombs during the last 72 hours of the war the previous summer. The majority of the cluster bombs found thus far had been American-made, a UNMACC spokesperson Dalya Farran told the *Daily Star*. Former U.S. President Reagan imposed a ban on cluster bombs for Israel for six years after the Jewish state used them in its 1982 invasion of Lebanon.

EVERYTHING BAD COMES FROM THE WEST

NYLA CONFIRMED THAT anti-Americanism was high. The United States of America is known as the United States of *North* America here—il wilaraat (states) muttaHide (united) isshamalayé (north). They also use "ameerka." Nyla laughed and said, "I don't say it but some people say, '*Min il rarb,*'—*Everything bad comes from the west,*" a perception exacerbated by the American movies' depiction of the opposite and the recent documentary, *Reel Bad Arabs*. Praying to Mecca, they face the sun (in the east—shark), which is why the name for the north is the same as the word for left (shmal). Even when you sleep, you have to face southwest in the bed—Arab feng shui—they can't put their backs to Mecca.

Television announcers speak classical Arabic but we were learning colloquial Arabic with gender dialects. Ladies are meant to say "wa ?t"—the word for time—with the glottal stop "?", considered more delicate than gentlemen's pronunciation with the more manly "q"—waqt. The verb, to publish, in Arabic, pronounced *unshor*, appropriately also means to put out the wash and also, interestingly, "to saw" (that old saw.) A publisher is "naser" (pronounced "nashair"). East and West share the proverb, "Every dog has his day" but the meaning here is exactly the opposite. Whereas in the U.S., every dog will have his day in the sun, (fifteen minutes of fame), the Arabs, (who hate dogs), say eventually you will have your comeuppance, and something will go wrong. Then there is "Ma tAraf hairy ta itjarreb rairy"—Better the devil you know than the one you don't, or literally, "you don't know my goodness until you try someone other than me." There is also a proverb, "East and West will never meet", hopefully proved wrong by another, "Iza fi iraade, fi tariq"—where there's a will, there's a way.

CHAPTER ELEVEN
February

CREATING A SENSE OF COMMUNITY

I TOLD EMAD, "I don't feel like a foreigner."

"No, you are one of us," Emad affirmed, not skipping a beat. For the first time since our arrival, I believed him. I felt drawn into the heart of the country. In a rare look at a closed culture without press freedom, Jordanians had generously shared with me their understanding of the status quo—social, political and cultural. Living in this more ancient civilization had made me feel innocent. The Orient is a lesson in elaborate courtesy and appearances—"welcome" is the first word of the desert where the thirst for conversation is as great as water but where detachment is taken to an art form. What makes Americans similar also sets us apart—we are a generous and courageous people but are unversed in subtlety.

In *The Clash of Civilizations*, Samuel Huntington wrote that the increasing power of non-Western civilizations internationally will make the West develop a better understanding of other cultures and that those cultures, in turn, will learn to coexist to shape the future world. Conflicts may ensue between relatives or the imposition of one culture on another; the Israeli Eretz expansionist culture, for example, conflicts with the Israeli culture of peace.

My hope is that this book will convince the Israeli-US axis of the inevitability of a peaceful transition toward living in the Arab world which would come with compensating Palestinians for their land, access to water, and freedom of movement throughout the area. But the only way to achieve this, according to Huntington's model, is for the more powerful Arab state on Palestine's western border, Jordan, to work with Israel to build impoverished Palestine into a nation-state. History is on their side for there is a cultural connection from centuries before the Bible was written—a common heritage of Christians, Muslims and Jews, whose myths and legends cross and crisscross one another.

What strikes me is how jingoistic and xenophobic some Americans are, unversed in other languages and cultures. Zealotry and fearfulness polarize the American view of the world into good and bad. Making money shapes the American mind-set, without examining the consequences for the planet or the historical context of their global adventures. The French, by comparison, live and breathe historical context and value the quality of life more than making money even at the cost of going bankrupt.

A poem on the NYC subway train brought back the Middle East:

> *An Old Cracked Tune* by Stanley Kunitz (1905-2006)
> My name is Solomon Levi
> The desert is my home,
> My mother's breast was thorny,
> And father I had none.
> The sands whispered, Be Separate,
> The stones taught me, Be Hard.
> I dance for the joy of surviving
> On the edge of the road.

A child reminded me that being direct and humble are qualities Arabs admire most. That day in a doctor's waiting room, I must have looked as though I were feeling the weight of my responsibility rather heavily, for a five-year-old girl with huge brown eyes looked at me and smiled. It was the sweetest, most loving smile and it made me think of the truth of the Arabic expression which is translated as "May God put light in you" (Allah ynawwer aleek), in English as "Let there be light," in French, "Que la lumière soit" and in Spanish, "La Luce Sea."

THE BEST SOLUTION

WHILE IN PARIS, we met Harold Kaplan, a former senior State Department official who had worked with my grandfather while he was Ambassador to Saigon. "Under what conditions could the Israelis and Palestinians live together in peace side by side?"

"The illegal settlements need to be disbanded and there needs to be a road built that runs north and south so people can travel the distance of the Palestinian territories easily, not this Swiss cheese that they have now with the Wall going every which way. That's very dangerous. As for a one-state solution, that's twenty years down the road. First they need to agree to two states. Everyone has declared they are in favor of a viable and livable Palestinian state; the important thing is to know if this state will be led by reasonable people."

THE DAY MARKED THE eighth anniversary of the death (Feb. 7) of King Hussein (1935-1999) and the assumption of Abdullah to the throne. Beginning on May 2, 1952, at the age of eighteen, King Hussein was one of the longest serving heads of state in the world. Throughout his five-decade reign, the king raised the living standards of his people, infant mortality declined by 50 percent and literacy rose 160 percent. He also struggled tirelessly to promote peace in the Middle East and to help the Palestinian people regain their legitimate rights.

A few days earlier, Jordan, the protector of the Al-Aqsa Mosque by treaty, demanded that the UN Security Council halt Israel's archaeological dig near (and possibly under) the ultra-sensitive security area of the Al-Aqsa Mosque compound. Meanwhile, the rival Palestinian factions formed a national unity government the previous day after marathon talks in Mecca. Palestinian President Mahmoud Abbas who headed the party, and the exiled leader of the ruling Islamist Hamas movement, Khaled Mishaal, signed the historic document named "The Mecca Declaration," with Saudi host King Abdullah also attending. Abbas swiftly asked Prime Minister Ismail Haniyeh to form a new government following the accord, calling on the future government to "respect international law and agreements signed by the Palestine Liberation Organization."

Jordan now has over 1 million Syrian refugees; the Zaatari refugee camp near Mafrak on the border is a city of 85,000. At the time of writing, Syria had 1 million Iraqi refugees and Jordan at least 750,000; inside Iraq, 1.8 million people were displaced out of a population of 26 million. The influx of migrants triggered concerns over inflation, job losses and ghettoization in this tiny desert kingdom still reeling from Al-Qaeda's 2005 triple suicide attack on Amman hotels. Many of Amman's Iraqis settled in the up-market neighborhoods of Rabiya and Khalda which taxi drivers jokingly renamed Karrada and Jadriya—two residential areas of Baghdad. Amman's shopping mammoth, "Mecca Mall" was re-baptized the "Baghdad Mall."

It's been reported that the influx of refugees has had a beneficial effect of bringing to life new neighborhoods and making Amman into a place that was more than a stop on the way to Petra. Once sleepy neighborhoods came alive thanks to restaurants serving tasty Iraqi meals such as Masguf fish and the so-called "Fallujah" meat kebabs as well as night clubs featuring Iraqi singers and belly dancers.

The Fondazione Mediterraneo (Mediterranean Foundation) which served to stimulate partnerships among the Mediterranean, European and the Islamic world, recognized the queen for her efforts to integrate different components of Arab society in the global process. Her speech was a glowing tribute to the values that America used to stand for: "As migration picks up pace, neighborhoods are transforming, societies are diversifying, and the challenge of maintaining social harmony and providing equal opportunity is greater than ever," Queen Rania, said, as she accepted the award. "We must reach out; we must learn about each other; we must support each other; we must stick together; and we must be good neighbors—not only at home, at school, and in our communities, but across the boundaries of geography, culture, age and race," she added, emphasizing the crucial need to foster dialogue. "We have to show by example that what humanity has in common is more powerful than anything that divides us and that means actions not just words, and it means raising the volume among the voices of moderation."

THE MAIDS

THE FILIPINO GOVERNMENT periodically shut down the market for Filipino maids, considered the best. At a local spa, I had the chance to get the inside story on life in the Middle East—that Filipino maids suffer physical and mental abuse but are powerless to change it (and also that Arab men don't like any body hair on their women at all). The worst was Saudi Arabia and many wouldn't consider working there. The year before here, six girls were raped and murdered and their bodies thrown off the bridge near the bus station at Ras Al Din. The cases were reported to the Filipino Embassy and nothing was done. One case *was* reported on Jordanian television because the girl survived. "They say she jumped from the third floor but we know she was pushed. The neighbors heard the screams. She was sent back to the Philippines in a coma and died there." Apparently, their sorrow and terror was common. Rental agents here said the reason why the windows in maids' rooms were light shafts with no view was because otherwise they jump. One hundred girls without papers were picked up by the police every day and languished in jails. The girls were charged 500JD for every year they were found to have gone over their residency limit. The police had a peculiar relationship with a woman named Elvi who was ten years over when she was caught and was allowed to reduce her 5,000JD fine by turning in girls without papers. Elvi continued to be widely known, feared and hated. (She has since returned to the Philippines).

PELLA

CERTAIN DAYS IN FEBRUARY were warm enough for a picnic and our expert picnicking couple, Nasser and Noor, took us to Pella, a gorgeous site not far from Umm Qays to the northeast of Amman. The next day, Dr. Stephen Bourke, research scholar at the University of Sydney, Australia, spoke at the Royal Cultural Center in Amman, Jordan, about his thirty years of work at Pella, sixty miles northwest of Amman at an event hosted by the Australian Embassy and King Abdullah's uncle, HRH Prince Hassan. With scholars from the New York Metropolitan Museum of Art in attendance, Prince Hassan spoke of a common heritage of the region without boundaries—a tribute to the interaction of cultures in the entire Fertile Crescent. These discoveries, he said, were important because of two kinds of truths, the truth of faith—Moses, Jesus and Muhammad—and "that which is less certain, the truth of historical enquiry, and the truth of our identity."

Archaeological discoveries were for the first time calling into question whether Mesopotamia was the only cradle of civilization or if perhaps the Jordan River Valley predates their neighbors to the east. Bourke began his talk by showing slides of the earliest free-standing sculptured monolith in the Middle East, dating from around 14,000 years ago. From the same Natufian village site came a tool kit containing flint pieces and a double-edged sickle. ("Gillette claims to have invented it but actually the idea dates to several thousand years ago.")

In 3400 BC, 1000 years before the pyramids, massive terrace walling and fortifications were crafted at the top of the nearby fortress hill of the Tell Husn, indicating it is one of the earliest complex urban centers known to the region. Maritime trade with Cyprus and overland trade with Turkey has been established as early as 2800 BC by carbon dating organic materials found in association with copper spearheads and axes. Pella's Middle Bronze Age city walls were built around 4000 years ago. They were four meters thick and over ten meters high, and over 1.5 km long. Large tomb deposits with over 2000 objects were associated with the city.

Probably the most significant discoveries relate to the appearance of new pyrotechnology in the sixteenth century BC, namely glassmaking and iron/mild steel working. *This predates previous discoveries in Mesopotamia and Egypt.* There is also alabaster and faience brought from Egypt, and from one tomb evidence of a musical instrument—a tortoise shell used as a sounding box for a lute, found laid across the body of a musician, one of the earliest such finds in the Middle East (1600 BC). From 1450 BC are embossed copper rams and bulls, ivory work, fragments of gold, and other indications of cult practices and, significantly, "the earliest known representation of a king in Jordan" dating to 1400 BC. There is lapis lazuli from Afghanistan indicating significant commerce eastward as well as painted ceramic vessels hinting at much greater east-west contact than generally acknowledged.

In 1350 BC, Pella was the center of Egyptian administration for the north Jordan region, and after a period of collapse, a new civilization grew up in the Iron Age after 900 BC. A massive mud-brick and stone building (probably a palace), had twenty-seven rooms for weaving, cooking, grain and oil storage. Associated tombs are wealthy, with bronze and iron weaponry, much pottery and ivory. Iron Age Pella was destroyed in 800 BC, probably by enemy action. In later times, Pella, re-named for the capital of Alexander the Great's homeland, may have been re-occupied by Alexander's Macedonians but the settlement certainly flourished again by 200 BC. Roman Pella is mainly known through its rich tombs featuring much beautiful glassware.

In the Byzantine period, a 6th century AD church—one of the three main churches at Pella—produced a reliquary under the altar still containing the relics that made it holy. On nearby Tell Husn, the Byzantine fortress was the place where Christian forces surrendered to the triumphant Islamic armies after the Battle of Fahl in 635 AD. In 749 AD a massive regional earthquake destroyed Pella and all surrounding cities, but preserved much evidence of daily life, including one tomb containing a man dressed in Chinese silk with gold dinars having fallen from the threaded garment, and much pottery and metalware.

In later Islamic times a 9th century AD caravanserai (an inn with a central courtyard for travelers in the desert regions of Asia or North Africa) and a 14th century AD mosque were uncovered before the site was abandoned in the early Ottoman period. Bourke's team continues the work begun by Professor Basil Hennessy in the 1970s and '80s. Bourke hoped to continue his work in Jordan, in particular, by looking for the city founded by Alexander the Great and the famous "City Temple" recorded on Roman Imperial coinage.

Hassan said that he hoped for "a cosmic oath" to create a heritage commission committed to what "binds us together—the children of Abraham, in such a way that the roots of civilization are recognized and the lessons learned, history being cyclical." He underscored his personal interest in the meaning and purpose of the Decapolis, the ten cities of the Roman period, linking, among others, Pella, Jerash and Amman.

A WEDDING

ONE NIGHT WE WENT to Majid's youngest daughter's wedding reception—formal dress for the women but not for the men who came in business suits or traditional Arab garb. The elegant wedding with thirty tables of ten set with white tablecloths was held in a large hall with a banquet of stuffed lamb among other delicacies. The dresses of the bride and the mother of the bride came from Beirut, Majid proudly told me. Majid's wife wore turquoise blue, said to repel envy. The bride, the youngest of four daughters and two sons, married a Jordanian-American and would live in Atlanta. Normally she wore a white hijab covering her hair with a little pin on the side, setting off her Audrey Hepburn beauty. But on that night her hair was done up with a diamond tiara and parure (earrings, necklace and bracelet). She looked ravishing in her white bridal gown with a full train, drawn together in points like a duvet quilt, and bustier of crepe de chine. The traditional bagpipe and drum greeting, no doubt a remnant of the British colonial era, ushered in the couple. They danced, cut their wedding cake with a saber and fed each other the pieces, and in between dances, sat on a small sofa on a stage decorated with flowers.

The eyes of Majid's eldest daughter appeared perky behind the full black face veil and dress (the only one so attired). When introduced to her, Bob as ever tongue in cheek told her, "You are looking particularly lovely tonight." The daughter's decision to "put it" was her choice after a trip to Saudi Arabia about five years earlier. May, the second girl, who lived in London with her Pakistani husband, was dressed in a vision of long black crepe, encrusted with rhinestones, and with a creme silk underslip. Majid took the hand of her three-year-old son and lovingly paraded him around the room.

After a seated buffet dinner, Mrs. Majid, whose dress was lined at the hips with some elaborate rhinestone brocade, drew me out on the dance floor, where women mostly danced with other women, and attempted to teach me how to move my hips and hands sinuously, humoring my clumsy attempts. Some of the women had long hair and their shimmery, floor-length dresses accentuated the art of their movements. Some of the more experienced dancers knew how to move both their hips and their breasts. But most of the guests were not so gifted and simply joined hands and danced in a circle around the couple. We were told we were liked because we were always smiling broadly and seemed to enjoy ourselves. Most of the evening, Majid stood serenely smoking his cigar, looking the part of Mr. Big. Once the bride managed to coax him onto the dance floor where he revealed a small fraction of his natural enthusiasm.

THE PRO-AMERICAN PERIOD

WE INVITED MARWAN AND Joyce, Anton and Salwa, to dinner, where Marwan spoke of the unpopularity of America. "After World War II," he said, "the Arab countries wanted the United States to be the trustee of mandated Palestine, in keeping with the Wilsonian tradition of the right of self-determination. Previously, the Arab peoples had been the victim of the British and French colonial interests. He mentioned that during the King-Crane commission visit to Palestine, it was obvious that the Palestinian people wanted the United States to act as trustee instead of the British mandate, so high was the credibility of the United States at that time.

Under the partition plan of 1947, territories assigned to Israel were much less than what was usurped between the partition plan and 1948, when the state of Israel was declared. (See Maps p. 303) In the post-war period of the 1948 Arab-Israeli war, Marwan told us, "George Marshall said to President Truman, 'This will create problems in the area.' Truman responded famously, 'I have a lot more Jewish votes than Arab votes.' " In a recent survey, President George W. Bush was named the least popular man and Nasrallah (Hezbollah's leader in Lebanon) the most popular. Hezbullah rouses region-wide cheers for bloodying Israel's nose. Marwan then treated us to an Arab proverb : "You will be a happy man, when you choose your friends and are not chosen by them." (Inta bitkun saide lama takhtar assdiqaak).

RUSSIA MAKES A MOVE

JORDAN AND RUSSIA SIGNED four bilateral agreements, including a 25 million JD purchase of six KA-226 Russian helicopters. Russian President Vladimir Putin left Jordan on that day for Saudi Arabia and Qatar, part of a three nation tour. Putin, who had launched a fierce diatribe against U.S. foreign policy, was given the red carpet treatment here. In Saudi Arabia, he was hailed by King Abdullah as "a statesman, a man of peace, a man of justice" while King Abdullah of Jordan, to his credit, couldn't go that far, and praised his "personal courage and leadership." An analysis by Karim Talbi of the *Jordan Times,* noted, "Such praise was music to the ears of Putin, whose country has traditionally had close ties with Washington's

Middle East foes, Iran and Syria."

A DEAL WITH THE DEVIL?

THE FRENCH GROUP MET the day before in the Kempinski Hotel where one of our members worked. The day's book topic was *The New Great Game*, the race to control oil fields in Azerbaijan and other parts of Central Asia, by the German journalist, Lutz Kleveman, who reminded the reader that Rudyard Kipling first wrote about "The Great Game" of the Russian Empire taking control of Central Asia. Aida said that it was not complimentary to the Americans who were described as neocolonialists. One woman cried out, "The Americans would make a deal with the devil!" (Later, Bobby said, "Of course they would!" I was so offended by the outcry that I vowed not to go to the French Club for a year, but friends made frantic phone calls and I ended up relenting.)

"They certainly wouldn't be in Iraq if it didn't have oil," another said.

I asked the speaker if the Americans were the only investors in the region. "Oh no," she said, "they are all there—all the Europeans—and the Rothschilds."

Since 1870 when oil was first discovered in Azerbaijan by the Russians, the problem of how to transport oil from the Caspian Sea to Europe has fired the imagination. Baku, Azerbaijan, on the Caspian Sea, bordered by Iran, Russian, Kazakhstan and Turkmenistan, had more KGB and Iranians spies than there were businessmen. The World Bank and the European Union were financing the new $3.6 billion 1,776 km pipeline under construction, Baku-Tbilisi-Ceyhan, (Azerbaijan-Georgia-Turkey). The pipeline would eliminate the need for 360 tankers that then carried the oil through the Bosphorus.

Seismic shifts in the area of the Caspian Sea—the largest salt lake in the world—endangered vast reserves of mineral water in Georgia. One of the five extensions to the pipeline passed through Chechnya and this was why, some were speculating, the Russians had been so brutal there. One of the women was speculating that another of the extensions would perhaps enable gas to be piped directly into Jordanian homes (at that time you hailed down the gas truck.) Yolaine asked why Russia, the second largest oil producer in the world, was still trying to dominate an area that gained its independence in 1995.

BOXED SET

THE PREVIOUS DAY, Kenneth, Prince Hassan's speechwriter, in preparation for my interview with the prince next month, gave me a press release issued in Rome, on February 1, when Prince Hassan presented his Holiness Pope Benedict XVI with of a boxed set of the three Holy Sources: The Hebrew Bible, The New Testament and The Holy Qur'an. "Sources of Wisdom and Shared Values: The Holy Books Offered as a Set for Peace; Faithfulness to the Roots and Commitment towards the Future." After the first stage, they would hopefully sponsor PhD students to do research on the concordance of values of the three faiths, to analyze the texts in which they have more in common than differences. The prophet's message of tolerance, forgiveness, and compassion has been lost in a sea of contradictory messages from religious or tribal leaders who cling to traditions or hadiths inconsistent with the prophet's original message. Naguib Mahfouz explains that the epicenter of the Muslim faith is the most tolerant and that the circles reverberating and widening outward from that center are progressively less so.

EX ORIENTE LUX

AS BACKGROUND FOR MY interview with Prince Hassan, I asked Kenneth why the prince was always talking about the Trans-Mediterranean. What had changed was that we traveled differently. For centuries, the easiest way to get from A to B was not by land or air but by sea. The Mediterranean was safe for shipping so, with trading, the area prospered. The Greeks colonized the Mediterranean, then the Romans and then the Byzantines, then the Ottomans. The centuries of cultural exchange that went on around the Mediterranean have been written over in recent decades. It is overly simplistic to say there's Europe and there's West Asia—the Middle East— and there's a line there that has always existed and that they are two different entities.

In Sicily, the Italians are very anti-Islam and yet Islam has had a strong influence in Italy. Arabs are very keen to identify themselves as Europeans, Italy being the whole birthplace of European civilization. The races have been mixing for centuries. The whole south of Italy was Arab and in all those islands, there was a constant mix to do with trade. Of course, there were wars but this was the theater of operation for centuries. So when you talk about Trans-Mediterranean, you are identifying the whole Mediterranean region.

"There is a theory that the European renaissance came from the East," Kenneth was saying. Ex Oriente Lux—from the East, light. *Reorienting the Renaissance*, edited by Gerald McLean, with an introduction by William Dalrymple, argues that the inspiration for the Renaissance did not come from Italy but was transported to Italy from this part of the world where there was still learning at a time when the Europeans were emerging from the Middle Ages. If you go to St. Mark's Square in Venice, you see in the architecture a very strong Arabic theme. Who owns culture? Who owns ideas? Nobody; they have always been there. It's just a question of where they survive and where they re-emerge, the Mediterranean being this pool of ideas with borders that don't exist."

Why we don't hear more about this golden age, when the Arabs basically took all of Greek learning and philosophy back into Europe in the Dark Ages is like "looking for crumbs from the master's table," Kenneth explained. "We preserved this for you." "Yes," they answer, "but we want you to concentrate on what we produce ourselves." Even though they produced many inventions, they seem to be better known for their translations. This is why you won't find information on the Arab Renaissance at the turn of the 20th century."

The Arab Renaissance pre-dates Laurence of Arabia by a few decades, in the one-hundred-year span in the 19th century. Arab nationalism, as espoused by the original Ba'athists from the first years of the 1900s until World War I, emerged in Damascus, Beirut and Egypt. It promoted the idea of one nation emerging from the ruins of the Ottoman Empire, covering the whole Arab world, with Damascus as the capital, the main Arab city at the time. They were harking back to a time when there was freedom of thought, when there was intellectual debate, when the sciences flourished; that period came to an end in the 12th and 13th centuries when the Mongols invaded and destroyed Baghdad, the primary city.

They wanted a renaissance of thought—a political alliance not based on religion because some of the protagonists of the whole thing were Christian Arabs—according to Michel Haflék, a Syrian Christian. It was to re-establish thought processes that had been shut down for centuries. The

Arab Renaissance never really had an opportunity to take root and that's a problem, Kenneth was saying. It wasn't the fault of the West. The Renaissance was trying to rediscover the spirit of inquiry in the arts and sciences but it never materialized. The political situation overtook it because when the Ottoman Empire fell, Britain and France moved in and they were worried about their own interests. At the time of the First World War, you had the notable families ruling in Syria, Lebanon and Jordan. After the second war, you had a series of coups all around the region.

"The prince is becoming very frustrated by the divisions which are new, becoming more entrenched. [And have become so much more so today.] On both sides—you have the fundamentalists gaining ground and people in the West stereotyping and generalizing about this region. So it works on both sides and one feeds the other. They couldn't survive without the other. It's the sort of thing that creates its own reality. If you keep saying on both sides that there's a difference, then there's a difference."

Chapter Twelve
March

Spring again

AT INTERSECTIONS AT THE beginning of spring poor children were selling bunches of yellow freesia for a (Jordanian) dinar ($1). When I bought three dozen for six dollars (5 JD), they were gleeful. Bob said I paid too much. "We have an obligation to share our bounty or risk losing it," I replied.

Getting robbed

IN THE COURSE OF OUR years here, stolen items include cash, all my gold jewelry, priceless family heirlooms, and of course the usual attempts in real estate, highway robbery, builders, and contractors. We were warned that however kind and efficient your household staff is, just before you leave the country, you are robbed of all your gold and your cash. And they feel justified in doing so. The first robbery occurred after six months of living in Amman when 500 JD ($800) was taken from Bob's wallet. The police inspector and his assistant came, questioned the garage attendant, the cleaning lady and other likely suspects. The inspector, a clean-shaven man with receding, short-cropped hair, wearing a white shirt and grey coat, had a cynical, sidelong, far-off look and the other man, young and casually dressed, took notes, and then did nothing.

THE THIRD INFLAMMATORY REMARK

THE BRAZILIAN EMBASSY HAD organized a large dinner the previous night in the garden of the Intercontinental Hotel; palm trees festooned with string lighting set off the climbing fuchsia bougainvillea. Inevitably, the conversation veered toward Palestine and Israeli-American intransigence. Next to me was Jabra Khoury, the honorary consul general for Cuba, who loved Fidel, cigars and Palestine and was quite vocal about it, raising a red flag for Bob who loves discourse. Dining across from us at our table was Elia Nuqul—short, wiry and slim—the influential Palestinian businessman who developed the vast paper company, *Fine*, from a small concern in the post-1948 period to a multi-million dollar business throughout the Middle East. Like most Palestinians, Nuqul is anti-Zionist but not anti-Semitic, and he and Bob were getting into the finer points. Suddenly, Bob brought up the controversial figure of Amin al-Husseini, the Grand Mufti of Jerusalem and Muslim leader of Mandatory Palestine in the late 1930s, who opposed the 1947 UN partition plan. Al-Husseini was well-known for having visited Adolf Hitler to request support opposing a Jewish national home in Palestine and for having made propaganda radio broadcasts during World War II to help the Nazis recruit Bosnian Muslims, many of whom had found their way to Palestine. When Bob brought this up, Elia threw his napkin on the table and stood up and motioned for his wife to rise, and they left the table. There was total silence and recriminating sidelong looks from the remaining guests. I whispered to Bob, "Let's go!"

YOU'VE GOT TO KEEP YOUR NERVE

MARWAN AND JOYCE INVITED us to another of their delightful Friday lunches with family and friends at their country house outside of Amman. The Jordan Valley was very green at that time. The grasses, grown tall around the olive trees, would turn brown in the summer sun. The fruit trees were giving forth white flowers, a fairy-tale of beauty, petals floating from the trees, filling the air and falling on the reddish brown earth. We noticed on our way southeast that picnickers had come here by the droves for the view of the Dead Sea and Jericho. We were at 750 meters above sea level compared to between 900 and 1,035 meters in Amman, so it was warm enough to eat outside all winter long.

Jane Taylor encouraged a visit to Azrak, a few hours from the Iraqi border where T.E. Lawrence spent a winter. The Roman fort made of black battle, a lava-like stone, from the reign of Diocletian in the 3rd century AD, is near a wetland reserve featuring the ibex (resembling a gazelle), which were reintroduced into the desert kingdom under King Hussein after a period of near extinction. The animal is commonly featured on their ceramics and jewelry. Finding the Dana Reserve between Karak and Petra was difficult as it was not well-marked—by the time we saw a sign, there was only a dirt road which didn't seem right. "It was right," Jane told us. "It becomes paved after a kilometer or so. *You've got to keep your nerve in Jordan.*"

Under the shade of Marwan's palm trees, he said quietly, referring to Iraq, "When the Americans occupied Baghdad, they were so happy that the Iraqis were giving them the thumbs up sign. What they didn't know is that in their culture using the thumbs up is the same as when you use the middle finger held up (f—you). Likewise when Bush, Sr. went to England and held up a victory sign, with the back of the hand out, it means the same thing. You didn't just take down a government, you destroyed an entire system."

Joyce, a wholesome and welcoming blonde, blue-eyed Roman Catholic from Michigan, met Marwan in their junior year at Eastern Michigan University, married and returned to Amman after graduation in 1962. She raised their two children and worked full-time teaching language arts and life skills at the Modern American School, an international, private, college preparatory school—50 percent Jordanian, 15 percent American and 35% other nationalities.

From the hills, we could make out the edges of the Dead Sea twenty kilometers away, and Jerusalem, (Marwan made a point of saying), only thirty-seven kilometers away—Jerusalem's eastern section had been the jewel in the Jordanian crown before the 1967 war. It was a sunny day on the terrace and about ten of us were enjoying the magnificent view of the Jordan Valley, whose gentle hills were dotted with olive groves. "On a clear day," Joyce said, "you can see the spires and battlements of the old city."

Never missing an opportunity to drive the point home, Marwan remembered, "During the '67 war, we felt the reverberations of the bombing of Amman. The Israelis used napalm. Would you like to meet the victims?"

Joyce said quietly, "When they bombed Marka Airport, the force of the blast blew out windows of our house in Amman. I crawled under the bed with the baby in case of shards of glass."

Just then, Mohanna, Jordan's prolific and brilliant artist, came in, wearing a polartec hat with the ears turned up and a short brown cashmere coat. "Do you know Umm Qays and Jerash? Gerasa, you know. Alexander the Great named it after his home town in Greece. Philodemus from Umm Qays taught in Greece. "

Umm Qays, the beautiful antique ruin overlooking the Sea of Galilee, was a source of well-known cynic philosophers who taught in Greece and Italy. Philodemus, or Philo of Gadara, was one of them in the 1st century BC. Born in Umm Qays, he then went to Athens to study and later to Rome to teach and he became one of the luminaries of the Greek- and Latin-speaking world. The Philodemus library was discovered in the house of the Papyri at Herculaneum. There was also an Arab mathematician from Umm Qays in the 3rd century AD who figured out a very close approximation of the value of mathematical pi.

Mohanna started the Royal Academy of the Beaux Arts in Amman and recently had an exhibition at the gallery, "Lines", where everything was sold beforehand because people were afraid they wouldn't get a painting. In 1964, Mohanna said, when one of his paintings was part of the Jordanian Exhibition at the World's Fair in New York, the Jewish lobby complained because it was a depiction of a mother and child with a poem attached to it, which told of the loss of the land and the destruction of an entire way of life. "I tried to find out what happened to the painting," the artist said, his voice trailing off. I liked his penchant for ambiguity and mystery. Mohanna's dark-haired Italian wife, Gabriella, as outspoken as she is beautiful, told me, hauntingly, "You are in over your head. " Gabriella was like artist Hind Nasser, inspired by Princess Fakhrinessa (Prince Ra'ad's mother).

Marwan came over to where we were standing and suddenly, "We need more statesmen like your grandfather, Henry Cabot Lodge." (Marwan knew my grandfather was Ambassador to the U.N. when he was a student at the University of Michigan.) "Now there's an American with ethical standards, someone of high moral stature." He reminded me that Congress chose James Baker to lead the study which recommended an honorable exit from Iraq instead of continuing the "deadly policy" of President Bush. My grandfather, I told them, admired Philip Habib. Marwan touched his heart, "Ah yes, the late great Philip Habib. I remember a conversation I had with him in 1983. Philip said, 'We want to give you $300 million to build a dam (on the Jordanian border near Syria). I said, 'As long as the Syrians, the Lebanese and the Palestinians are in on it too.' 'Oh you're no fun,' Habib responded."

"Later," Marwan remembered, "the king summoned me and asked, 'What do you mean by refusing the aid to build the dam?' and I said, 'Do you realize that, in doing so, we would be implicitly recognizing the Israeli right to the Golan Heights?' 'Oh,' said his Majesty, 'then you were right.'"

Marwan said, "Bush really should follow the advice of the Baker-Hamilton report and give priority to the Israeli-Palestinian conflict, since it is the most serious problem in the region with far-reaching implications."

Talal, a lawyer there told me, "The Palestinians' land is still by law under their name. I am working with a group of lawyers to sue the Israeli government for unlawful confiscation of property."

I said, "There is so much talk and frustration about Israel. Some say with a one-state solution only the extremists would go home; others say a policy allowing everyone to go home would prevent extremism. What do you think of one-state?"

"Of course," Talal said, "it's the only logical solution. It will happen. It's not a surprise to anyone but the United States. Terrorism in the Middle East springs from a sense of helplessness."

I said, "But you are not saying that all the Israelis should go back where they came from—to Belorussia and so forth, are you? You *are* speaking about peace between the Arabs and the Jews, aren't you? If everyone could go home, and if a parliamentary system were in place, giving both parties representation, the violence would end."

"Yes," Talal answered.

I asked, "I understand that George Soros is the lobbyist for the Palestinians ?"

"Yes, I kicked one of his people out of my office," Talal said.

"Why was that ?" I asked.

"Because he wanted to start an Arab MTV with a lot of naked women."

Bobby's interest suddenly perked up, "Really? Where can I watch it?"

"I don't get it," I said.

"They think it will calm the Arab world and distract them from the real issues," Marwan explained.

After lunch, we were seated around the fire—Marwan, Joyce, Mohanna, Talal and his wife. "It occurs to me," I said, "that the philosophical tendency of the Arab peoples has to do with the influence of the Greeks."

"Oh no," Mohanna said, humorously, "that has more to do with the fact that we are people of the desert and, as Leonardo da Vinci said, exertion is inversely proportionate to the level of contemplation in societies. A state of confusion is actually a state of life—research is life—if everything were understood, we wouldn't be alive."

Bob asked, "Are you an Arab nationalist?"

Mohanna replied, "No, I'm not any sort of ism—socialism or communism have done horrible things. Sometimes I'm even ashamed to be a human being." Bob decided Mohanna was his new best friend.

Talal's wife and I swapped stories about New York, where their daughter, a graduate of Harvard Business School, and our sons, Max and George, were living. When I told Mohanna that our younger son, George, was pursuing a degree in geography, he responded, "As Montesquieu said in *L'Esprit des Lois*, everything relates to geography because it's what makes us all different."

Toward the end of lunch, I told my partner what Ambassador Dorin had told me, that Saddam Hussein was the worst dictator since Stalin and Pol Pot. Joyce turned to me and asked, "What did you say, Emily?" And I repeated what seemed to me a statement of fact (i.e., without emotion) to everyone's amazement. We were never asked back.

Over dinner that night, I told Bobby Marwan's Philip Habib story about Israel giving back the Golan Heights. I asked, "Don't you remember when we looked out over the Sea of Galilee and saw the dark hills of the Golan Heights looming over it, ominous and sad, as if the hills themselves wanted the return of the sound of laughter?"

Bob responded, "Peace came in Ireland only after each side was granted a state. One-state isn't realistic. They can't live together."

King Abdullah gave an impassioned plea before a rare joint session of Congress for the United States to take the lead in the active pursuit of an Israeli-Palestinian peace, imploring Congress to exert "leadership in the peace process that delivers results not next year, not in five years, but this year." He pleaded for the Palestinian people, a theme rarely heard in Congress, Brian Knowlton reported in the *International Herald Tribune*.

"Sixty years of Palestinian dispossession, forty years under occupation, a stop or go peace process—all this has left a bitter legacy of disappointment and despair on all sides," the king said. Palestinian grievances were the "core issue" underlying violence throughout the region. If this issue was not resolved, he warned of three civil wars in the region—in Iraq, Lebanon and between Hamas and Fatah in Palestine. Abdullah said that the Palestinians "ask whether the West really means what it says about equality, respect and universal justice… Thirteen years ago, my father was here to talk about his hopes for peace. The next time a Jordanian, a Palestinian or an Israeli comes before you, let it be to say, 'Thank you for helping peace become a reality.' Help fulfill the aspirations of Palestinians and Israelis to live in peace today. "

Unfortunately, of course, the situation is much worse.

DINNER WITH A PRINCE

BOB AND I WERE INVITED to another wonderful dinner at the Brazilian ambassador's residence with His Royal Highness (HRH) Prince Hassan and Princess Sarvath. During the aperitif, HRH came and sat next to me, perhaps knowing that my interview with him was on his schedule. He mentioned House Speaker Nancy Pelosi's visit to Syria and how he hoped that she would press the question of Arab-Israeli peace. He seemed to perk up when I told him I thought the Arabs were ingenious, having invented, among other things, the wheel, the water pump, and algebra. I mentioned that, according to one of his researchers, per capita, Iraqis and Palestinians have the highest number of PhD students in the world.

"How strong the Arabs have been historically in the sciences!" I said. "Perhaps they could help the West resolve the trade-offs between energy and the environment, necessity being the mother of invention."

"Don't forget the Chinese invented the compass," he bellowed, with his trademark belly laugh, deep and straight from the heart. I told him what his friend Adnan Pachachi had told me about Arab unity as the only way to end the Iraqi civil war. We discussed the need for an Arab defensive force with peacekeeping capability. At dinner, he spoke of the concept of the Middle East as Western Asia and the links between the Greek world and the Hindu civilizations in ancient times.

What would it take, I wondered, to bring about another Arab renaissance, as exhibited so strongly in the ingenuity of the time when the Arab nations ruled the world in the 8th to the 12th centuries, when inventions in the sciences—the water-pump, algebra, algorithms, optics, and heat—and translations of Greek texts were passed on to Europeans, then in the Dark Ages? When the Ummayads reached Poitiers, what was the reason why they fell back? Was it because Charles Martel knew enough to kill the caliph? Does the pyramidal system—one of the great symbols of the Middle East—discourage creativity? I returned to see Humam Ghassib who has pushed for funding for research, greater freedom of thought, and greater discipline.

It is no accident that Palestinians are among the most scholarly in the world. It goes deep into the structure of the value system, not just in books and on paper but by the work ethic, a value system with a hierarchy, and discipline. It requires a change of mind-set. The Qur'anic verse meaning swords or "anphos" means the same as mindset.

"Even in the worst days of totalitarianism, there were great scholars," Ghassib answered. "In the Soviet Union, under Stalinism, there were great achievements even on the worst days, so the question is open. How do civilizations progress? The ruler of Baghdad, Harun al-Rachid and his sons and descendants, the Caliph Ma'mun, encouraged scholars by giving them the weight of their manuscripts in gold and even supervised the translations directly. Then there came a time when caliph or first man in the land was not like his predecessors about encouraging scholarship.

"China was responsible for the compass and the printing press. The same question can be addressed to them: Why did they not manage to achieve this industrial revolution? It's a multi-faceted question and needs to be looked at from different perspectives. With the fall of the Roman Empire, after Marcus Aurelius, the leaders lost their vision. In mathematical physics, we have the so-called catastrophe theory. Things combine like a cusp, reach a critical point and then they collapse. It is not one single factor but hidden factors to be seen from far away by an encyclopedic historian. In theology, when freedom of expression is closed, that is the beginning of the decline. We have to revisit Arnold Toynbee's *How Civilizations Rise and Fall*. As a general rule, any civilization, even the present American civilization, could also reach that point."

"Do you believe in the notion of a clash of civilizations?" I asked.

"If the American press wants to be objective, they must recognize that the great works of Islam, Christianity, Buddhism and the Upanishads are universal, that they speak the same language. Prince Hassan is part of that great humanitarian tradition, whether for Gandhi or Martin Luther King. Extremists don't have a wide view of humanity, a vision of humanity at large. Extremists are affected psychologically by their own bitter experiences. One can understand but not tolerate extremism because they can never see the other.

"If you think of any major challenge, the Arab world is not dealing with that challenge. Science and technology is a major example. In general, there are various levels—Jordan might be more advanced than Libya in some respects, for example, but not compared to the West or other Arab states. We are struggling with this issue of modernism—how to tackle the phenomenon of life in this day and age."

ISRAEL AS A NEIGHBOR

DR. SULTAN BARAKAT, of the Royal Scientific Society, was asked to revive the Human Security Center that existed in 2000 and aimed to resolve security through individuals, issues of migration, access to basic services and poverty. I asked him if he is Jordanian. He answered, "That's very interesting—in the United States, you wouldn't ask the question, right? But I'll answer it. We have very complex layers of identity in Jordan. I would best be described as Palestinian Jordanian. I was born in Kuwait, one of my parents was born in Jerusalem, the other in Karak (Jordan), my grandfather was from Hebron and his great-great grandfather from Hijaz and so on. If we ask too many questions, without knowing what we are going to do with the answers, we will have very uncomfortable data."

"Is Jordan an oasis of stability in the region?" I asked.

"So far, yes." (Long pause. He looked at me steadily.) "It is relatively stable," he began. "The state sovereignty and politics are stable but if you are talking about people, the same dynamics are going on everywhere," he told me in a soft, calm, bass voice. "We have a lot of people who feel unsafe and insecure and they leave."

"Iraqi refugees?"

"Even the Palestinian refugees. There are waves of people. We export a lot of people out. We try to attract finances in. We have 750,000 to 1.2 million refugees, though no one knows the exact figures. You can see how the U.S. reacts to boats coming in from Cuba, or Spain, for that matter....1 % of population causes strain. You can imagine if 20 percent of the population suddenly arrives. The government has commissioned a study with FAFO, a Norwegian academic research institute that is doing an assessment of the conditions of the Iraqis in Jordan."

"It's a sad situation," I said.

(Long pause.)

"What is sad about it," Barakat replied with some emotion, "is that it was man-made, driven by the U.S.'s stupid, one-sided foreign policy, and it could have all been avoided. What is modestly sad is that we are unable to cope with it in a way that guarantees our own stability for the future. The way the whole issue has been handled ranges from trying to deny it to trying to control the Iraqis' work permits—to physically controlling them. The answer lies somewhere in-between.

"[As if to predict the development of ISIS] So far it's working—this culture of tolerance that the government has extended to the Iraqis. But I think that, judging from my experience in other countries—and I've worked in many countries on the influx of refugees with cross-migrants—it's inevitable that whatever drove them out of their country will reach them here. They will start settling accounts of the politics they left. It will spill over and the politics that drove them out will catch up with them. The export of the conflict is what we saw in Bosnia, Rwanda and with the Palestinians.

"Now it falls back to us to do something about it before it happens. This is where the international community is not doing enough. They dangle some money to spend on the Iraqis but there is no vision."

"What would you like to see happen?" I asked.

"Well, personally, I would like to see everybody observing international standards of human value. Americans should put the same value they place on the Iraqi as they place on each other. From that point on, you start developing policies that are inclusive. Designed for country by country, problem by problem, as opposed to a blanket response to problems, one size fits all. I think one very good example is the way the international community in Jordan now is insisting on finding out the exact number of refugees. The Minister of Foreign Affairs commissioned the study to find out how many Iraqi refugees there are in Jordan without having a vision about what we are going to do with them. It could be as harmful, if not more harmful, to start digging up how many Iraqis are here without knowing what you are going to do with the information.

"Jordanians already live under an exhausted infrastructure—I'm talking about east Amman, the poorest areas. This is where the fallout will come. They will start to feel the injustice developing, as is normal everywhere, in schools, hospitals, everywhere. With statistics comes location, comes identity—Shia, Sunni, Christian, etc. The breakdown of identity is helpful if you have a plan but unhelpful if you don't and can be manipulated by all sorts of people. Grand visions need to be matched with a plan. The U.S. and U.K. who led the war in Iraq, had neither a plan for the country nor a plan for the region. They should take the primary responsibility and lead the way to bring the region together—to face the fallout of this war and come up with some serious resources. Compare what they spend on winning the war in Iraq with what they spend on refugees. They are trying to make $100 million available now—negligible if you want to do something in a creative way.

"The history of Jordan shows that a temporary displacement of peoples always becomes permanent. Although the majority has come with peaceful intentions, a lot of them are having to live underground. Not being able to renew their residency and become active citizens of the society, causes them to become more and more illegal. Ultimately, the line between illegal residency and crime is thin. Then in two to three years' time, at the age of 14, the line between being a criminal and becoming a terrorist is even thinner. In a year's time, we risk self-destructing as a society if we don't address the issue. I fear that the international community will give you all the right nods and support but it's not genuine."

"So you are concerned about Jordan's stability," I concluded.

"I think we have to do a lot more about the social infrastructure," Barakat answered, "to guarantee a minimum level of stability and we need to go beyond Amman in a big way. Otherwise we risk developing two systems of social infrastructure, one system recognized by the government that requires a certain allegiance and the other will be underground, their activities scrutinized, their banking, internet, layers of connections. The way it is being tackled now is not the right way to go about it.

"The Jordanian government should recognize them so they don't feel that they are illegal. To say outright, 'You are legal.' ... One of the positive aspects of the way Iraqis have settled in Amman is that they were hosted amongst the Jordanians. They were able to penetrate society in a very low profile way and find flats, and the elasticity of the city has actually coped with that influx. The idea that they [Saddam's daughters, for example] have driven up the price of property applies largely to the rich in West Amman. I suspect that they are using Jordan as a stepping stone to move elsewhere. The problem is not with those. The problem is with the poor who have integrated into East Amman.

"The way is to invest in infrastructure that serves both societies. I know one case where a boy from an Iraqi family had severe eczema from his being exposed to some chemical agent in a shelter in Baghdad. Radiation cases from weapons are horrors that Jordan has never had to deal with before— that requires serious support. The medicine here is good with cases they are aware of, but things that have developed with the war—since '90-'91, levels of cancer and chemical-related issues, are traceable to the wars in Iraq. The same is true with education. Jordan provides access without building schools for them. We need to subsidize the government schools so they can expand and hire Iraqi schoolteachers. We need creativity. The history of the camps since '48 or '67 is not entirely positive.

"There is too much focus on the physical security aspect—on the wounded American pride in Iraq and how can we restore the elections. There is not enough about the regional solution to what has happened and recalculating the mistakes that were made and saying, 'Sorry, this is how we can make it right now.' Slowly we are sliding into a chaotic situation. It is in the U.S.'s interest to keep Jordan stable and to widen the stability beyond Jordan.

"The international community shouldn't be stupid and limited; they need to understand what the fallout of the war has been. Too much fixation on number crunching will not help as much as looking at the fallout qualitatively. The Jordanians are as much part of a future solution as they are part of a problem. They have had fifty years of experience of dealing with the Palestinians here in the Middle East and should know better. One solution would be to investigate the way the victims of the holocaust were dealt with and follow the same pattern. Before they counted how many people died, foundations were set up, action was taken. We need to follow the same pattern. We need to be pro-active without waiting to identify whether they are Shia-Sunni-Christian-Kurd, with lots of divisions and subdivisions that cannot be calculated. We should get beyond that."

CHAPTER THIRTEEN
April

EASTER

A S WITH CHRISTMAS, many Muslims celebrate Easter with the Christians out of respect for the prophet Muhammad's recognition of Christ. Groups of Palestinian ladies have special baking parties to roll dough to shape tiny crowns while others fill it with a delicious fig paste topped by powdered sugar. Painted Easter eggs and chocolate ones are ever-present and elaborate Easter lunches are planned. Everywhere is a sense of the numinous.

On Good Friday, the previous night, the church bells near our house tolled endlessly, stopped, then started again, in the darkening air. Today was the mystical day of transformation, the time between Christ's death and resurrection. At 7:22 am the church bells were tolling again.

As if commiserating, the springtime weather of brilliant blue skies returned again to winter with gray skies clouded with sand and wind—so much sand that it scratched my eyes and made me style my headscarf the male way with an open flap to wrap around my eyes. That night, the night before my interview with Prince Hassan, as I was praying for the continued stability of Jordan, I opened my prayer book and read, "I will guide you with my eye."

I must ask my reader's indulgence in changing the format to a Q and A with the prince as the most accurate way of communicating his views for a Middle East peace ; similarly with the subsequent one with Israeli

Ambassador Rosen. Their answers are best understood in their own words. In Hassan, I found my falcon who casts his eye from high above and views the region as his territory. In this interview, he suggests a new way to resolve the Middle East crisis, creating a Benelux confederation of Jordan-Israel-Palestine with a development bank to aid Palestine and to create a Union of West Asian countries to oversee issues of water and oil. The first is widely judged to be inevitable and the second, ideal.

INTERVIEW WITH A PRINCE
A Benelux for the Middle East

A DRIVER IN MILITARY UNIFORM drives me to Raghadan Palace. At this time of year, the fields are lush green and dotted with blue and red wildflowers. The palace is located near the huge flag in the downtown area that some claim is the biggest in the world. Inside the palace gates, security checks my name—"Miss Emily" is sufficient—"an ancient Roman name," my driver remarks. The prince's office, next to the palace, resembles a large square villa with an interior court of orange trees, one still in flower, the other burgeoning with fruit, open to the skies; the sound of the birds mingles with the booming laugh of the prince. The sun is shining on the white marble floors. Nart Hammed, a tall protocol officer, greets me and a guard takes my cellphone.

Prince El- Hassan bin Talal, 60, son of the late King Talal and Queen Zein al-Sharaf, brother of King Hussein, was Crown Prince, the heir to the throne, from 1965 to 1999, and uncle to the present King Abdullah II of Jordan. After graduating from Oxford University in Oriental Studies, he married Princess Sarvath whose mother was the first female Member of Parliament in Pakistan; her family includes, variously, a Pakistani Secretary of State, a Prime Minister, and a Vice-President of India. The prince is president of the Club of Rome, presides over inter-faith dialogue, developmental planning, regional water and energy and refugee issues via the Royal Institute for Inter-Faith Studies, the Royal Scientific Society (1972), the Arab Thought Forum (1981), and the Jordanian Higher Council for Science and Technology (1987) which he founded. Fluent in Arabic, English and French, he also understands Hebrew, German and Turkish, and is author of *A Study on Jerusalem* (1979), *Palestinian Self-Determination : A*

Study on the West Bank and the Gaza Strip (1981) and *Search for Peace* (1984). Prince Hassan is the 42nd generation direct descendant of the prophet Muhammad through the male line of the prophet's grandson El-Hassan.

PEOPLE THINK JORDANIANS LIVE IN TENTS UNDER TREES

AN ELDERLY BEDOUIN MILITARY guard in an impeccable uniform serves coffee in small cups from a brass Arabic pot with a tiny piece of ginger in the spout. He wears a long brown wool caftan with a triple belt of bullets, a holster with a gun at his side, a knife in his belt, a magnificent red and white checked headdress swathed in gold braid. The protocol officer explains Jordanian coffee is clear and sweet, and milder than the muddy Turkish coffee. I tell the officer I am writing this diary. He responds, "People judge the Middle East without knowing it and only believe the media. The main problem is the Israeli-Palestinian question. People think Jordanians live in tents under the trees. They can't imagine it is safe. We are a small country to be playing such a large role in the region and we are safe thanks to the wisdom of the late King Hussein."

As I enter the Prince's office, I try a little Arabic—"Marhaba, As-salamu alaykum," (hello, peace be with you)—and present him with my father's recent speech, *"What's Happened to Globalization?"* which explains, among other things, the World Development Corporation, my father's brainchild. Hassan's brilliant mind is widely recognized. I was forewarned he might answer all my questions at once, that one doesn't control an interview with Prince Hassan. In the prime of life, of average height with a huge head, he bears on his shoulders the weight of his responsibility not only for his country but for the region; his remarks are punctuated by prolonged sighs along with a few of his famous guffaws. Prince Hassan is embarking on a study entitled, *Arab Thought at the Crossroads of Civilization.*

EL: *"Why is the idea of a Trans-Mediterranean Region a constant theme of yours? Do you mean we must not talk about a clash of civilizations, rather a common heritage of achieving peace?"*

PH: "The concept of the Mari Nostrum, or shared sea, the Medi Terra, or

Frontera Meda, the middle ground, is a concept as old as history. One speaks of the importance of what Karen Armstrong would describe as the influence of the axial age, of all the Asian civilizations. Civilization moved for centuries from east to west, in the context of Asia Minor, the Near East, the Levant. The Renaissance, of course, depended on the Hellenistic age, on the Ptolemies, on the Phoenicians, on the Sumerians. It's about time that we started associating the peoples of this region with a common heritage, whether Arab, Kurd, Turk or non-Arab, Persian, the Jewish Arabs or Sephardic Arabs, who were expelled from Spain at the same time the Muslims were expelled from Spain."

"When I speak of region, I think of West Asia, so as to include the Near East and the Levant [mostly referring to Syria and Lebanon, but sometimes also to Palestine, Jordan, part of Turkey, Iraq and Egypt]; if you take the issue in the context of security, for years we have heard the expression, 'the soft underbelly of NATO' and one author has produced an endearing title, 'Let's go from NATO back to Plato.' Cy Vance, Cap Weinberger, and other prominent Americans were always willing to listen to my suggestions that the Mediterranean should be a nexus not a divide, should be a bridge between the Western hemisphere and this region that is particularly poignant when we speak in terms of migration.

"In the Roman Empire, after all, half a dozen of the generals were of Arab origin and the whole of the Arabian Peninsula was regarded as the province of Arabia. The Decapolis was the granary of the Roman Empire, and made up what one author described as 'the frogs around the Mediterranean Sea'—meaning the great cities who spoke in Greek, Latin, and Arabic."

The prince cited the 1994 Middle East-North Africa Conference, immediately after the signing of the Jordan-Israel peace treaty. The signatories, Jordan and Israel, suggested that twenty-four countries from Morocco to Turkey should be regarded as having the potential for destabilizing Europe if a healthy infrastructure plan were not put in place to pre-empt illegal migration.

"The figure mentioned was $35 billion for a decade," His Royal Highness told me. "Unfortunately when we went to the EU—I recall Shimon Peres was involved in this exercise—the answer was first come, first serve."

EL: *"That's unfortunate since you already have the Palestinian refugees,"* I *interjected.*

PH: "Exactly," said the prince, "but the idea has always been that a peace treaty opens the doors to investment possibilities. In 1993, at the EU meeting in Copenhagen, they delivered the so-called Copenhagen shopping list. 'Germany will take this industry, Austria will take this aspect of tourism, etc.,' rather than saying, 'We'll go away for nine months, develop a vision, a concept, in concert with the countries of the region.'

"Unfortunately, no one looks at the critical mass; it's always unilateral and bilateral. But the result is that when 9/11 took place, it was imperative to find the money to build Homeland Security and by sheer coincidence it was $35 billion. So to keep potential enemies out—as President Bush said—to keep our country stable, we have to fight them outside our borders, rather than fight them in our streets. I would suggest that what we should do is not only fight our enemies—which is what we all do, we are all part of the alliance in the global war on terror—but at the same time, we need other alliances. We have many acronyms—an alphabet soup—Partnership for the Mediterranean, Partnership for Peace, Organization for Security and Cooperation—but who has actually sat down and looked at comprehensive security needs to focus on human dignity?"

EL: *"Dr. Barakat explained to me the pressures on infrastructure as a result of the Iraqi war. Will the Iraqi refugees' visitor visas be extended? Will they become legal? And will Jordan become a breeding ground for social problems that the U.S. and the U.K. have placed on your doorstep?"*

PH: "The question is not whether or not we are prepared to recognize the refugees, but whether the world is prepared to support a regional conference on demography—on human resource planning related not only to employment but economic and natural resources. If you take this situation, and add the Palestinians in Syria, Egypt, and Lebanon, Jordan has tried to integrate but not to assimilate. I am not saying the Palestinian presence in Jordan has been at the expense of the Jordanian economy; on the contrary, I think the Palestinians have contributed hugely to the Jordanian economy. But the fact remains that Jordan is the principal supporter of the UN Relief Works Agency—300 million dinars a year—and the biggest host country.

"When you add the 750,000-1 million Iraqi displaced persons in all their different categories, it stands to reason that the issue of stability in the region is simply not realizable without a clear understanding of what, within an eighty-kilometer diameter of conflict, the Palestinian-Jordanian-Israeli end-game for peace will be. Our region was once described as "Benelux"—how can you develop this Benelux concept of intra-independence without understanding what Paul Volcker [chairman of the Federal Reserve under Presidents Carter and Reagan] puts forward in his report on the Middle East Development Bank in which he calls for a period of asymmetric development. He says to the Israelis, 'You have benefited so much from international support, economic and so forth, if you want to talk about building confidence, then your vision has to accept that parity and equity have to be developed. If Jaffa oranges are benefitting from over a third of the ground source water from the Jordan tributaries in the '67 territories, if your settlers are using seven times more the amount of water than the Palestinians, can you accept that there will ever be a hope for peace?' Leaving the emotions aside, just on a practical side, the issue is how to develop peace with a human face."

EL: *"Security remains the great barrier for most moderate Jews and Americans. Once there is a peace, with the water issues resolved and the land returned, could there be another Arab Renaissance or are some Middle Eastern countries using this anti-colonialist, anti-Israeli position as an excuse for weak governance? True, the Wall is going into those areas where the water is most plentiful—but there are these other issues as well. Which comes first, the practical or the security issues?"*

PH: "In 1949, tools were created for two states—the custodianship council, the trusteeship council, and the international council which led to the UNSCOP, the International Special Commission on Palestine which led to UN Relief Works Agency which only looked (inadequately) at the temporary status of the refugees. 39 percent to 46 percent of the land on which the settlements have been built is actually privately owned. The dispensation has been made very clear by Israeli law—if you are a Palestinian land-owner dispossessed of your private land, you can raise these issues legally through the courts. This category of people should be encouraged to do just that... There should not just be a lip-service recognition of the genuine desire of millions of people all over the world for a better deal—systemic change, clean government, good government practice should actually start from the bottom up as well.

"You need to generate a text that you can put into a context, a two-state solution that is flexible enough where you can invite the participation of people in the legal process where they can re-acquire their land, address the question of intra-independence, accepting that in certain instances, asymmetric investment is required, particularly focusing on politics where people matter, anthropocentric rather than security centric, then the concept of human security will begin to prevail over security at the end of a gun. We simply have to change the mindset that the only good Arab is a dead Arab, the only actions that an Arab will understand are force and violence."

EL: *"Is that why Jordan is a stable country in the region, because Jordan has been governed wisely?"*

PH: "As far as stability is concerned, we are all doing second best in this region. If you can't hold regular elections, if you can't take a regular census, then you are saying, 'I am keeping the lid on, I am fighting the war on terror, I'm accepting a certain level of public debate and criticism but only so much.' We have tried to maintain that stability by developing what Paul Volcker has called an understanding of our five challenges—our neighbors: Iraq, Syria, Palestine, Israel and Saudi Arabia—in the eye of the storm as we are. How do you maintain this balancing act?

"I have a great admiration for Finland; the Helsinki Process could start in Jordan because we understand what it is to have difficult neighbors. We also understand what it is to try to develop a pluralist society. But when you say stable—and I say this publicly—I do not believe that stability can be maintained through security services. Since 9/11, the security services have taken the issue of democracy and human rights in the context of the war on terror to extraordinary powers in all the countries of the region, including Jordan. Of course, in terms of the eyes of the public, this is justified because when sixty innocent people are killed in weddings at three hotels in Jordan by Al-Qaeda, then of course, there is an uproar and the demand for the death sentence which of course, until now, still is applied. But the moment comes when building from the bottom-up, re-asserting what I used to call, in the days of my late brother, 'a good bedside manner'—developing channels of conversation with all sections of society, inviting Christians to talk to Muslims, Palestinians to talk to Jordanians. Deliberately preventing the ghettoization of society is hugely important if we are to avoid the coming storm which I think is going to be populist Islamic fragmentation of the region."

EL: *"To what do you attribute the growth of Hamas?"*

PH: "They have their separate sources of funding, despite the global war on terror's attempt to stop them. Money is getting through. In that context, I think they are closer to the titles of the issues—poverty, dispossession and so forth. The former Minister of Morocco wrote a brilliant book called *The Bearded Government* about Islamic parties all over the world. In terms of actually improving governance, there is not so much to be said. They think that they can create a new calipha by sweeping away governments. Absolutist caliphas, they say, will rule benignly. It is absolutely specious to say that anybody today can have the integrity of a prophet of 1400 years ago or of his companions."

EL: *"Is there separation of religion and state here?"*

PH: "It is essential to accept that religious organizations make legitimate, transparent contributions as opposed to just pontificating from the pulpit—all we have is fire and brimstone preachers—everything is wrong—in the mood of general malaise as a whole whether it is climate change, ghettoization, economic depression and decline—many of these things hit a chord. In Iraq, we are talking about five million orphans, according to the UN, for the last three to four regional wars. We have 200,000 Iraqi students we have to find places for in the beginning of the next academic year. These issues need attending to. We can't sweep this under the carpet or count people just by security measures."

EL: *"You've looked deeply into the inter-faith dialogue. How can we counter the notion of the jihad which starts out as a struggle of the soul to overcome the sinful obstacles that keep a person from God, in Reza Aslan's words, and which ends up as a struggle against injustice? You recently gave the three Holy books—the Torah, the New Testament and the Qur'an—to the Pope in Rome. You also recently met with Iraqi religious leaders."*

PH: "The three books were to develop standards to which we can all adhere, particularly the question of equity. We have over fourteen recognized Eastern churches. Many of them prefer to apply Sharia law to family matters whereas criminal justice is supervised by civil law. Jordanian civil and criminal law is dealt with by civil courts. You don't cut off a person's hand to rehabilitate him. This applied 1400 years ago, not today. Try putting yourself in the shoes of the other. I always say I learned English history from a French point of view. In Europe they have this wonderful series where students were obliged to study their history from the standpoint of the other side. I wouldn't have thought that Israelis and Germans would be visiting Auschwitz together were it not for the fact that people have a lot of work to do together. There is psychological rehabilitation to do. This is why when I sat with my brother Prime Minister Rabin after the signing of the Jordan-Israel peace treaty, and they asked me what I thought, I said, 'This is a wonderful day but at the same time I am worried that this is not going to turn into a people's peace.' We need a warm peace or it won't endure. I didn't mean it to be a self-fulfilling prophecy."

EL: *"From the 8th to the 12th centuries, Arab scholars translated classical texts and created new inventions and introduced them to Europe, still engulfed in the Dark Ages. The question many people ask themselves is: what allowed the West to pull so far ahead of Arab and Ottoman societies? Because Western Europe adopted a pluralistic approach and the Arab countries still had the pyramidal model? Why did they lose control of half the world?"*

PH: "You are asking about the Abbasid calipha that straddled half the world? They were part of the outlying region. After Istanbul, after the fall of Constantinople in the 15th century, there were centers of learning in Cairo, Baghdad and Damascus, but the powerhouse was the Ottoman state, centered in Asia Minor, and it became the swing vote between the Hapsburgs working on one side, the alliances of the Bismarck period against the French [who were allied with the Ottomans]. They chose the wrong ally. I would recommend to you strongly this essay by Nabil Matar, a Christian historian, in "Re-Orienting the Renaissance.""

EL: *"Dr. Ghassib, from the Arab Thought Forum, told me that in the Arab Renaissance, those 8th century Arabic leaders who promoted education— Mamoun and Harun al-Rachid, who supported scholarship—made the difference—that those were the periods when Arab civilizations thrived".*

PH: "Injustice cannot just be addressed by writing or widening capabilities. The institutions that exist are motivated against the tradition of merit and competence. If you consider the brain drain from this part of the world and that half of NASA are foreign, the lobotomy of a region is horrifying. If you consider the graduates of (INSEAD at) Fontainebleau which is now twinned with the Wharton School, and you say to the Arabs there, 'Will you come back?' They say, 'No, we want to work in a merit-based system.' Cronyism is not a way to develop a self-sustaining career. This was [also] part of our conversation with the Iraqis [religious leaders]. They felt that the 35 billion dollars in oil were not being put back into the system on a well-sharing basis. To go back to what your father [George C. Lodge, "The Corporate Key: Using Big Business to Fight Poverty", July-August 2002, *Foreign Affairs*] was saying, quoting Jeffrey Sachs who is a colleague of mine on the Prague Forum, 'Until the poor are brought into the international financial system with real power, the global economy cannot be stable for long.' Markets are social rather than economic institutions and the test is: do they improve the quality of life? For an Arab Renaissance, we need Paul Volcker's Regional Development Bank with a lending window or a donor facility which includes Islamic banking."

EL: *"Do you see the Arab League as being a new force in the Middle East?" I asked.*

PH: "Only if the Arab League or the UN were to recognize the importance of an 'eco-soc' region for the sub regions—an economic and social council for North Africa, for West Asia. You already have an effective council for the Gulf, which is largely based on oil production but now there is talk of a new council to include Uzbekistan, Russia and Qatar for gas production. So the question is: is the theme just commodities— oil and weapons?! The instability goes up, weapon prices are more lucrative, more people buy weapons. $60 billion is set aside in Congress for the purchase of new weapons. Oil prices go up and Iran's economy lifts. It's a vicious circle, this purchase of weapons. When will people develop an 'eco-soc' which looks at empowerment in the true sense, a culture of participation rather than cultural futility? The cycle of violence is just the culture of futility."

EL: *"Is the Arab League capable of acting to remedy this?"*

PH: "In its present structure, no. In 1980, when the Arab Thought Forum came together, Saleem Al Has, prime minister of Lebanon and member of the Arab Thought Forum, presented a study of the sixteen organizations of the Arab League. Like Neal Kinnock, when he was asked to reform the EU, he asked, 'What is the mission of this regional body?' There was no real definition of their mission possible because the heads of state had not given their imprimatur. The Secretary General of the Arab League and the Arab League countries, like the UN, maybe even less so than the UN, are a reflection of the whim of the individual countries. The Saudi-inspired peace plan was the first time that they got together in a long time."

EL: *"Could the regional conference idea proposed by Olmert take place, perhaps in East Jerusalem, the jewel in the crown of the new Palestinian state?"*

PH: "I would personally recommend that it is not only the final document of a conference that is important to discuss, as has been the case with many Arab League meetings, but to have break-out workshops that look at the whole process. If you talk about five years to have this realized, like an advent calendar if you will, why can't we look at the security issues—basic security issues like nuclear, WMDs, current security, terrorism, criminality in all its different kinds, exposing the mafias and start addressing these issues in a criminal context? Today we are talking about bombing targets in Afghanistan from the air. Sicily has the largest concentration of mafia in the world. Would the Italian air force bomb the 'capos'? Did the British use the air force to bomb Belfast? Why is it that a regional conference cannot be structured in such a way that the interconnectedness of that advent calendar takes security first—the voices of people from the region and from the West on a range of social-cultural issues—and develop for every meeting a timeframe and a continuation. Where is the ownership of this process? Who is participating in it? Where is the awareness program? When will the Israelis know a bit more about what the details are, for example, concerning the right of return and compensation?

"My approach with Yitzak Rabin—and I had the privilege of meeting him in 1971, long before it was safe or fashionable—was that an unspoken gentleman's agreement—because that's what gentlemen normally do—was that, 'You will continue to say no to the right of return and I will continue to say yes until we can come up with something more creative, more imaginative, more along the lines of a *règionale aménagement du territoire*.' All of this can be done if we develop the collective institutional means to do it rather than everything being bi-national, uni-national, and unilateral. What frustrates me is that you sit behind closed doors and you can discuss chemical weapons bans, everyone agrees, then the militarists step out of the door and it's every man for himself. Mediocracy is ruling everywhere. Nobody seems to able to break away from the pack mentality, and don't consider me a maverick when I suggest—blinding flash of the obvious—that to get from here to there, we need a systematic approach, what Kissinger used to call 'step-by step diplomacy.'"

EL: "*With the regional wars all around you, Jordan is as valued an ally as Israel. When we met with President Bush Sr. last summer, he mentioned how much he admired you. He asked me, 'Do you think they [the Jordanians] like us [the Americans]?' I said, 'I think they would appreciate more of a dialogue.' He replied, 'They should have more of that.' How would you respond?*"

PH: "If the concept of 'Benelux' is acceptable, then what you are saying is right and if there are certain aspects of asymmetry—given that they are stronger in many fields—then these should not be impediments. It's not a question of a rich man's club or any man's club, it's a question of creating a future for generations to come. I've known George Bush Sr. for many years and I said to him one evening, 'When David Rockefeller called us together, along with Javits and McNamara, and Simone Veil, Eric Roller, of the Bank of England, among others, you could have a conversation and step out the door without someone saying, 'he said this or that' or, 'he is pro this or that.' I hate the idea of a '*groupe de savants*' but at least somewhere there needs to be a collegial approach."

EL: "*Is this administration different from past administrations?*"

PH: "I haven't met a single official. I'm not complaining. Once I called on the Vice President in Bethesda and it was, 'I only have fifteen minutes and I'm really very sorry I have to go,' leaving me sitting there with three heavies and the door open. How can you have a conversation? Maybe it's partly because of the embarrassment of talking to this side and how it will be seen but I'm not going to give you an infectious disease if I have a conversation with you. I would be happy to have you tell me your opinion to my face."

EL: *"That's a shocking remark, given the importance of Jordan to the future of the region."*

PH: "I am a member of the Council on Foreign Relations, the Nuclear Trade Initiative, and so many international groups. Often I am asked when it will be convenient for me to go to Saudi Arabia or would I go to visit Sudan as a member of the global leadership foundation, which I just did. I've become a sort of international consultant in my own backyard rather than at least being a friend at court, at both courts."

EL: *"What would you prefer? What is the alternative?"*

PH: "The alternative is that when Nancy Pelosi traveled to Damascus, ostensibly we were told that the administration doesn't approve of it, at least she is briefed. I am not briefed by anybody. I am not in the loop. In terms of the functional aspect in Washington and in capitals all over the world, they have never been so exclusionary as they are at this particular time. You can go to Brussels and ask European heads of state and government. You can have access but nobody is listening so even if I had access, nobody would be listening."

EL: *"The Bush administration is not listening to you?"*

PH: "Not to me personally."

EL: *"To Arab governments?"*

PH: "To world governments. There is no conversation. I am calling for a new Berlin Congress; the Westphalian system is not working. The time has come to recognize that we need pluralism, not narrow nationalism, to bridge the gap between cultural identity and economic worlds. Then people would really feel elated because they would feel you are beginning to address the real issues. It could start as a forum and then if it had confidence, it could become a negotiation in the future. That's why I am heading this coexistence council initiative which will present its report to the European Parliament to try and address these issues in the absence of a framework in which we could all be doing something useful instead of sitting on our hands worrying."

EL: *"In the World War I period, when your great uncle led the charge of the great Arab revolt with T.E. Lawrence against the Ottoman Empire, the British and the French promised a larger Arab state based in Damascus. Would that be the kind of pluralistic, regional approach? You were recently named a champion of the earth for your regional approach to water issues."*

PH: "The only hope for this region is two axes, both of which are developmental, and need to be recognized as potential facilitators of peace and stability. One is the Great African Rift Valley from Lake Victoria through the Jordan Rift Valley all the way to Anatolia [Turkey]. It is shorter than the Indus Valley. You have the Rhine Valley development plan, the Mekong Delta development plan, all supranational concepts. In terms of the Great African Rift, Lake Victoria can provide more hydro-electric power than the needs of the Nile Valley Basin.

"We need a supranational concept—what Robert Schuman and Jean Monnet and George Marshall brought about after two world wars—maybe it took two world wars to bring that about. There are enough of us in this region to bring about a similar relationship that focuses on a supra-national concept that would be able to '*gerer*,' which is a better word than 'manages', blue and black gold—water and oil.

"In 1980, when people were talking about the Iran-Iraq war, I was talking about the importance of the whole of Africa. The two are related. The killing continues. From the Red Sea to Cameroon, corporations are taking oil out of the region. At the northern end of the second spine, the energy ellipse from the Caspian to the Hormuz, we have the new pipelines from Borgash in Bulgaria to Andreanopolis taking the oil out of the region, from the Black Sea to the Adriatic. So the basic question is, if the United States of Arabia is no longer possible or desirable, what you need, given the fact of the new pluralism, is the United States of West Asia, just as you have ASEAS—Association of East Asian States."

EL: *"Wouldn't that be the same as the Arab League?"*

PH: **"My point is it would include Israel,** in the context of peace and regional development. After my great uncle met Chaim Weizmann [the Zionist leader at the Versailles Conference and first president of the state of Israel], a shot had not yet been fired in anger between Jew and Arab so the idea is to bring in Jewish know-how, and the international connections of the Jewish lobby into the region with the Arabs to develop new horizons. In 1918, this was entirely acceptable and was not at the expense of anybody. Nationalism had not yet raised its head. As you know, Aldous Huxley describes nationalism as a common hatred of your neighbor and a common misreading of history. The renaissance I would like to talk about is an Arab renaissance that includes Jews, Christians and Muslims—all Arab. Incidentally, in the revolt against the Ottoman Empire, in 1909, when the young Turks entered Gilder's Palace, the Empire had ceased to exist. At that point, there was no Jordan. We didn't fight as Jordan in the first war, we fought as Arabs, for our identity to be recognized and respected at the peace table. The diaries from the time record that these people fought with us as allies, they should be treated as allies, not colonized."

EL: *"People in America are concerned and interested in notions of jihad, the Sunni-Shia divide, and Al-Qaeda. Dr. Barakat, your new Human Security director, told me that if the U.S. wasn't realistic about the war, we could at least now be realistic about the aftermath of the war. Freeing up funds for refugees and for infrastructure in Jordan are preventive measures against extremism. What would you say to America about jihad?"*

PH: "It was Kierkegaard, the Danish philosopher, who said you should always look at other people subjectively and yourself objectively. Remember that 9/11 killed 400 Muslims and I was the first person to say it. In my capacity as the moderator for the World Conference for Religion and Peace, I apologized, on my own initiative, to the Buddhist world after the destruction of the Bamyan Temples; in the same way, I say to Al-Qaeda, 'What you are contemplating is un-Islamic.' As far as jihad is concerned, it is unfortunate that both sides have used [the words] *jihad* and *holy war*. The president of the U.S. used the word, 'crusade.' The evangelists who support him had every idea of what that meant. This is why the whole idea of a clash of civilizations develops and continues to fester. I don't think there is anything civilized about war, however it is produced and in whatever coinage. So yes, there is a clash within any family over different approaches between you or me or our children, for example, but it doesn't mean it's the end of the world. You need a civilized framework for disagreement. This is why we took the three books for example, to the Holy See, to try to develop a standard of behavior that applies to all people so that issues like jihad are understood in their correct context and application.

"Fighting against injustice should not extend to violating the sacrosanct nature of human existence. Two wrongs don't make a right. You don't kill innocent people no matter how bitterly you feel. I wish more of this would be understood in the West but you've got a lot of fear-mongers. For example, Bernard Lewis, [with whom I share a picture on the front of his book], basically says that we [the Arabs] didn't catch up with the Industrial Revolution. Well, actually the Ottoman Empire was on the verge of its equivalent with major reforms—the tanzimat (the reformation of the Ottoman Turkish Empire between 1836 and 1876) was a pluralist system. But just because this region was not visited by the Industrial Revolution, (meaning we did not progress) is blinkering the fact that this region was the extension of India, under the auspices of the India office. When the British withdrew from India, they didn't withdraw from 'oil' India, from Iraq all the way to Hormuz. They stayed there until the gold standard was stabilized in London, and became the financial capital of the world and then they withdrew. And who replaced them? Not the Americans in uniform at that time—the corporations entered and the corporations have to develop some kind of understanding of human security even to do business in this region. If you look at films like *Syriana*, or *Blood Diamond, A Constant Gardener*, these are pretty blinding flashes of the obvious to all of us.

"You have this oil-producing region which is not a paragon of democratic achievement, but a milk-cow. Then you have the Fertile Crescent region where you have Syria, Egypt, and Iraq which were all following the Soviet model like Romania and Albania. So you hear the Arabs have two heads or they are mentally handicapped, behind the world—the Arabs are no better or worse than anyone else in the world but they haven't been given a break.

"Don't tell me that Albania is so far ahead of Syria, or Romania has done more fantastic things than Egypt, for example. These are all former provinces of the Ottoman State. The Turkish parliamentarians invited me as a grandson of a member of the Ottoman parliament—my grandfather represented the Hijaz—and they asked me, 'Why is it that the British always talk about their commonwealth and our Empire?' It was called the Ottoman State but when did they have ministers from India sitting in Whitehall?

"This is the *carrefour* [crossroads] where we are, at the moment—either we go to pluralism as defined as a process of democracy where you recognize the rights of the other and you respect them within the state and beyond with the development of the regional council and parliament as in the Parliament and council of Europe, or...."

EL: *"Or you have a populist Islamic fragmentation of the region, you mean. During the first Gulf War, your brother, King Hussein, tried to convince the U.S. and the UN not to defend Kuwait against Saddam's invasion. How might Jordan have dealt differently with Saddam Hussein?"*

PH: "During the uproar over the Iraqi invasion of Kuwait [in 1990], we were being called upon to join a Western alliance to evict Iraq from Kuwait. I would disagree with your wording because the first Gulf war [the one starting in 1980] was between Iran and Iraq. My late brother [King Hussein] was the head of a quadra-partite alliance including Egypt, Yemen, Jordan and Iraq. So when the Arab League foreign ministers met, they made the recommendation for a regional solution, i.e. leaders from the region should travel to Iraq to lay on the table a very clear notice of eviction, if you will, of Iraq from Kuwait. It never happened because Egypt became a part of the alliance with the U.S. Even Syria was part of the coalition in 1990. Syria and Iran were required to be part of a security structure that was durable because you can't afford to have spoilers in Iraq. Concerning the invasion of Kuwait, we didn't see ourselves as spoilers or mavericks. [Jordan was acting in a local alliance that they felt should be treated locally.] We were calling for the Iraqi eviction from Kuwait. For that matter, in 1961-62, tiny Jordan sent forces [on behalf of Britain] to Kuwait when Kuwait was being threatened by another dictator." [It was resolved without a shot being fired.]

EL: *"Which leads to my final question: if you had one single piece of advice to give the government and the people of the U.S., what would it be?"*

PH: "Firstly, I'm not presumptuous enough to give anyone advice." Prince Hassan smiled and inclined his head, and quietly said, "Please look at the region in terms of **a regional approach which focuses on human dignity**. You have been responsible for the Marshall Plan that rebuilt Europe. You have supported the ESCAP region, the Economic and Social Commission for Asia and the Pacific. The West Asian and North African Region are no different. I know it is easier to continue with unilateral approaches, and Israel and Saudi Arabia are our best friends and Egypt is our best friend. That's all very well but there is a moment when you have to look, as the Europeans did, at coal and steel, at something more important, and human dignity is extremely important, particularly in the context of the needs and requirements of the region both of which are available but both of which are sadly misused—oil and water.

"I don't think it's a question of being pro- or anti-American or pro- or anti-Arab, it's a question of being pro-human. Anthropo-centric as opposed to oil- and security-centric which means all of us living up to the same standards and defining, as my brother said, the future of our children and our grandchildren."

I left his office feeling elated. His assistant murmured to me that it was one of the best interviews he'd ever given. I came away impressed by his powerful mind—the breadth and depth of his thinking—and hopeful that the Israeli ambassador with whom I was due to speak only two days later would be sympathetic to the Prince's policies and to his plea for dignity.

INTERVIEW WITH THE ISRAELI AMBASSADOR

AT MARWAN KASIM'S LUNCH in the country a few weeks earlier, Anton was talking to Jane Taylor about the former head of tourism bringing the Israeli ambassador, Jacob Rosen, to the Jordanian General Assembly and how disappointed he was by the negative reception. I told Jane I would like to interview him.

"He's a very nice man," she said.

I was lucky that the interview date with Ambassador Jacob Rosen followed so close on the heels of the prince's remarks—only two days later— so he could respond to Hassan's ideas, and give a complete picture of the stakes in the region.

The Israeli Embassy in the Rabi'a section of town is an apartment building surrounded by empty lots and perched on a hill behind the Days Inn Hotel, one of the hotels bombed by Al-Qaeda a year before. A hundred meters away, there is a guardhouse and roadblocks but the guards from the diplomatic corps, positioned in tanks, had not been warned of my appointment. There was a light rain falling and my dark blue crepe de chine pantsuit was not enough to protect me from the chill. The soldiers sent a guard ahead to check to see if I was expected and I managed to convey in my beginner's Arabic that I had an interview with the ambassador (*mowad min safir*) at 2 p.m. (*issaha tinein*) and that they had already kept the ambassador waiting fifteen minutes. I call Heba, Jacob Rosen's secretary, to help guide me in. Finally, I was given the okay and ran in the rain to the apartment building. Finally inside, I went through security. They tried to take my tape recorder—no electronic devices—but Heba, an attractive blonde, intervened again. I left my cellphone with security, customary procedure, and finally, after running the gauntlet, I reached the ambassador's office.

Ambassador Rosen, in his fifties, with amber eyes and a welcoming smile, generously found an electrical outlet in which to plug my recording device. He told me he loved Jordan, that he "came for a month and stayed five years," opening the embassy in Amman in 1994 and that in the time that he had been away, from the years 2000 to September 2006, Amman had changed dramatically from the impact of the 800,000 Iraqi refugees.

"When we were first here, there were 500,000 Iraqi refugees, mainly Shiites who had escaped from Saddam, some very educated and talented people. My wife's art teachers were Iraqi, for example. But after the downfall of Saddam, there were three waves of refugees—I prefer the word 'guests,' because the word refugees brings up loaded memories."

EL: *"Of the Palestinians you mean."*

JR: "Some, the oligarchs, came with a lot of money."

EL: *"How have you found your welcome back here compared to your welcome in the beginning?"*

JR: "It's a mixed bag. I wrote a book, *Crossing the River Jordan*. At the beginning, I was the first Israeli here and it's funny how people here perceive the Israelis. There was a lot of curiosity, a lot of loaded feelings, a lot of suspicion. In the Arab world, when an Israeli comes, they think he's a Mossad agent. Why else would I take the trouble to learn Arabic? They thought I was a spy and people were afraid to give me their business cards. After a while, people started to get to know me. My landing was quite light the second time because people had formed an opinion about me and that takes time. If I had been new, it would have been very difficult."

EL: *"So you feel welcomed?"*

JR: "Not exactly welcomed but many people know me. Luckily, they have not changed their opinion about me; they may have changed their opinion about my government. They say 'We hate the politics of your government but you are a friend.' So in a way, personally, I am still borrowing from previous credits. That's life."

EL: *"Why don't we start with the most recent news—the criticism that Prime Minister Olmert did not engage with the Saudi initiative. How do you feel about this? Have you received any of the details from that initiative about the right of return and the compensation?"*

JR: "First of all, I regard myself to be as a graduate of peace agreements. I was stationed for two years in Cairo, Egypt in the late '80s. I was also moonlighting in Doha, Qatar for two months. It so happens that I am the Israeli diplomat with the longest tenure in Arab countries, more than eight years. I know the Egyptian, the Jordanian, and the Palestinian approach. To make peace in the Middle East, you need a lot of courage. It's very nice to make the initial contacts in a clandestine way, and sometimes necessary. Since you are the granddaughter of such a great diplomat, I presume I do not have to tell you what is an open channel and what is secret. We have never had a breakthrough before there was a formal, open statement by countries, either by President Sadat of Egypt or by the late King Hussein or even by Arafat. Until they came out of the closet, nothing happened. Having a conference in Riyadh and telling us, 'Go to this website and download what we have to say,' and then asking what is our proposal? Sorry, this is not the way. Normally, as a professional diplomat, you cannot expect governments to respond by saying, 'Oh, we have seen your final communiqué on the website or read your proposals in the newspaper.' You have to come to us and say, 'Listen guys, these are our proposals.'

"It's nice that the Saudis hosted the conference and came up with a program but the marketing is tough. It is not enough to tell me, 'This is good for you.' You also have to package it. Now they are speaking about working groups to go to different places to explain, to send an Arab League delegation to the US, the EU, and maybe, to Israel to explain. You must consider the impact and timing. You had a conference two weeks ago. Nothing has happened so far. You need to hit when the iron is still hot. After a month, two months, the delegation starts roaming. It is losing all its impact."

EL: *"On that note, I spoke to Prince Hassan a few days ago. He said what a wonderful idea it would be to have a regional organization, an Association of West Asian Nations, the way there is of the East Asian Nations, which would include Israel, the Near East and the Levant which would have a regional council, a parliament and a defense system, rather than this unilateral and bilateral approach."*

JR: "First of all, let us see the proposal. We know that many countries in Europe were fighting each other for centuries. After the disasters of World War II, less than fifty years ago [now sixty]when seventy million people were killed, they decided to think about unification and just now we celebrated fifty years of the establishment of the EU. In the U.S., you had thirteen states."

EL: *"Three hundred years ago."*

JR: "It's a process and with mass communication, processes can be accelerated. It took quite a lot of time before it dawned on everyone that it's easier to do it together than if everyone is doing it on his own. But it takes time. People like to learn things the hard way."

EL: *"They have been learning it the hard way for fifty years".*

JR: "Prince Hassan has a very progressive mind. He promoted this idea of West Asian nations in Islamabad six or seven weeks ago. I would say there are some in the Arab world who are thinking along those lines. The question is how much impact they have."

EL: *"Israel and the U.S. are such close allies. It has been suggested to me that perhaps it is in Israel's interest to turn eastward and engage with its neighbors—that Israel is too dependent on the U.S. How would you see the relationship evolving?"*

JR: "I would give general advice, whether from India or from an Arab country or from the U.S. Don't tell the Israelis what's good for them. Let the Israelis, who are intelligent enough, decide for themselves. Some Israelis tell the Arabs what is good for them. Don't tell the Arabs what to do. Let people reach their own conclusions. Let people decide what they want to be, with one block or another, about that or another proposal. Every country has its own internal dynamics of reaching a conclusion, even if those dynamics are wrong. But we learn by trial and error."

EL: *"In 1994, the year of the peace with Jordan, there was a conference, the North African-Middle East peace conference, attended by Shimon Peres and Prince Hassan. Hassan told me it was decided that $35 billion was needed for the Arab world to achieve stability, not through security services but through what Paul Volcker has called 'asymmetrical development'—to renew the infrastructure of Arab areas, displaced from the wars. Since Israel has already got so much money behind it, in the context of a peace settlement, to what extent would Israel contribute to this infrastructure?"*

JR (Drawing a long breath): "Israel is full of displaced people. I was born in Poland to holocaust survivors. About 600-700,000 people in Israel came from Arab countries. They were displaced from war. Let's be more open-minded. It's true there are Arab refugees that left Palestine following 1949, but around the same time about 600,000 Arab Jews also had to leave property behind them because of situations which had been created, so… I think it wouldn't be bad to be a little bit critical and not to absorb this theory but to consider that Israel produced all these riches through our human resources. It's very easy to say Israel has got so much. Where did Israel get so much? Did we discover oil? Do we have huge gas reserves? How did we reach $39 billion annual export? Now that the Israelis have so much, they have to help the displaced people; we are part of this same displacement tradition."

EL: *"But the Americans helped you a lot."*

JR: "American Jews and non-American Jews helped a lot because they felt sympathy. Unfortunately, the Arab countries did not feel sympathy for the Palestinian refugees. You want me to be cynical? After every war, you see people donating money. I haven't seen people here donating money for their brother. Charity starts at home. [Not realizing that Israel, by sitting on Palestinian land, is the one who is obliged to pay out; the way we, as occupiers, did in Japan after WW II.] To preach to others, you have to… I am sorry to use those terms, it's very nice to come with this over-arching idea, but… I was recently in Qatar, I saw how much wealth there is and I was told it is nothing compared to what you see in Saudi Arabia, the United Arab Emirates. It's not only the Israelis and the U.S. who are going to solve the problems of the displaced people, not that we should not be part of the arrangement of the settlements. But come on— the whole onus is on Israel and the U.S.?"

EL: *"From the standpoint of security, because there has been a growth of Hamas and Hezbollah in the region, the question is, to what extent can these movements be moderated and their fanaticism tempered? In Israel, there are settlers who have shown signs of extremism. Can your respective silent majorities prevail over the extremists, or will there be a continuation of extremism and the refusal to compromise? The infrastructure issues might help temper the fanatical elements."*

JR: "Mmm, I saw where Al-Qaeda was born. I don't think there was a problem of money there. Let's be a little critical. In Saudi Arabia, there was no financial problem there. The idea is, if Israel were less aggressive, the extremism would not flourish. If there were no settlements on the West Bank, Hamas or Hezbollah would not flourish. This is the argument—let Israel dismantle its settlements, Hamas will fade away."

EL: *"But you are in favor of that, aren't you?"*

JR: "First of all, Israel withdrew from all of Sinai. So, we do not owe the Egyptians one grain of sand, so to speak. We settled our problems of borders with Jordan. I speak from a position of responsibility. After signing the peace agreement, we had to sign seventeen different agreements about water, security, vegetation, electricity, transportation, veterinary services, etc. Two years ago, we withdrew from Gaza. There was not one Israeli soldier in Gaza. We dismantled settlements in the

Gaza Strip, removed 10,000 people. We thought with no Israeli presence in Gaza, we had turned the page, that the irritant, the sore point, was removed and, what do we get every day, missiles from the Gaza strip to our cities and there is no one in control in Gaza. To say Israel extremism is the cause, when you know Al-Qaeda was born in the most affluent country, is not looking into the facts. There is extremism, and Israeli policy is not perfect, we commit mistakes, some disturbing mistakes, but what are the Arabs doing to mellow the Arab extremism?"

EL: *"The world admires Israel for withdrawing from Gaza."*

JR: "We started withdrawing from four settlements in the West Bank and we stopped it because we haven't found someone to… you see again, here I am speaking from a position of experience and knowledge since I was in Cairo for two years. When we identify a strong leader on the other side, a responsible government, you realize you can cut a deal with him. Sooner or later, we all become human experts. You meet a lot of people in your life and after a while, this is a serious person, you can cut a deal with him. Israeli leaders, when they identify a strong leader like Sadat or King Hussein, even Arafat we thought he was strong enough, he is able to deliver, with all the hesitations and all the pains, we did it. But when you face a situation on the other side, where for a variety of reasons, there is no strong counterpart with whom you can cut a deal, it's difficult.

"I remember when I came here in December '94, until Rabin's assassination in November '95, Rabin and the late King Hussein were meeting on the average of once every six weeks. There is a big, big hole there. Hussein and Rabin would sit around the table at the Hashimiya Palace, and all the advisors were sitting twenty to thirty meters deep, eating peanuts and almonds and drinking juice. They would sit for three hours, the ashtray would be full of cigarettes because both of them were heavy smokers, and we solved all the problems that the head of the negotiating teams, which has a limited mandate, could not decide. No one took notes. Maybe there was a microphone hidden under the table, I don't know. By the end of the meeting, they brought their people:

'OK, we agreed about this or that, go ahead.' There was a feeling of doing things without signing any paper—never! Nothing was written. Royal Jordanian started flying Airbuses over Israeli airspace without any agreement. We opened a border crossing without any agreement. We opened a letter of communications agreement so you could pass the dead from one country to another. Later they were incorporated. Prince Hassan was there with his brother. He knows what happened. There was a lot of trust."

EL: *"Prince Hassan was also reminiscing about the '94 accords. He told me, 'When I sat with my brother Prime Minister Rabin after the signing of the Jordan-Israel peace, they asked me what I thought and I said, "Well this is a wonderful day but at the same time, I am worried that this will not turn into a people's peace. We need a warm peace or it will not endure."' About an eventual Palestinian state, what will it take to make relations if not warm, at least less glacial?"*

JR: "At the beginning '95-'96, it looked promising. Terrorist attacks, by the way, under Prime Minister Rabin, did not stop for a day when he was discussing things with Arafat. Several suicide attacks happened in Jerusalem and Tel-Aviv—one hundred victims. Then Rabin was assassinated not by an Arab but by an extremist Jew—a black hole. In Lebanon, a bomb went astray and killed about one hundred Lebanese, and then Netanyahu came into power. He did not find common language with Arafat as Arafat had had with Rabin. Rabin and Arafat didn't like each other but they could work together. It wasn't a perfect marriage but at least they still lived in the same home.

"The sad thing is it didn't work until President Clinton came into the picture at end of 1999 with Camp David and tried to bridge the difference. But because of internal Israeli politics, Ehud Barak was running out of time and when you address delicate issues under time pressure, you are bound to commit errors in any profession. He was sure he was offering Arafat something he thought he could not refuse— a golden, once in a lifetime opportunity—98 percent of the West Bank and Gaza, and so on. He went back to Ramallah and after two or three weeks, the intifada started."

EL: *"I always hear that Israel over-reacts, that the Palestinians or Hezbollah in Lebanon do one small thing and then Israel responds too forcefully. Hezbollah may have started the war last summer with a kidnapping but wasn't Israel's response overkill?"*

JR: "Mischievously, I ask in response to those questions, could you recommend a desired dosage of response?

EL: *"The response was geared to getting rid of the arms trafficking in from Iran,"* I said, but sensing I would not get anywhere with this sensitive topic, I changed to another one, only slightly less so. *"The land border crossings are perceived by many Jordanians and Palestinians as humiliating. Crossing the Allenby Bridge last winter with my husband and son, there were eight checkpoints that lasted two hours. In the West Bank one hears of strip searches of elderly people. To what extent do you feel that these measures are justified by security concerns? What is your answer to those who feel that this is a form of moral harassment?"*

JR: "Just two to three months ago, a seventy-year-old woman in Gaza exploded herself. Yesterday a woman in Baghdad exploded herself killing twenty people. It is a burden, it is humiliating, do you want me to shout it into the microphone? The Israeli ambassador admits that some of the procedures may be perceived as humiliating. Former Prime Minister Ehud Barak, escorted by Israeli police, entering JFK airport and being asked to take off his shoes, is humiliating. It costs a lot to maintain the security, twenty-four hours a day, seven days a week, with roadblocks. It has to do with suicide bombers."

EL: *"Which is why now the Wall has gone up, of course."*

JR: "Before I came here, I was the diplomatic advisor to the mayor of Jerusalem. I was spokesman for the security Wall that is cutting the city. I was explaining the municipal problems it creates. How do you provide municipal services on that side of the Wall. How do you send someone to repair a water pipe when the water company says they are afraid to go there without an escort, fearing they will be killed. The commander of the police has to escort a garbage truck to pick up the garbage."

EL: *"Harold Kaplan, a retired senior State Department official who worked for my grandfather when he was ambassador to Vietnam, told me what Palestine needs is not this Swiss cheese patchwork approach, if you will, but a good road running north and south. Most moderates—Jewish, Arab or American—are in favor of going back to the '67 borders but that would involve taking down the Wall."*

JR: "Why was there a war in 1967? Until 1967, Israel was not ruling the Golan Heights [Syria[, Gaza [Egypt] and the West Bank [Jordan]. All those countries never bothered to establish a Palestinian state—**why?** Three to four years ago there was no Wall. The amount of suicide bombers was too much to take. In the beginning, Sharon was against it but with the reality on the ground, there was no other way. We had no one to talk to—Arafat was either sick or uninterested. Things had gotten out of his control. Sometimes when you release the dogs, they don't come back; they start attacking the policemen. Things are complex. We are spending a lot of money and resources on things which basically are a waste because you are building a Wall which one day you know you will have to knock down. It costs money, creates plenty of problems, humanitarian problems, environmental problems, and wildlife problems—birds and some animals and their habitat. Until I came here, I was taking senators and congressmen and showing them the problems the Wall creates. Thirty kilometers of Wall within the city have so far been built, and it is not yet completed. There are pressures from churches: Catholic students who can't go to school. The school is telling us if they can't get to school, they will close and, 'You are weakening the Christian presence in the Holy Land.'"

EL: *"Is there no way to stop the Wall?"*

JR: "On the other side of the Wall, you don't have a government which is able to govern. Three or four years ago, there was no Wall."

EL: *"Let's take the issue of water because that's a hot button, because the Wall is now cutting into water-rich post-'67 borders. Since '49 it's been a problem. In the context of a resolution with the Palestinian authority, what compromises do you see as being fair and practical?"*

JR: "To move to Mississippi. There is a big river there." [Admitting that compromise concerning water is not possible, that the West Bank expansion plan is based on water acquisition.]

EL: *"You are both Semitic people. The Arabs and the Jews are both descended from Abraham. You are brothers."*

JR: "Sometimes there are feuds in families. I am up to my neck in meetings on the Dead-Red project. On the 17th we had the first meeting of the three parties—Jordan, Israel and Palestine. The populations are growing steadily. In a pace of growth in population in Israel and in Jordan with the 700,000 refugees, pressures on drinking water and patterns of consumption are changing.

"What do you do when the other side says I am not interested in solutions, I am defending my honor and I don't hesitate to lose my life to safeguard it. [When the other side has nothing left to give but their lives.] The Americans say, 'Just withdraw to the '67 lines and xallas [translation: *finished*], that's it.' Unfortunately, the water aquifers that provide water to Israel are where the Palestinian Authority is today. If we withdraw without any agreement with them, they will start digging water for their own needs and Tel-Aviv and Haifa will be left more or less without water. Sewage, if you don't treat it, will start going down the hill. [A racist remark] In the U.S., a couple divorces, normally they sell the property, split the money, and move to a different state. In our case, we continue living in the same property and share the same utilities. So you need to have an agreement which can hold, with someone you can trust. We trust Mahmoud Abbas but unfortunately, he has no executive capabilities. He is a very practical, sensible, wonderful man who says all the right things, but when it comes to application, implementation, he is unable to stand behind his promises. He promised to confiscate all the illegal arms in the West Bank and

Gaza and he hasn't done it."

EL: *"I have been told that when the Israelis give back the Palestinian land, they uproot the olive trees so the Palestinians will be deprived of their source of livelihood."*

JR: "Wolfowitz mediated with Israeli settlers, paid them money so they would leave their land with the orchards intact because he had the American money—$30 million—so Israelis would not uproot the orchards and greenhouses. The Palestinians went into the orchards, cut out the trees, and now there are no more trees. [Untrue] Go to the Gaza Strip and ask what happened to the orchards and the greenhouses that the Israelis left them? They always say all the problems—'Kullho, kullho' [translation: *everything, everything*]—is due to the Israelis and the Americans."

EL: *"Jordan's King Abdullah went before the U.S. Congress and said the solution to the Iraqi problem is a Middle East peace. What is your reaction?"*

JR: "I don't think they are related but if the king thinks that by solving the Palestinian issue, it would help in Iraq...I don't think he convinced many people in Congress. Was there any condemnation of terrorism? Was there any shadow of admission that maybe something on the Arab side was not perfect? Just to push the Israelis to withdraw? Despite the standing ovation, I don't think Congress was convinced. We and the Jordanians understand each other on what is vital and critical. At least we trust each other. Finally, they manage to squeeze out a promise or a commitment but once they do, they know we will do it. And vice versa. Same with the Egyptians who are also tough negotiators but we understand each other. We know the limits of our power. Haram [translation: *pity*] that there aren't more of that sort."

EL: *"Let's assume there is a Middle East peace. Israelis might scale back on the production of Jaffa oranges, which drain the area of water, and the other water issues are resolved, the settlements are returned, the fanatics are removed from the borders and the '67 borders returned, and the Wall comes down. At that point, to what extent will the Arab League or another league of states, perhaps Israel included, have the governance to keep the region strong and free from infighting?*

JR: "We are not sure what the Arab League is doing. Americans think tools, marketing, packaging. The conference ended two weeks ago, what happened? They thought Olmert had rejected it. Send us a delegation from the League! We understand that it might not meet all the requirements but OK… They say they are going to establish working groups to market it… to whom? You need a strategic plan. Nothing. To tell us to look at the website or news agencies, haram [translation: *pity*], this is not the way you do business. You do not negotiate through computers. You sit around the table, you sit in a lobby, you exchange jokes. In Egypt at least two hundred people have spent hundreds of hours negotiating with Israel; same in Jordan. So far, whatever the Syrians have achieved has been by violence and by squeezing your arm, or your ear; nothing by positive dynamics the way you and I know it."

EL: *"We went to Umm Qays, and saw the darkened hills of the Golan Heights facing us with Israel across the Sea of Galilee on the other side. We imagined the sound of laughing children on those hills—Syrian and Israeli—with the whole area completely free and open."*

JR: "In December '91, following the Madrid conference, after the Gulf war, the Israeli team talked with a Syrian, Palestinian, Jordanian delegation. I remember when the Syrians came into the room and said, 'We came here with one purpose—to get rid of Israel from the Golan Heights.' We said, 'There are still a few outstanding problems we have to negotiate beforehand.' This is the issue of leadership.

"King Abdullah, seven years in power, has not committed one mistake. That is an achievement. Slowly he is gaining more experience and you can trust him. You need a personality that can capture the imagination of the other side. We have scandals non-stop."

EL: *"That's a free press."*

JR: "So we need something that will make a breakthrough that will capture their imagination."

EL: *"Can I make a suggestion? Hold the regional conference in East Jerusalem."*

JR: "Who will come?"

EL: *"Everybody."*

JR: "You think so?"

EL: *"They want East Jerusalem to be the jewel in the crown of a new Palestinian state; they will go."*

JR: "This should be negotiated. You have three countries, each of them feels, and rightly so, that they are the leaders of the area, three centers of learning and historical accomplishment—Cairo, Baghdad and Damascus. [The Palestinians have one of the highest literacy rates in the world.] When the Mongols invaded Baghdad, the Tigris was black for a month from the ink of all the books they threw in the river. Damascus was the cradle, the center of modern nationalism. The Hashemites, because they have never been the leaders of the Arab world, are very realistic. They know the limits of their own power so they look at reality from a normal perspective, not the grandeur of the Pharaohs, nor the grandeur of Nabucco or Saladin. You see what happens in other countries of the Gulf, with killings and internal intrigues—normally the son would depose the father. There has never been any intrigue from within the Hashemite family trying to overthrow their own government. Now you ask all the Arab nations to think the same way."

EL: *"They are certainly united on the Palestinian question."*

JR: "This is the only thing they manage to unite about."

EL: *"I'm not so sure they are too happy about Hamas either. "*

JR: "So let us hear them saying it loudly. The point is King Hussein never executed one person who tried to make a coup d'état. He always pardoned them. They went into exile, he pardoned. This was why he was so loved. In the '50s and '60s, every few months there was an attempt to overturn the kingdom—communists, Ba'athists. Crown Prince Hassan was ready to become king and Prince Hassan accepted the verdict. Abdullah would become king and Hamzah, the son from Noor, would be regent. Two years ago, Abdullah decided the guy was not ready. He continues to go abroad with him. This is the Hashemite discipline. This is what gives Jordan the stability. They are devoted to their people and aware of the strategic situation."

EL: *"Do you think that the Israelis could borrow a page from the Jordanians in terms of treating the Palestinians equally?"(I noticed with this last remark that it was the only time in the interview that there was a pause, and when the ambassador started speaking again, he seemed to have something caught in his throat as if he were almost speechless.)*

JR: "We started doing it and then things got out of hand. There is no central Palestinian government. If you had been here five years ago and I told you there would be a war between us and the Palestinians, you'd have said I had had too much to drink. You learn by trial and error. Sooner or later, the thing will fall into place. How long can we drive each other crazy? I am on record that we are driving each other crazy. In the Gulf states and in Jordan, the Palestinians run huge economic and civil systems—real nation-building. The frustrating thing is that the only thing they cannot manage to do is to build their own nation. Look how successful and ingenious the Palestinians are in business in Jordan. I know some Palestinians quite well to whom I can ask this nasty, dirty question—'You have built this big enterprise, how come your cousins in the West Bank and Gaza can't imitate what you are doing?'"

EL: *"Are you ready to invest in the infrastructure of Palestine?"*

JR: "If we propose to invest in their country, in their infrastructure, it will be perceived as Zionist influence. When Israel gave an intensive care unit to Jordan, they thanked me and said, 'Sorry, Jacob. We can't put a plaque on it,'" Ambassador Rosen said quietly.

He accompanied me downstairs and out to the front door and,

standing in what was now sunshine, I told him how wonderful our stay was at the American Colony Hotel in East Jerusalem, not far, it turns out, from his house there. As a parting remark, I said, with a smile, "See you in East Jerusalem!" He smiled back. But it wasn't a happy smile. His comments left Jordan little room to maneuver; in fact they were almost diametrically opposed to Prince Hassan's and left no room for hope. I left the embassy feeling constrained and reduced. Here was the opposite of Hassan's generous and expansive vision. As I was walking back to my car, Yeats' oddly prescient poem came to mind.

> "The Second Coming"
> "Turning and turning in the widening gyre
> The falcon cannot hear the falconer;
> Things fall apart; the centre cannot hold;
> Mere anarchy is loosed upon the world,
> The blood-dimmed tide is loosed, and everywhere
> The ceremony of innocence is drowned;
> The best lack all conviction, while the worst
> Are full of passionate intensity.
> Surely some revelation is at hand;
> Surely the Second Coming is at hand.
> The Second Coming! Hardly are those words out
> When a vast image out of Spiritus Mundi
> Troubles my sight: somewhere in the sands of the desert
> A shape with lion body and the head of a man,
> A gaze blank and pitiless as the sun,
> Is moving its slow thighs, while all about it
> Reel shadows of the indignant desert birds.
> The darkness drops again; but now I know
> That twenty centuries of stony sleep
> were vexed to nightmare by a rocking cradle,
> And what rough beast, its hour come round at last,
> Slouches towards Bethlehem to be born?" ~WB Yeats

CONCLUSION

CONSIDERING THE ILLEGAL expropriation of land post-1967, Prince Hassan's request for the Israelis to give the Arabs back their dignity does not seem to be asking too much—a proper peace with the institutional backing to ensure its stability. Although we spent eight years in Amman, this diary of our first year, 2006-2007, revealed to me the anger and frustration of the millions of Palestinians forced out of their homeland, some refugees living in camps for decades. At the time of my writing, several thousand Israeli housing units were planned for East Jerusalem and Ma'ale Adumiin, strategically severing connection to the West Bank. In the decade after this diary, 2007-2017, Israel has dramatically swallowed up even more territory within East Jerusalem and the West Bank, the occupied territories the UN has repeatedly declared would become the new Palestinian state (see Maps p. 303). How can the United States continue to tolerate this unlawful occupation?

For twenty-five years, the Palestinian Authority has endorsed a two-state solution on twenty-two percent of their original land. Meanwhile, in the West Bank, lack of freedom of movement, access to water, health care, and employment, are everyday challenges, and discrimination and trauma daily occurrences; in Gaza, thirty percent of the people are without water due to the continuing electricity crisis. Seventy years ago, on November 29, 1947, the UN voted to partition Palestine into two states, a Jewish state and an Arab state, and yet, on November 29, 2012, the U.S. was one of only nine UN member states to vote against recognising the official status of the State of Palestine on the territory occupied since 1967 and upgrading Palestine's status at the UN from observer entity to observer state.

Although the 1967 UN Resolution 242 affirmed the inadmissibility of the Israeli acquisition of territory by war, most Americans don't realize that the Israel that they support is a rogue state that continues to violate international law. When I suggested to one Israeli scholar visiting Jordan a one-word solution to the West Bank occupation—"Leave!"—he was shocked, as if my recommendation were an attack and not a clarion call for justice and mercy. My American friends ask, "How could Israelis be outlaws since Israel has near unanimous Congressional and Presidential support?" (Rep. Darrell Issa, a Lebanese Christian Arab, being the sole exception). The U.S. Congress knows that injustice fuels terrorism, and that Al-Qaeda and its offshoots are influential in the region.

In 2012 my husband and I were among the three hundred people in Amman, invited to view Lubna Dajani's film, *My Safed* about the village in northern Galilee during the 1948 war with Israel. At the urging of the British and Jordanian army, 12,000 Palestinians, 100 percent of its inhabitants, were forced to flee their village never to return. Mahmoud Abbas, the current president of the Palestinian Authority was born there in 1935, and his family had wanted to stay and fight. During the screening, the audience cheered when the elderly inhabitants vowed to return and regain their land. The hatred and desire for revenge were palpable. But the prospect of return is unlikely; even Mahmoud Abbas's recent concession on the right of return saying he would like to have the right to visit but that he no longer had an automatic right to return and live in Safed, was ignored by the Israelis. ("It's my right to see it but not to live there.") All my Jordanian Palestinian friends have the modest hope of being able to freely visit all of Palestine/Israel, to smell the Mediterranean Sea again, but not to live there. Meanwhile, Netanyahu and right-wing Likuders have their eyes set on the *acquisition* of all of ancient Samaria and Judea.

We need structures to achieve a real peace. The answer is to adopt Prince Hassan's idea of a United States of West Asia extending the entire length of the Jordan Rift Valley from Lake Victoria (Uganda, Kenya, Tanzania) to Anatolia (Turkey) to deal with the key issues of water and oil, blue and black gold; it would have a regional council, a parliament and a defense system. Another key piece of the puzzle is a Benelux arrangement for Jordan, Palestine and Israel—a Mediterranean Union—with a Middle East Development Bank. An international borrowing-lending institution could balance the asymmetrical development and satisfy the ancient yearnings for a true Arab renaissance by reducing the corruption that paralyzes business in the region and alleviating the ghettoization of societies.

We need a Middle East Marshall Plan for Palestine so she can live side by side with Israel with serenity. One high-ranking businessman suggested that a $40 billion payment might cut the heart out of the terrorist threat and give the Palestinian people—ridiculed, mocked, scorned, forgotten, abused, tortured or killed—the rights they deserve. Billions of dollars of aid to Israel doesn't help the relationship; in any case Israel, with $39 billion in annual exports, doesn't need us. We have a duty and an interest in helping to strengthen the sagging infrastructure. But if a Marshall Plan for Palestine isn't possible, then at the very least, omit the military aid package to Israel, which already has the Iron Dome and nuclear weapons, and get out of the way, to allow the region to find itself again.

The original trusteeship councils set up in 1949 for two states that Hassan referred to need to be dusted off to build an infrastructure for Palestine, so that the current despair will eventually dissipate, since despair leads to religiosity and fanaticism. Israel needs to cultivate Palestine as a partner rather than an adversary. It needs to take the high road and help to create a state that runs from the Sea of Galilee to the Negev and Gaza, with a good road north and south. With Palestinian dignity restored and their economy booming, Israel would have an incentive to turn eastward and set up a trading partnership with its neighbor which could eventually lead to one state. Currently, it is the exact opposite. Out of desperation, sane people and institutions favor the boycott, disinvestment and sanctions against Israeli goods coming out of occupied Palestinian territories. By banning people and organizations that support BDS, Israel is testing the limits of its status as a democracy, which enshrines the right to free speech and free assembly.

If we don't solve the Arab-Israeli problem, foreign aid is just a painkiller to a disease that encompasses Lebanon, Iraq, Israel, Jordan, Palestine and now Syria. Some experts say that of all the issues of the Middle East, Palestine is one that can be resolved because there are no winners and no losers. Israel realizes it can't win by force. They want to live in peace. Two states will be created. But one state might be more practical since Israel has annexed most of the West Bank already, but only if equal rights and compensation for lands are the norm. Why, in a democratic country, should this be considered utopian? A good starting point would be direct Jordanian-Israeli bi-lateral talks, but as long as Israel looks westward instead of eastward, as long as she ignores and humiliates her neighbor and is subsidized by the U.S., this horrid stalemate will continue. For Israel to truly prosper, it needs to live in the neighborhood. If the U.S. were really Israel's best friend, it would help it to become an adult and act responsibly by engaging its neighbors instead of treating it as its spoiled child.

I never thought I would enter the Palestinians' and Jordanians' world, nor that they would enter my heart. But my hope is that Israel will see their interest lies in reversing its racist, apartheid state policies (that I personally experienced at the border checkpoints). Respect for Arab generosity, wisdom and complexity should create the conditions toward building a functional modern state of Palestine. My husband and I have come to love the Arab world, the language (in which "to have a change" is "to smell the wind") is beguilingly whimsical and fascinating. There is a strong mysticism here and a spirituality that may account for the gentleness of the people—their generosity and patience and immense goodwill and funny quirks, born of crisis and adversity. We have learned to see the West from the East where civilization began and we have come to have enormous respect for the Arab people and their complex history.

Growing up, not knowing any Jews or Arabs, it took time for the vastness of the injustice against the Arabs to sink in, just as the tales of the Holocaust took time as well. I came to understand what a terrible thing the Israeli ethnic cleansing of Palestine (aided by the British) really was by talking to the people who were forced from their homeland. No matter how much we want it to, the racist repercussions of what happened in colonial Palestine, a post-World War I gift from Lord Balfour to Lord Rothschild, cannot be forgotten and filed neatly away—the losses are too raw, too flagrant and within living memory—unless there is adequate financial compensation, some fraction of what we give Israel annually. This ridiculously obvious solution, coupled with a new institutional framework for implementing change, *will* allow Palestinians to forget. They want peace more than anyone. Ironically, the Israelis' biggest enemy is fear. Most Israelis believe all Arabs are terrorists; as Hassan put it, *the only good Arab is a dead Arab*, a riff on General Custer's remark about the American Indian. As Miko Peled wrote in *The Israeli General's Son*, "During a trip to the West Bank, I confronted what emerged in my mind as the greatest obstacle to peace: fear of the 'other,' a fear I had never realized I possessed... I knew if ever there were to be peace, the fear that ran inside me like a virus had to be conquered." The vast majority of Palestinians have already faced the reality of the two-state solution; over centuries, the majority have been tolerant and merciful toward their neighbors; they are also natural merchants.

Unfortunately, some Israelis, believing the lie that they have been taught, feel justified, for example, when they cruelly gather on a mountaintop to watch the horrific bombardment of Gaza, as did the residents of the Israeli village of Sderot on July 14, 2014. Contradicting what everyone here has told me about Palestine when the Jews arrived, Golda Meir, former Prime Minister of Israel, famously said—*no one was there.* "Land without people for people without land" was the Israeli propaganda at the time. Even now, the Israelis act sometimes as if they are trying to make it so. Indeed prior to his death in 1981, General Moshe Dayan chillingly asserted, "There is no more Palestine. Finished." On the contrary, as the U.S. did with the Japanese after World War II, Israel, the victor, must extend the hand of peace to Hamas. Hamas would then recognize Israel and they could live in peace. America also has an obligation to treat Palestinians with the same respect they do the Israelis. These are perilous times: if our greatest sin for Muslims is pride, our current president is our greatest threat, a powerful magnet for radical Islamic terrorism. It is a truly crucial time for the region—with Amman in the bull's-eye and Al-Qaeda and ISIS in the backyard.

CHAPTER FOURTEEN
Postscripts: 2007 – 2012

SAYYID AL KHASAWNEH

IN APRIL, 2010, a year after the release of the Goldstone Report, the UN fact-finding mission on the Gaza conflict which accused the Israeli Defense Forces and Palestinian militias of crimes against humanity, I was lucky to be granted an interview with Awn Al- Khasawneh, a graduate in International Law from Cambridge University, former prime minister, and now one of the fifteen judges of the International Court of Justice at the Hague. Awn Al-Khasawneh, first elected by the UN General Assembly and Security Council in 2000 for a ten-year term and re-elected in 2006, represents the Middle East, (West Asia), is an expert on Arabic and Islamic legal systems on the Court (composed of three Asians, two Africans, two Latin Americans, four or five from Europe, the US and Canada). I asked him about the Wall in Palestine's occupied territories and the Goldstone Report, (April 2009)

"Ten years ago, when I was first elected, we declared the illegality of the Wall but the Court did not ask for a vote before the Security Council because they assumed the U.S. would veto it." I wondered whether he thought the Goldstone Report would encounter the same difficulty. "Because Palestine is not a state, it is unlikely that the Goldstone Report will be sent. In any case, I read recently that the U.S. and the Israelis are trying to stop it from going."

Khasawneh gestured for me to sit in the elegant living room of his Amman villa. "I am a farmer," he began, encouraging a taste test of his olive oil that is of such high quality it is sold at Harrods. Prior to his current status on the Court, he was legal advisor to King Hussein in 1994 during the peace treaty with Israel and then to Prince Hassan and Chief of the Royal Court, 1996-98. Khasawneh spoke of the time two decades ago when peace was so close at hand.

"In 1994, we had hope. At long last we felt we had come to a defensible scheme that everyone accepted—even by those people we now think of as extremist—Hamas and the Muslim Brotherhood and to a large extent, Israel. The opposition by Israeli extremists proved to be much stronger than we thought. They issued the equivalent of a fatwa against Rabin. Leah publicly accused Israeli leaders, notably Netanyahu, of having her husband's blood on their hands. The peace unraveled.

"None of the thorny questions were settled. The American technique was that of creative ambiguity which turned out to be destructive because it worked in favor of the stronger. If you leave the thorny questions until the end, you can be disappointed and small groups intent on power can take control, as we have seen with the rise of the Likud. Since the death of Rabin the area has been sliding toward anarchy and the window of opportunity has been lost.

"In 1982 with the rise of Reagan, the neo-con strategy with its strange relationship with fundamentalist Christian groups came to the fore. The reconstruction of the temple of Solomon was seen as necessary for the coming of Christ. In the middle of this, Rabin comes along, with the right credentials, a successful general in the '67 war. He knew we couldn't go on fighting forever. He was part of a generation of Jews who recognized that.

"There were even those extremists who felt because ancient Israel extended beyond the east bank of the Jordan River that Churchill in creating [Trans-]Jordan had betrayed them. Even Ben Gurion was a traitor to the Jewish cause by accepting a Jewish state that was confined to the west of the Jordan River. These people are not interested in boundary limitations. From the Euphrates to the Nile, God said to Abraham, goes to your seed and it doesn't matter that Arabs claim descent from Abraham too. So Rabin's blood was kosher because he had compromised Israel's sacred rights to the Temple Mount.

"The Jordan-Israeli peace was always meant to be part of an overall peace with Palestine and Syria. We always felt we couldn't divorce it from a wider peace. It really was these two men—King Hussein and Yitzhak Rabin—who made it possible and their death was another blow to peace."

Consistent with Arab hospitality, I was invited to join the family brunch where we feasted on all kinds of delicious breads with olive and thyme, pastries with date sauce and other delicacies. I told him that privately many in the West tell me that peace would be possible if there were a Mandela figure in the Palestinian leadership. "You know," Khasawneh answered, "I once met [Frederick Willem] De Klerk [president of South Africa, 1989-1994, credited with ending apartheid, and who shared the Nobel Peace Prize with Nelsen Mandela in 1993]. I asked him why he gave up his power in South Africa and he replied, 'Because I am a Christian and I knew there would be more bloodshed.' We don't have this in the case of Israel."

CHORAL DIPLOMACY

2010 WAS A BUSY YEAR with the choir. In the spring of 2010, Shireen brought Dozan Aw Watar to Syria to sing with our Christian and Muslim counterparts at a special event in the very church in Damascus where St. Paul was lowered in a basket to escape capture by the Romans.

Then in the fall, in Sept 2010, Bob arranged with the Israeli Embassy to get visas for the choir to visit Israel. Shireen brought the choir to Jerusalem where we sang Mozart's "Ave Verum Corpus" *à l'improviste* at the Sea of Galilee and joined a Catholic choir in Jerusalem for a special event. As we were leaving, many in the choir—of Palestinian origin—were in tears as they knew how difficult it would be for them to return. We heard stories of those Palestinians who betrayed their friends by selling property to the Israelis.

Members of the choir were offered the chance to return and sing in Bethlehem at the Church of the Nativity on Christmas Eve, December 24, 2010. That was an experience I was not going to turn down. I came and stayed in a convent a few days before to rehearse. Our son, Maxwell, was flying into Amman for the occasion but his plane was delayed. Bob called a (twice) former prime minister who had negotiated the peace treaty between

Israel and Jordan to ask if our son could hear his mother sing in Bethlehem. "That's such a touching story," the PM said. "I will make sure the bridge remains open." Bob and Max were in the audience in Bethlehem in time, along with Mahmoud Abbas and other Palestinians leaders. The church was full of light, and peace, an unmistakably spiritual moment.

At the beginning of the Arab spring in May of 2011, the musical discipline of the Syrian Christian tradition showed its true colors. Shireen had organized a joint Syrian-Jordanian production of the Mozart *Requiem*: half the choir, three out of four soloists, and the entire orchestra was Syrian. Even though the musicians were promised a government escort, they were stopped at Daraa near the border. In an incredible act of generosity, Shireen's father chartered a plane and brought them into Jordan. The musicians arrived thirsty and famished. All Amman came to the Mozart which, for me, will always remain the music of the Arab Spring. Of all the Mozart *Requiems* I have sung this one was the most moving.

VISITING HEBRON WITH A FRENCH DIPLOMAT

JEWS AND MUSLIMS have many things in common—similarities in language and diet— and also the belief that Jesus Christ was a man and not the son of God; both faiths believe in the coming of their Messiah (whereas Christians believe in the Second Coming). So it is ironic that the city of Hebron, cherished by both Jews and Muslims as the final resting place of the Patriarch Abraham and his wife, Sarah, has become a place of rivalry, hatred, violence and mistrust. The Israeli government pays the Jewish settlers to occupy Hebron as well as the other illegal settlements within West Bank territory, such as the suburban city of Maade Adumiin. In 2012, we took a family visit to Hebron courtesy of our friend, the French diplomat, Jean-Philippe, since taxis no longer dare to take tourists here.

The Church is divided in half but on Feast days the compartments are removed and Muslims can worship the Patriarchs freely. Even in the Muslim section, Israeli soldiers operate checkpoints into places of worship in order to check for guns. The day we went was the anniversary of the prophet Muhammad's birthday so the mosque, which enshrines the tombs, was closed to Jews; there was only a small corner on the outside where the settlers were praying guarded by twice as many police.

The old city is claustrophobic and has the feeling of an armed camp with the Israeli authorities surrounding the souq to protect the two hundred Israeli "settlers" living there cheek by jowl. A wide sidewalk is reserved for a tiny minority of Jews—bicycling, jogging, and strolling in pairs—while a narrow path is reserved for the 100,000 Arab residents. The poverty is evident from the sad expressions and feeling of resignation in the market place (souq). So it as a welcome relief to make friends with a woman selling beautiful scarfs and to buy a delicious glass of fresh pomegranate juice from a smiling Palestinian vendor inside the old city, a roofed alleyway where Israelis dump their garbage! A few years ago, Jean-Philippe told us, the Israeli authorities closed the sewers in Hebron to prevent Muslim residents from escaping, with the inevitable disagreeable effect of the sewage backing up into the streets.

Palestinian Loss of Land 1947 to Present

Jewish Settlements
Palestinian Land

PALESTINE

1947

Israeli Land
Palestinian Land

PALESTINE
Jerusalem (UN admin.)

ISRAEL

Partition Plan, 1947

Israeli Land
Palestinian Land

PALESTINE

ISRAEL

1949-1967

Israeli & Occupied Land
Palestinian Land

ISRAEL

Present

Courtesy of Fosna.org

https://interactive.aljazeera.com/aje/palestineremix/maps_main.html

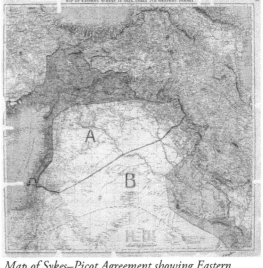

Map of Sykes–Picot Agreement showing Eastern Turkey in Asia, Syria and Western Persia, and areas of control and influence agreed between the British and the French. Royal Geographical Society, 1910-15. Signed by Mark Sykes and François Georges-Picot, 8 May 1916.

CPSIA information can be obtained
at www.ICGtesting.com
Printed in the USA
FSHW020054220719
60252FS